CHRISTIANITY 101

Your Guide to Eight Basic Christian Beliefs

CHRISTIANITY 101

PHOENIX FIRST PASTORS COLLEGE
13613 N. Cave Creek Rd.
Phoenix, AZ 85022

Gilbert Bilezikian

Foreword by Bill Hybels

ZondervanPublishingHouse
Academic and Professional Books
Grand Rapids, Michigan

A Division of HarperCollinsPublishers

To Maria
and other former students
who urged me to preserve in writing
what we learned together
in the classroom.

Christianity 101
Your Guide to Eight Basic Christian Beliefs
Copyright © 1993 by Gilbert Bilezikian

Requests for information should be addressed to:
Zondervan Publishing House
Academic and Professional Books
Grand Rapids, Michigan 49530

Library of Congress Cataloging in Publication Data
Bilezikian, Gilbert G.
    Christianity 101: your guide to eight basic Christian beliefs / Gilbert Bilezikian.
      p.   cm.
    Includes bibliographical references and indexes.
    ISBN 0-310-57701-2
    1. Theology, Doctrinal—Popular works.   I. Title.   II. Title: Christianity
one hundred one.
  BT77.B49   1993
  230—dc20   92-38543
                                                    CIP

Scripture quotations are taken mainly from two versions:
1. THE HOLY BIBLE: NEW INTERNATIONAL VERSION® (North American Edition). Copyright © 1973, 1978, 1984, by the International Bible Society. Used by permission of Zondervan Publishing House. All rights reserved. ("NIV" and "New International Version" are registered in the United States Patent and Trademark Office by the International Bible Society.)
2. The New Revised Standard Version of the Bible (copyright © 1989 by the Division of Christian Education of the National Council of Churches in the USA); used by permission.

Edited by Leonard G. Goss and Verlyn D. Verbrugge
Cover design by PM Graphics

Printed in the United States of America

01 / DH / 13

have materialized without the persistent urging and encouragement of Pastor Bill Hybels. The title of the book itself was
borrowed from one of his sermon series—although the idea for its
use was suggested by daughter Liliane while brainstorming with
John-Marc and Jane, Christiane, and Lionel.

My thanks go also to Mrs. Jean Blount, who typed my handwritten manuscript, and to test readers, such as Dr. John H. Augustine
and his father Harold E. Augustine, church elder Steven M. Bartz,
Rev. Winnie Jackson Houwen, Rev. Mark Mittelberg, and Dr. John
C. Ortberg, Jr., who all made valuable suggestions. My friend Mike
Topel juggled family and professional responsibilities as the CEO
of a dynamic high-tech video post-production company in Chicago
to invest enthusiastically large amounts of time in the finalization
of the project. His laser-sharp scrutiny subjected the manuscript to
an unforgiving quality-control treatment in both form and substance.

Multitudes of Christians revere the Bible as God's Word, but
they have little personal interaction with it. They may carry a Bible
with them to church, memorize verses from it, and even read it for
devotional purposes. But the secret of getting at the great truths of
the Bible escapes them. Because Bible scholars frequently dis-
agree on what the Bible teaches, ordinary people think that they
lack the qualifications for ever coming up with a correct understanding of the contents of the Bible.

This book is intended to meet the needs of such people. Used
properly, it will help Christians understand what they believe and
develop thoughtful ownership of their faith. Inquirers about
Christian truth will find here a convenient summary of the most
important teachings of the Bible. This book will also help
nonbelievers obtain a first-hand acquaintanceship with what
Christians believe.

The best method for using this book is to study it in conjunction
with an open Bible so that biblical references can be checked as
the reading progresses. A short bibliography is included at the end
of each chapter to suggest additional reading. Such listings are
intended to add breadth to the reader's inquiry. They do not
necessarily constitute an endorsement of the contents of the books
indicated or of the views espoused by their authors.

Engaging in any theological discussion is like tiptoeing one's
way through a minefield of controversy, since a bunch of differing
interpretations crops up with practically every topic that is approached. in order to avoid such confusion, people who do
theology often choose to interpret the Scripture on the basis of
predetermined theological frameworks that provide them with

systematic grids for the interpretation of the Bible's content. This is not the method that was followed in this book. Here, it is assumed that God's truth is always greater than any human systematization that may be applied to it. Consequently, for the purpose of conducting this study, the Bible was approached on its own merits and allowed to speak for itself in accordance with rules of interpretation derived from its own structure (see pp. 14–20). As a result, the contents of this book do not follow any one particular school of thought. Rather, truth is recognized in various theological traditions, wherever they seem to reflect accurately the thoughts of God inscripturated in Holy Writ. The learned reader will perceive that this methodology has led to a broad-spectrum centrist evangelical position that avoids the pitfalls of cultic, narrow allegiances on one hand, and of nondescript, uncommitted generalizations on the other hand. In this vein, mention should be made for the comfort of concerned vigilantes of creedal rectitude that access to retirement status allowed me freedom for the exploration of chiliastic alternatives beyond constringencies imposed by institutionally stipulated confessional norms. Most of my readers will have no clue as to what this disclaimer meant. I call them especially blessed and wish them happy reading.

G.B.

Outline of Chapter One

I. The Forms of Revelation
   1. General Revelation
      a. Revelation of God in nature
      b. Revelation of God in humans
      c. Revelation of God in history
   2. Special Revelation

II. The Authority of the Bible
   1. External Evidence
   2. Internal Evidence

III. The Writing of the Books of the Bible

IV. The Gathering of the Books of the Bible

V. The Transmission of the Text of the Bible

VI. The Interpretation of the Bible
   1. The Principle of Thematic Interpretation
   2. The Principle of Testamental Differentiation
   3. The Principle of Hapax Identification

VII. Current Views on the Bible as Revelation
   1. Low Views on the Bible as Revelation
      a. Secular approach
      b. Bibliolatry
   2. Mediating Views on the Bible as Revelation
   3. High Views on the Bible as Revelation

CHAPTER ONE

The Bible As God's Revelation

Preface

Most books of this kind are written in the quiet seclusion of the theologian's ivory tower. This one was born in the heat of action, on the battlefields of the Kingdom.

Several years ago, I became involved in the founding of a church dedicated to reaching unchurched people with the gospel of Christ. As unbelievers were converted to Jesus Christ by the thousands and developed into devoted disciples of his, they often came to pastors, elders, and other leaders of Willow Creek Community Church with profound questions about the Christian faith and its relevance to their lives—questions that are more easily discussed in seminary courses than from the pulpit. It was natural to refer such inquirers to several excellent theological reference books that were available on the market. However, they found that such books were generally written in a language that the average person could not understand—the specialized language of theological research and scholarship. As a result, the elders of Willow Creek Community Church commissioned me to write a summary of Christian beliefs in a style that would be accessible to the ordinary churchgoer, a person whose education did not include formal theological training.

At the same time, generations of students whom I had been teaching at Wheaton College were insisting that I commit to writing one of my general education courses entitled "Christian Thought." Thus the idea was born of a textbook of Christian doctrine specifically written for people who had never received specialized theological training. The basis for such a manual would be my Christian Thought course, presented in simplified and condensed form and written in language simple enough to be understood by people without prior theological education.

The opportunity to write this book came with the granting of a sabbatical leave by Wheaton College, followed by a term of reduced teaching made possible by the elders of Willow Creek Community Church. I am grateful to both institutions for having made this endeavor possible. However, this project would never black and white, young and old could minister freely to one another out of the richness of their diverse giftedness.

For over twenty years Dr. B. has mentored me, both in my personal spiritual journey and as a pastor. I cannot overstate the role he has played at Willow Creek Community Church. It is ironic that behind Willow Creek's laser-age persona, with its high-tech methods, its youthful energy, and its sometimes controversial creativity, beats the heart of an aging Bible professor who carries himself with quiet, European dignity.

I am delighted that this long-overdue book is about to hit the bookstore shelves. My only regret is that you can't read this book the way I have read it, with the distant echo of a heavy, melodic accent rising and falling in a cycle of passion, righteous indignation, and quiet longing for his students and readers to grasp the relevance of what he has to say. Even without the echo, however, I think you will "hear" a man who believes deeply what he says. With the historical perspective of a true scholar and the cultural perspective of a man who has lived throughout Europe and the Middle East, as well as in the Western world, Dr. B. speaks with sensitivity and understanding.

Having devoted himself for a lifetime to the careful study of Scripture, Dr. B. offers us a treasure chest of information. Yet he is careful not to wrap his gems in a stodgy, professorial style. His words are generally simple, and when they aren't he provides clear and concise definitions. The simplicity of his words, however, does not take away from the profundity of his thoughts. This is one of those rare books that can effectively inform spiritual seekers or new converts by offering a careful explanation of the basics of Christianity, and at the same time challenge veterans of the faith by offering unexpected insights and fascinating nuances of Biblical interpretation.

I love the man and I love his book, but I would be remiss if I did not end this foreword with one caution: Beware of the content of these pages. Two decades ago it changed my life. Today it may well change yours.

Foreword
Bill Hybels

Growing up, I was fascinated with stories of the ancient pyramids of Egypt. Who built them? How did they accomplish such a task? What would it be like to walk inside them? When, as an adult, I did ascend the narrow stairway into the inner sanctum of the Great Pyramid, the structure far exceeded my youthful imaginings, both in size and in mystery. I left that experience with even greater awe of the people whose vision, gifts, and sweat had created these wonders of the human world.

From my youth I listened to teachings about God, Jesus Christ, the Holy Spirit, the church, and the other great doctrines of the Christian faith. And I did more than passively listen; I was intrigued by these truths; I imagined their transformational power. But it was not until college, when I sat through my first class with Gilbert Bilezikian ("Dr. B.," as he is affectionately called by students and friends), that those great doctrinal truths took on personal, life-changing significance for me. Listening to the words of this passionate Frenchman, I began to experience the transcendent God of the universe as an intimate, nurturing Father; the Jesus of the cross became my ever-present companion and the Christ of the masses my personal confidant; the Holy Spirit, whose presence and work I had never understood, became the affirmer of my adoption into God's family, the administrator and energizer of my spiritual gifts, and the whisperer of personal leadings that changed the course of my daily life.

And it was Dr. B.'s revolutionary teaching about the church that ignited and fueled my passion for the ministry. As he painted, in brilliant detail, the picture of the church described in Acts 2:42–47, I realized that such a church was the world's only hope—and my only hope. I longed to be part of a community where people were genuinely responsive to God and compassionate toward each other; where people felt free to take off their masks, reveal their sin, and receive forgiveness and healing; where the excesses of the rich could meet the needs of the poor; where men and women,

vi

Contents

The Bible As God's Revelation

The Need For Truth

What is this world?

Who are we and what are we doing in it?

Is there any purpose to it? Can we make sense of our lives?

Is there an explanation for things and people? If there is, where is this explanation to be found?

These are basic questions that we all raise in one form or another. We want to know what life is all about, how we fit in the scheme of things, and what will be the outcome of it all.

Some people believe that there is no purpose to life and that there are no answers to their basic questions. They think that each person is left to oneself to make sense of life as best as one can.

Others believe that there exists a source of truth apart from the human mind and above it. Their reasoning goes like this: "I know I did not create myself. As a matter of fact, no human being could have created himself or herself. Only a Higher Power could have brought about human life on this planet." And, going one step further: "Just as I did not create myself, I cannot create the explanation for my own life. But the Higher Being who has created us can provide the explanation for our lives."

This explanation for life is what Christians call "truth." Obviously, truth is not something humans can imagine or invent on their own. Only the creating Higher Being, that is, God himself, can make truth available to us.

This is why Christians believe that the Creator is also the Revealer, the God of truth. He makes available to his creatures the truth that they desperately need to understand the meaning of their lives. Since they cannot find truth on their own, God gives it to them. This truth that comes from God is called "revelation."

I. THE FORMS OF REVELATION

It is generally agreed among Christians that God reveals himself in two different ways. These are called general revelation and special revelation.

1. General Revelation

General revelation is the knowledge obtained from God in a roundabout way, by watching what he does. Just as you can discover something about the skills and the mind of a craftsman by examining a piece of jewelry he has made, in the same way you can know something about God by watching the world he has created. It is customary to define three areas where general revelation is available: nature, humans, and history.

a. Revelation of God in nature

From the writings of King David, we can tell that he was a lover of God's creation. He had been raised as a shepherd and was used to living outdoors. Once he became so overwhelmed by the beauty and the majesty of the universe that he exclaimed:

> The heavens are telling the glory of God;
>   and the firmament proclaims his handiwork.
> Day to day pours forth speech.
>   and night to night declares knowledge.
>   (Ps. 19:1–2 NRSV)

Notice the words "telling," "proclaims," "speech," and "knowledge"—all used to describe truth about God that is available in his creation. Yet David realizes that there is no direct communication from God in nature, for he goes on to say: "There is no speech, nor are there words; their voice is not heard" (v. 3). But, he cannot give up the idea that nature communicates a message, so he adds: "Yet their voice goes out through all the earth, and their words to the end of the world" (v. 4).

The apostle Paul reinforces the same idea as he writes, "Since the creation of the world God's invisible qualities—his eternal power and divine nature—have been clearly seen, being understood from what has been made" (Rom. 1:20 NIV). Such expressions are in agreement with the awed response of many thinkers, poets, artists, scientists, and ordinary people throughout history to the grandeur and complexity of our natural world.

b. Revelation of God in humans

The first thing stated in the Bible about humans, and also the most important, is that men and women are made in God's image (Gen. 1:26–27). If the image is at all reflective of the original model, this implies that something of the nature of God is apparent in the personhood of humans. Taking into account the inherent limitations of humans (their finiteness) and the destructive results of sin upon the human race (their fallenness), we can assume that

4

the qualities that set humans apart from the rest of creation point to the identity of the Creator. Without being divine, humans bear a resemblance that evokes their Creator. As a result, the study of humans (psychology and anthropology) and of their institutions (sociology, economics, political science, etc.) should tell something about the works and the nature of God.

c. Revelation of God in history

If God has a purpose for history, its unfolding should also tell a story about God and his ways. History may sound like a "tale told by an idiot, full of sound and fury, signifying nothing." But within its cycles of confusion, one can trace a pattern of redemption as the ancient community of faith brings forth Jesus, who launches the new community of the people of God. History's continuation despite the forces of destruction at work within it points to the compassion of God; a *new community* (the church universal) emerging out of the chaos of history points to the love of God; and the drive of history itself to a climactic finish points to the ultimate sovereignty of God.

Each of the areas of general revelation deserves to be closely examined and appropriately interpreted. This task belongs to Christians who are scientists, social scientists, and students of the humanities and the arts. Much of what they discover can be helpful in pointing to the necessity for the existence of God. But as important as such information may be, it alone does not have the compelling power to convince unbelievers. Otherwise, every thoughtful skeptic would become a believer in God. Neither does the information provided by general revelation answer our basic questions about life, about its purpose, and about the truth issues that we raise in the face of loneliness, suffering, and death. Life creates problems that it does not resolve. Life also creates problems that only death seems to resolve. But then, the very presence of death is itself a haunting mystery that calls for a divine explanation. Beyond the broad strokes of general revelation, we need truth focused more specifically on the issues that make us yearn for certainty and aspire for fulfillment. Hence, the need for special revelation.

2. Special Revelation

Christians believe that God's intentional revelation is to be found supremely in Jesus Christ and therefore in the Bible, for the Bible is the original book about Jesus Christ. The Bible is a collection of sixty-six sub-books. Of these, the first thirty-nine comprise the Old Testament, called that because it deals mainly with the period of the beginnings of history, the story of the fall of humans, and the narrative of God's preparation through the people of the old covenant for the coming of the Savior.

Christians consider that Jesus Christ was God present in person, but in human form, on this earth. As such he was the very expression of God, God's best self-revelation. People who knew him well recognized him as the bearer of God's truth and called him the "Word"(John 1:1–14). Not only did he teach the ways and the will of God, but he also demonstrated in his person and ministry the real nature of God. By looking at Jesus and by listening to him, we can know exactly who God is.

But Jesus Christ stayed on this earth physically among humans for a relatively short period of time—about thirty-three years. This means that after his departure, the body of revelation he had brought to humans would have been lost for later generations. Fortunately, sensing this danger and eager to prevent it from happening, Jesus' followers carefully recorded in writing the life and teaching of their Master. They also kept the documents that his early followers had written concerning him and his work. These writings were later collected in the twenty-seven books that comprise the New Testament. Because most of what we know about God's supreme self-revelation in Jesus Christ is contained in the New Testament, it is also considered part of God's special revelation.

As a result, the church's ultimate spiritual authority is found in Scripture. By writing the New Testament, the apostles surrendered to it the authority that Christ had vested in them, thus making their own office obsolete. No person, leader, priest, prophet, teacher, minister, or spouse may claim for oneself the spiritual authority that belongs to Christ and that was committed to Scripture under his command and under the guidance of the Holy Spirit. For Christians, the locus of spiritual authority is to be found always in the Bible—never in fallible human beings.

Thus the Old Testament, the documents of the community of preparation, and the New Testament, the documents of the community of fulfillment, combine together to form the Bible, which Christians hold as God's special revelation. The main beliefs that Christians draw from the Bible will be discussed in the remainder of this book.

II. THE AUTHORITY OF THE BIBLE

The claim that the Bible is God's revelation raises the question of trust. How can we be really sure that the Bible is reliable as

God's Word? Too much is at stake to take a chance on a matter as important as committing oneself to the Bible as truth. Indeed, if the Bible is God's Word, it will shape our beliefs, our values, our moral choices, and our lifestyle decisions. In other words, the Bible will be the supreme authority in our lives as Christians. Consequently, we had better make absolutely sure that the Bible can be received as fully trustworthy.

1. External Evidence

Some people try to establish the reliability of the Bible on evidence outside of it. For instance, they cite the fact that archaeological discoveries have often confirmed the accuracy of the biblical text; that much scientific research agrees with statements of Scripture; that prophecies contained in Scripture have been accomplished in history; and that the Bible has had positive impacts upon society in such issues as the abolition of slavery, the recognition of women as human beings, the protest against cruelty to humans and animals, and the establishment of charitable institutions for orphans, the sick, and the helpless.

These are interesting arguments; but are they strong enough to convince the unconvinced? Indeed, opponents of Christianity are quick to counter that many archaeological and scientific discoveries do not confirm scriptural data; that because the Bible contains so many predictions some were bound to happen, but that many of them have not been fulfilled during the periods that were seemingly targeted; that terrible crimes have been committed in the name of the Bible (such as the Crusades in medieval times and the wars of religion and the tortures inflicted by the Inquisition in sixteenth-century Europe); and that racial and male dominance are still being defended and practiced by people who quote the Bible as their base. Such objections notwithstanding, there is enough external evidence that supports the reliability of the Bible to justify probing further and going to the Bible itself for affirmations of its truthfulness.

2. Internal Evidence

When we look *inside* the Bible for affirmations of its authority, we do much better. Indeed, the Bible is filled with claims for it to be God's Word. Time and time again, Moses and the prophets present their messages with introductions such as the familiar "Thus says the Lord. . . ." In the New Testament, Jesus declares repeatedly that he speaks with the authority of God, while his followers claim to speak and write under his authority as those commissioned by him to do so.

7

At first sight, this self-validation of the Bible as divine word sounds like a good argument. But upon reflection, it proves again to convince only the already convinced since it is based on circular reasoning. It's as if someone would say, "I must be telling the truth because I claim to be telling the truth." Obviously, such self-contained logic carries little weight. However, you can strengthen the same argument immensely by making Christ your starting point rather than the Bible itself. That argument runs as follows:

1. Consider Christ as Savior and Lord of your life. There are sufficient reasons to do so on the basis of information available in the Bible, even if the Gospels should be considered, at this stage, only as historical records about Jesus Christ.

2. As a result of accepting the lordship of Christ, recognize his authority upon your beliefs.

3. As you consider the Bible, discover that Jesus Christ endorses the Old Testament as truth. He quotes it as truth, cites Old Testament events and persons as being true, and affirms its content as divine revelation (for instance, Matt. 5:27–29). Therefore, your commitment to Christ requires that you also follow him in recognizing the Old Testament as revelation.

4. As for the New Testament, discover that Jesus committed his teaching to his disciples and commissioned them to pass it on, promising them his continued presence in the form of the Holy Spirit as his teacher (for instance, Matt. 28:18–20; John 14:25–26). In other words, Christ approved in advance the witness that his disciples would bear to him under his spiritual guidance. Since this witness has been carefully recorded in the New Testament, we can say that Christ also endorsed the New Testament as revelation.

This approach, which makes acceptance of the authority of the Bible dependent on a prior commitment to Jesus Christ, is in full agreement with his own teaching. Jesus promised that those who believe in him will be able to verify the truthfulness of God's revelation (John 7:16–17).

Sometimes, unbelievers are asked first to accept the divine authority of the Bible so that they can then become Christians. This puts the proverbial cart before the horse. To appeal to the authority of the Bible as divine revelation is irrelevant and meaningless to unbelievers who do not hold the Bible to be God's truth. For them, the Bible is at best a book of ancient religious literature that establishes the existence of Christ as a historical event. It is preferable to encourage seekers to build on their concept of a historical Christ so that they can encounter the living Christ. Then, on the basis of their experience of Christ, they will come to recognize fully the Bible as God's revelation. Note that because of the reality of Christ, countless people have become committed Christians without having had access to a Bible. This was especially true during the first centuries of the Christian era when the New Testament did not exist as a canon of twenty-seven books. Trust in the Bible's authority is indispensable as a *second* phase for Christian growth and learning—to make possible, for instance, the kind of endeavor that this book is all about. Belief in Christ is the best reference point for the recognition of the authority of the Bible as God's revelation.

III. THE WRITING OF THE BOOKS OF THE BIBLE

The very idea that the Bible is revelation suggests that God was involved in the making of the Bible. But evidently, the Bible is also a very human document. Its authors, people such as Moses, David, Isaiah, Luke, John, and Paul, were much involved in the writing of their works. Their books bear the marks of their peculiar choice of words, their individual ideas and beliefs, and their cultures and personalities. The books express their convictions and their emotions, their fears and their hopes. Often they present themselves in their writings as being engaged in dialogue with God himself. The Bible contains a divine element, but just as important, it also includes a human element, if for no other reason than because it was written by human hands under the control of human minds.

God's part in the composition of the books of the Bible safeguards its integrity as revelation. But the same cannot be said of the contribution of humans. Often, their knowledge is faulty, their understanding warped, and their means of expression limited. How can we be sure that human errors did not creep into the Bible to corrupt God's revelation?

Obviously, God did not simply dictate the text of the Bible to warm bodies who transcribed it passively. If this had been the case, all sixty-six books in the Bible would show exactly the same style, the same vocabulary, the same rules of grammar, and the same concepts in the same wording. This is far from being true. On the other hand, neither did God only put ideas in the minds of the authors and leave them on their own to write them down as best they could. If that were the case, we would have no guarantee that

God's truth was spared distortion between the receiving of the ideas and their transcription on parchment or paper.

In order to explain the unique character of Scripture as God's truth in human words, Christians have adopted the doctrine of divine inspiration, often called verbal or plenary inspiration. Some simple definitions are in order: (a) "inspiration" refers to the divine influence on the human authors during their writing of the text of Scripture; "all Scripture is *breathed out* by God" (2 Tim. 3:16); (b) "verbal" (from the Latin *verbum*, which means "word") indicates that the very wording of the text is affected by inspiration, not just the ideas contained in the Bible; (c) "plenary" indicates that inspiration concerns the "full" extent of the Bible, not just certain parts of it.

A formal definition of this doctrine might go like this: Verbal or plenary inspiration refers to the divine activity that surrounded the writing of the books of the Bible, without infringing on the autonomy of their authors, so that the resulting autographs (that is, their original documents) inerrantly expressed the thoughts of God in their very wording.

In plainer language, this means that the writing of Scripture resulted from a cooperative activity between God and human authors, whereby God exerted enough influence in them without controlling them completely, so as to guarantee that the original manuscripts that came directly from their hands (the "autographs," not later copies or translations) rendered the thoughts of God without errors or contradictions.

The concept of "inerrancy" cited in the formal definition above refers to Scripture's quality of being free from error. Obviously, misleading statements cannot be upheld as a standard for knowing truth. If the Bible is to be regarded as revelation, it must be free from error in what it affirms or teaches. This much is recognized in those passages of the Bible that refer to its own inspiration in relation to its intended usefulness (2 Tim. 3:16; Heb. 4:12–13; 2 Pet. 1:21). The implication of such texts is that a faulty revelation would be of no value in correcting human thought and behavior.

Admittedly, the Bible contains difficulties that still need to be resolved—such as the differences as to who actually spoke to Jesus in the two accounts of the believing centurion (Matt. 8:5–13 and Luke 7:1–10), and whether the disciples who were sent on a short-term mission took staffs and sandals with them (Matt. 10:10 and Mark 6:8–9). With research, similar difficulties have been resolved in the past. Therefore, we may legitimately suspend judgment on such problems. On the basis of the vast amount of material that has proven to be reliable in the Bible, we may justifiably exercise patience with such relatively few difficulties and continue to believe in the trustworthiness of its message.

IV. THE GATHERING OF THE BOOKS OF THE BIBLE

Although the Bible presents much evidence that their authors were conscious of writing under divine guidance, they did not suspect that their works would eventually be collected as Holy Scripture. Most of these were action documents written to meet urgent needs in times of change and crisis. Eventually their lasting value came to be recognized, they were collected and protected, and the Bible was formed.

The thirty-nine books of the Old Testament had already been gathered before Jesus' time by a process of accumulation, although they were not set in the Hebrew Scriptures in the same order as in our Bibles. These were the Scriptures that Jesus and his apostles used and quoted in their teachings and writings. The Christian church simply adopted them as the "Old Testament" Scripture.

The story of the formation of the New Testament *canon* (a Greek word for the collected books of the Bible as "standard" or "measure of truth") is immensely complicated. A rough oversimplification goes as follows:

First century A.D. The books of the New Testament are written to meet a variety of needs in the early churches.

Second century. The books travel from church to church in an improvised exchange program and are used to define Christian beliefs.

Third century. The books are gathered into groupings (called "lists") of Gospels and Epistles—not necessarily the same from place to place. These mini-Bibles were needed to provide authoritative guidance for faith and practice.

Fourth century. Worldwide representatives of churches come together (in "Councils") and recognize the twenty-seven books of the New Testament as divine revelation, thus confirming and bringing to a close the biblical canon.

The question may well be raised as to the responsibility that those Councils of the fourth century took upon themselves to shape for generations to come the nature of the Christian faith and the church by selecting only those twenty-seven books. The answer of those church leaders would be that they did not select the books as much as *recognize* them under God's guidance as inspired writings on the following bases: (1) They were written by apostles of Christ or by their immediate associates. As a result, the authors of those writings were covered by the authority that Christ

11

had given them to teach in his name. (2) The content of each book was in accord with the teachings of all the other books taken together; thus there was consistency of teaching among them. (3) They had been used by the churches since the time of their writing and had proven their value as God's word in the life and worship of the churches throughout the Roman empire.

With the work of those Councils done, the Christian quest for a written revelation came to a close. The recognition of the canon indicated its sufficiency—all that God wanted to make known as special revelation was contained in the Scriptures and nowhere else. It also indicated the finality of the canon so that nothing should ever be added to Scriptures as special revelation.

In addition to the sixty-six books of the Bible, some church groups also recognize as inspired a collection of fifteen writings called the Apocrypha. It includes several types of literary works such as historical accounts, novels, letters, proverbs, and devotional material. These have immense value in relating the beliefs and the history of the Jews between the time of the Old Testament and the New Testament. But as valuable as it is, the Apocrypha was never included in the canon of the Hebrew Scriptures (the Old Testament), and no book of the Apocrypha was ever directly quoted by the authors of the New Testament, although they did quote abundantly from practically every book of the Old Testament. In reaction to Protestant criticism of some of the content of the Apocrypha, the Roman Catholic Church adopted it as inspired Scripture at the Council of Trent in 1546. Therefore, the Apocrypha is included in Bibles sponsored by the Roman Catholic Church. Since neither Jesus nor the apostles quoted from the Apocrypha or endorsed its teachings, and since it was considered as Holy Scripture neither in the Hebrew tradition nor by the early church, most Protestants do not recognize the Apocrypha as divine revelation. However, it is a fascinating document of great historical and devotional value that all Christians can read with profit.

V. THE TRANSMISSION OF THE TEXT OF THE BIBLE

The books of the Bible were written a long time before the invention of printing and electronic copiers. Yet even then there was a public demand for the text of the Bible. The only method of duplication was the tedious and unreliable process of copying by hand. Consequently, during the centuries when the Bible was being passed on from generation to generation in handwritten form, many changes and alterations crept into the text.

Thousands of ancient handwritten manuscripts of the Bible or portions of it are still available today. When compared to each other, they show great numbers of differences or discrepancies (called "variants") from one to the other. Most of those variants are insignificant, though some affect the meaning of words, sentences, and even whole sections. The most notable ones in the latter category are found in Mark 16:9–20 (about which the New International Version states, "The most reliable early manuscripts . . . do not have" this section) and the story of Jesus' forgiveness of the woman caught in adultery (about which the NIV states, "The earliest and most reliable manuscripts . . . do not have John 7:53–8:11," and the New Revised Standard Version gives a more extensive explanation: "The most ancient authorities lack 7:53–8:11; other authorities add the passage here or after 7:36 or after 21:25 or after Luke 21:38, with variations of text; some mark the passage as doubtful" ["authorities" means "ancient manuscripts"]).

The realization that such uncertainties surround the very text of the Bible may seem to be devastating to Christian faith. Indeed, we may wonder what happens to the integrity of God's revelation when we cannot even be sure of what the text of the Bible was like originally.

This question has, of course, been faced by biblical scholars. As they have studied ancient documents written during the same period of history as the Bible, they have discovered that, in comparison to other ancient writings, the text of Scripture has enjoyed miraculous protection from alterations so that none of its major doctrines is affected by the variants. For example, a copy of the text of Isaiah found in the middle of the twentieth century among the Dead Sea Scrolls was estimated to have been written about a thousand years earlier than the oldest text of Isaiah available at the time of the discovery. The comparison of the two manuscripts showed an amazing degree of preservation of the text during this gap of almost a millennium. Moreover, as additional ancient manuscripts of the Bible are being discovered and processed, scholars are able to eliminate the effects of variants on the text and to establish a text of Scripture that resembles increasingly and reassuringly what the original autographs must have looked like.

A matter of equal concern is what happens to Scripture when it is translated into our modern languages. The Old Testament was written mostly in Hebrew and the New Testament in Greek. Since most people do not know these languages, it is necessary to translate the Bible in order to make it available to the public. But as anyone who knows more than one language understands, there is no such thing as a perfect translation because a translation is often a mutilation.

Nevertheless, several good translations (also called "versions") of the Bible are available in the English language. Most of them are the result of scholars working together as teams, taking into account the most up-to-date manuscript research and writing in current English. These translations avoid either a loose paraphrase of the original text or a rigid word-for-word rendition. Because of the inevitable shortcomings of the translation process, you should study the Bible by using several versions in order to obtain a balanced perspective on the richness and the difficulties present in the original text of Scripture. In order to make that text understandable to modern readers, some translators have rendered it as a paraphrase. When using a paraphrased Bible, always remember that it doubles as an interpretation and is therefore to be followed with a great deal of caution.

VI. THE INTERPRETATION OF THE BIBLE

Because God's special revelation occurred a long time ago in the lives of people like Moses, David, John, and Paul, it is time-bound. This means that, although God's truth is always relevant, it is conveyed in languages, cultural mind-sets, and literary forms that belong to ages past and to peoples who have long disappeared. This cultural gap between their time and ours compounds the difficulty of understanding the text of the Bible.

In order to bridge the cultural gap, we need to agree on ground rules that will help us interpret Scripture correctly. Otherwise, the quest for Christian truth becomes a free-for-all. Any person who comes along can pull bits and pieces out of the Bible and claim them to be God's truth. Indeed, the Bible is a very large book—some 1,500 pages on the average, depending on the printing format. The very bulk of the Bible makes it vulnerable to misinterpretation; one can pick and choose from the Bible while ignoring the totality of its message. For instance, the text that permitted "an eye for an eye, and a tooth for a tooth" is often misused to justify revenge and punishment, whereas a more thorough reading of the Bible would favor extending forgiveness, compassion, and a chance for renewal to the offender.

The definition of standards for the interpretation of Scripture (called "hermeneutics") is highly debated among scholars. Indeed, whose rules are we to follow? From which century and what culture? On whose authority? Ideally, the Bible could have contained a few chapters defining principles for its own interpretation, but it does not. As a result, the theological landscape of the church is like a battlefield. For every belief, there is a counter-belief. For every doctrine, there is its opposite. For every set of verses, one can gather another set of verses that seems to say the contrary. For people who are not trained theologians, all this is confusing. They feel like giving up ever knowing for sure what the Bible says, or they limit themselves to read the Bible only devotionally while committing themselves to the authority of someone who claims to be qualified to tell them what the Bible teaches. This lack of a broadly accepted method for interpreting the Bible is frustrating. What use is it to have an inerrant revelation from God if there is no agreement as to how to understand it?

Fortunately, the situation is not as hopeless as it seems because the structure of the Bible, if not its contents, suggests three principles for its interpretation.

1. The Principle of Thematic Interpretation

Most people who approach the Bible in order to study it regard it as a collection of mainly individual verses. Indeed, at first sight, the verse appears to be the basic unit of the Bible. But the basic unit of the Bible is neither the verse nor the chapter but each of the sixty-six books that compose it. The sixty-six books form the original structure of the Bible; the verses have nothing to do with it. The chapter and verse divisions form a convenient reference system that was added to the Bible between the thirteenth and fifteenth centuries of our era—only a few hundred years ago and long after the writing of the Bible was complete.

Therefore, the verse division is neither sacred nor inspired. While it makes it easier to find our way in the Bible, it should not be allowed to dictate how we study it. The common practice of singling out verses and cross-referencing them with each other from one book to another is a hazardous method of doing Bible study. With little verses taken from here and there and brought together, one can make the Bible say almost anything and everything. This scissors-and-paste method of Bible study is to a great extent responsible for the theological chaos that reigns among Christians and for the splintering of the church into so many denominations.

According to the principle of *thematic interpretation*, the contents of the Bible should be interpreted one theme at a time, in one book at a time. This principle is based on the fact that the Bible comes to us in sixty-six distinct books written by a number of different authors, all of them inspired by the Spirit. But they also brought to their work their ideas, their vocabularies, and their theological perspectives. Thus, Moses did not write like David, David like Isaiah, Isaiah like Matthew, Matthew like John, and John did not write like Paul.

Sometimes, biblical authors may even use the same word but give it different meanings. For example, the basic word "faith" has different connotations for the authors of the New Testament. For Matthew, it means simple trust, a childlike confidence in the ability of the Father to meet human need. For John, the concept of faith means relational commitment, "believing in" someone. For Paul, faith generally means saving or justifying faith, although in the letters to Timothy and Titus the same word refers to "sound doctrine" or correct teaching. In Hebrews, it refers to a commitment of the mind, like seeing through spiritual eyes what is not visible to the eyes of flesh. And in James, faith refers to resulting action, for "faith without works is . . . dead" (James 2:26 NRSV).

As a shortcut to Bible study on the topic of faith, we might be tempted to gather from a concordance a few scattered verses that contain the word "faith" with no concern for the shades of meaning it has in the specific books where it is found. Then, brought together like a collage, those verses can be made to teach fabrications of our own invention that are foreign to the Bible. A much better approach, suggested by the very structure of the Bible itself, is to trace the meaning of the word "faith," as a sort of word-study, in just one of the sixty-six books of the Bible. Then, the results can be summarized as a definition of the theme of "faith" in that particular book. When the procedure is repeated with additional books of the Bible, the resulting summaries may be brought together to show with accuracy the richness and the diversity of the biblical teaching about that theme or subject.

This procedure may be followed for the study of any topic in the Bible: one theme at a time, in one book at a time. This method certainly requires more homework than picking a few random verses. But it is infinitely more rewarding and God-honoring, since it keeps us from shredding Scripture into a mass of disconnected verses. Moreover, it protects from the danger of "prooftexting" Scripture, that is, singling out one verse from the Bible and presenting it as if it were the totality of what the Bible teaches on that subject, without regard for additional teaching that may be available on the same subject in the rest of the Bible. Nor should we jump all over the Bible and pull out isolated verses to prove a point. Any verse singled out should be a representative summary of the theme contained in the book in which the verse is found, and it should be understood that the verse does not necessarily represent the totality of the teaching of the Bible on that topic.

2. The Principle of Testamental Differentiation

Besides the fact that the Bible comes to us in sixty-six distinct books, the other noticeable feature about its structure is that the Bible is composed of two sections, the Old Testament and the New Testament. Those two parts are called "old" and "new" because they represent different stages in the process of God's revelation.

From the third chapter of Genesis on, the Old Testament represents the phase of promise and preparation for the coming of Christ. The New Testament tells the story of the fulfillment of the Old Testament promise with the coming of Christ and the establishment of the church, the new community of faith. Therefore, the difference between the two Testaments has great significance for the understanding of Christian truth.

The Old Testament is the collection of the documents of the community of preparation. It was only the beginning of God's revelation to humans, and its truth yearns for completion. The old covenant could offer salvation only in anticipation of the ministry of Christ. Of itself, it produced fractured community and condemnation (Rom. 8:1–4). Although it was necessary as the first phase of revelation, it was intended to be replaced by a new covenant that would be better than the first because it would be built on better promises (cf. Heb. 8:6–13). The Old Testament anticipated and pointed toward the fullness of revelation that would be brought in Christ and revealed in the New Testament.

The New Testament is the collection of the documents of the community of fulfillment. The truths revealed dimly in the Old Testament came to fullness in the New. Indeed, Christians regard the Christ of the New Testament as the fullness of God's revelation to humans, as the eternal Word expressed in human form. In him, all the promises of God find their fulfillment. Christ gives—and in fact is—God's full and final Word, God's ultimate revelation. Although what is contained in each Testament is equally true, the New Testament is more truth-intensive than the Old. It reveals more truth and does so more completely, since it is the fullness of divine revelation.

Obviously, this difference between the two Testaments is of considerable importance for the interpretation of the Bible. Since the truth of the Old Testament is partial and incomplete, the Old Testament cannot have the final word on any aspect of revelation, unless it is confirmed as such in the New Testament. In other words, the full meaning of the teachings of the Old Testament is to be found in the New Testament. It is the New Testament that controls the meaning of the Old Testament, never the reverse. This rule obviously excludes Genesis 1 and 2, since they reveal God's original creation prior to the Fall, in a state of sinless perfection that did not require the redemptive program described in the New Testament.

A simple example will illustrate the principle of testamental differentiation. Suppose we want to find the Bible's teaching on how to obtain salvation. If we go to the Old Testament, we discover that it was necessary to sacrifice animals on an altar as an expression of repentance and of a desire for divine forgiveness. However, in the New Testament we find that God himself provided the perfect sacrifice in the person of Jesus, since he more than fulfills the requirements for the Old Testament sacrificial offerings. Moreover, his death on the cross explains the necessity for the old covenant sacrifices as predictive signs pointing to their perfect and final fulfillment in the new covenant. The Old Testament teaching on animal sacrifices does not control the doctrine of salvation; rather, the New Testament teaching on Christ's sacrifice does. The full meaning of the Old Testament sacrificial system is to be found in the New. This model, based on the finality of the new covenant over the old, applies to all beliefs and practices of Christians. For followers of Judaism, the old covenant has finality. For Christians, it is Christ and therefore the New Testament that have the last word in defining Christian beliefs and practices.

The validity of the principle of testamental differentiation is widely recognized in the New Testament itself. Jesus declared that the old covenant Scriptures continue to stand as divine revelation since they testify about him. Nevertheless, it was necessary that he should come in order to fulfill them and give them completion (Matt. 5:17–19 and John 5:39 illustrate this theme that runs through the Gospels, often with the notation that "this happened in order to fulfill that which was written. . ."). The apostle Paul likewise affirms that the key to the understanding of the Old Testament is the gospel of Christ. According to him, the minds of the people of Israel remain hardened and covered with a veil when they read the old covenant Scriptures, because only through Christ is that veil removed and the Old Testament made intelligible (2 Cor. 3:4–18). Much of the argument of the letter of Hebrews is that since the old covenant institutions could not permanently meet human needs, the new covenant takes precedence over the old and renders it obsolete (Heb. 8:6–7, 13 summarizes this theme). And the apostle Peter states that the purpose of the prophets of the old covenant was focused on the gospel of Christ, and that they were not ministering to themselves or for their own times but for the church (1 Pet. 1:10–12).

Thus, the theme of the subservience of the old covenant to the new runs throughout the New Testament. It requires that every time we go to the Old Testament for a teaching, we also find how it is redefined and completed in the New Testament. All the promises of God find their final word, their "yes" and their "amen," in Christ (2 Cor. 1:20).

3. The Principle of Hapax Identification

Hapax is an ancient Greek word that means "once." Applied to the Bible, it refers to statements, ideas, or words that appear only once in it. Within the structure of the Bible as a whole, several stories are told only once and never cross-referenced again; some facts are recorded once and never again; certain ideas are expressed once and never again; a few Hebrew and Greek words are used once and never again. Each one of these is a hapax. The following principle of interpretation should be obvious: Never build a doctrine on or draw a teaching from an unclear or debated hapax.

If the hapax is clear (and most of them are) and if no debate over its meaning has occurred in the history of its interpretation among Christians, then you can use it and incorporate its teaching into the belief and practice systems of the church. However, if the meaning of the hapax is not clear (and some are difficult to understand) and if there is controversy among Christians over its meaning, then it is safer and preferable to leave it alone. Indeed, so much clear non-hapaxic material is available in the Bible that we do not need to press into service difficult texts that are better left aside when not understood. Those texts had meanings when first written, but such meanings are now lost because of our ignorance of ancient languages and customs. God does not hold us responsible to explain and use everything found in the Bible. We are accountable only for that which we can understand. Therefore, humility before God's revelation requires that we recognize our limitations, using well what we do understand and admitting our ignorance for the rest.

A few examples of hapaxic statements may help clarify this principle. The account of the visit of the Magi who came to worship the infant Jesus in Bethlehem is a hapax (Matt. 2); this event is confirmed nowhere else in the New Testament. Yet the text is clear and believers do not debate its meaning. Therefore, we may appropriately use this hapaxic story in the worship and teaching of the church.

On the other hand, while defending the doctrine of the resurrection in his first letter to the Corinthians, Paul tries to show the inconsistency of their beliefs by making a passing reference to the "baptism for the dead" (1 Cor. 15:29). He neither endorses the practice nor explains it. The allusion is unclear; its meaning has been debated among scholars for centuries, and it is never confirmed elsewhere in the Scriptures. Despite these difficulties, some groups have elevated this debated hapax to the status of doctrine. It should have been allowed to remain untouched because of our failure to understand it.

A hapax may also be a single word never used again in Scripture. For example, while Timothy was pastoring the church in Ephesus, Paul wrote him a letter that dealt with problems within the Ephesian congregation because untrained women went from house to house, "saying what they should not say" (1 Tim. 5:13 NRSV). To resolve the crisis, Paul lays down rules for the proper conduct of the Ephesian women. In particular, he tells them not "to have authority" over men, as rendered in several translations (1 Tim. 2:12). The Greek word for "authority" in this text is a hapax. Thus, there is no control text to determine its meaning; no one knows for sure what the word means and what exactly Paul forbids. Scholars have proposed a number of theories, but without being able to reach an agreement. Since the word is unclear and its meaning debated, it should be approached with a great deal of caution. The principle of hapax identification requires that no teaching or practice be based on such uncertain texts.

The science of interpreting the Bible is too serious a matter to be left to the ingenuity and to the whims of fallible human beings. The proposed rules derived from the structure of the Bible itself provide guidance for a respectful and God-honoring use of his Word. These rules have been observed to establish the teachings discussed in this book. The many verse references it contains have been carefully interpreted within the thematic context of the biblical books where they are found.

VII. CURRENT VIEWS ON THE BIBLE AS REVELATION

A quick survey of current attitudes toward the Bible suggests three basic positions that we shall describe as low, mediating, and high views of the Bible.

1. Low Views of the Bible as Revelation

a. Secular approach

In this view, the Bible is treated as a merely human document reflecting the developing religious consciousness of humankind, without any element of divine inspiration. The Bible is a book of ancient religious literature and selective history to be treated as any old book from antiquity. From this perspective, the Bible has no revelational value.

b. Bibliolatry

Another low view is reflected in the approach of those who believe the Bible to be inspired and inerrant and who may even cherish it, read it faithfully, use it in worship, and memorize it, but who do not allow the dynamic of its message to affect their lives or change their values and prejudices. For them the Bible remains a revered object, like a sacred relic or a magic charm; it is reduced to the status of a much admired antique. Reverence for the Bible without obedience to its message is, in practice, no better than rank secularism. Jesus rebuked the Pharisees mercilessly for such use of Scripture. Bibliolatry is the attitude of Christians who worship the Bible instead of worshiping God and obeying the Bible.

2. Mediating Views of the Bible as Revelation

The people in this group believe in the revelational value of the Bible, but they subject its contents to selective human judgment. They deny that the Bible resting on a desk is the word of God, saying rather that it is a dead object made of paper, ink, and glue—though it does hold the potential for becoming the word of God. For them, the Bible *contains* the word of God. Should the message of the Bible when it is read or preached speak to someone, then the Bible becomes subjectively revelation for that person. For this school of thought, revelation is something that happens in an experience of personal encounter with truth; revelation cannot be objective truth committed once for all to the pages of a book. The obvious problem with this position is that it reduces revelation to subjective, personal perceptions which, in turn, make truth relative to each individual. On such premises, the writing of a volume such as this one about basic and normative beliefs is an impossibility.

Another approach that falls within this mediating category is that of people who hold the Bible as inspired and authoritative but who claim that in order to be complete revelation, the Bible must be interpreted in the light of their church tradition, consisting of the writings of early Christian thinkers and of the pronouncements of their chief leaders to whom infallibility is attributed. This approach also subjects the truth of the Bible to authoritarian human determinations.

3. High Views of the Bible as Revelation

As stated earlier, commitment to Christ requires a high level of respect for the Scriptures as God's revealed truth. Such an approach is best attained with the recognition of the inspiration and authority of Scripture as the divine Word, the objective nature of the truth of Scripture that can be defined in clear statements or propositions, and the dynamic impact of divine truth upon human lives.

When God's truth is not activated in human life, it remains a dead letter, and the dead letter kills (2 Cor. 3:6). But when God's truth is released from the Book and becomes translated into real-life experience, then it actually fulfills the ministry for which it was intended by its divine Author.

RESOURCES

In addition to these, the following resources are helpful:

Alan F. Johnson and Robert E. Webber. *What Christians Believe: A Biblical and Historical Summary*. Grand Rapids: Zondervan, 1989, pp. 17–55.

F. F. Bruce. *The New Testament Documents: Are They Reliable?* Grand Rapids: Eerdmans, 1959.

F. F. Bruce. *The Books and the Parchments*. Old Tappan, N.J.: Revell, n.d.

Chicago Statement on Biblical Inerrancy

Leon Morris. *I Believe in Revelation*. Grand Rapids: Eerdmans, 1976.

DISCUSSION QUESTIONS

1. What can be known of God and his will through general revelation?
2. Does the inspiration of the sacred authors necessitate the inerrancy of their writings?
3. How can interpreters of Scripture keep their own prejudices to a minimum?

CHAPTER TWO

The Doctrine of God

Outline of Chapter Two

The Doctrine of God

I. DOES GOD EXIST?

Ever since humans have been thinking about themselves, their lives, and their world, they have been haunted with questions about God. People who make a commitment to Jesus Christ as the source of truth find answers to such questions, though they do not suddenly get to know everything that can be known about God, nor are they free from doubts. That would be impossible since God is always greater than our highest thought of him. But Christians have access to enough information about God to satisfy their life-needs and their quest for meaning. Christians believe that the most accurate and complete information about God is found in the Bible. Consequently, in this chapter, we will confine ourselves to the consideration of a few of the most important teachings in the Bible about God.

Anyone who knows Scripture has discovered that the Bible never tries to prove the existence of God. It simply affirms that God exists. From the first line of the Bible, it is evident that a world without God is inconceivable since, in the biblical mind-set, God is the reason for creation and the backdrop for all of life.

Throughout history, however, some people have expended energy and time trying to prove the existence of God. During the Middle Ages, Christian thinkers put out a whole line of so-called "arguments for the existence of God": the existence of the world, the existence of purpose in the world, and the presence of rationality and conscience in humans all point to the source of those realities, that is, to God as the necessary source of all things. Such arguments seem to help some people while they leave others unconvinced.

The Bible assumes that one who seeks after God will find him because God is already present, eager to meet any who search after him (see Heb. 11:6). And Jesus cut through all the philosophical arguments by claiming that the best access to belief in God is through commitment to himself (John 14:6–9). While the ques-

25

tions of both seekers and unbelievers have to be answered honestly, the biblical assumption concerning God's existence suggests inviting such people to approach first the "historical" Christ as the revealer of God. Countless people who become acquainted with the Gospel in this manner witness to an awakening of the spirit, a deep stirring of the soul that leads them to face seriously the claims of Christ as Savior and Lord. Their ensuing commitment to Christ provides a better and more direct access to the knowledge of God revealed by him than engaging in endless arguments about his existence.

II. WHO IS GOD?

The only one who knows the complete answer to the above question is God himself. Human thought falters and human language fails at defining God. But fortunately, God has revealed enough of himself to enable humans to understand some aspects of his being. While the whole Bible is a long commentary about the nature of God, the first two chapters of Genesis are especially helpful in providing basic definitions, since they describe the relations of God with creation and with humans before sin and death entered this world. They offer an appropriate starting point for an attempt to define some aspects of the divine being. The three features discussed below stand out in the narrative of these chapters.

1. God is a Transcendent Being

In majestic tones, the opening words of the Bible announce that before time began and all things were created, there existed nothing and no one but God. Before anything else, God was. Human life cannot exist outside of time and space. We need time to breathe, to think, to work, and to play. We need places where we can move, rest, and rise. Not so with God. He created time, space, and everything that exists within them. He was before creation. When Moses tried to pierce the mystery of the identity of God, he was given this mysterious name for him, "I am the one who is" (Ex. 3:14)—as if God were saying, "Moses, you cannot see me. But I am more real than anything you can touch and see, because I am life original from whom all other life derives. I am dependent on nothing and no one for my existence. I am pure being, discrete and autonomous."

This quality of God that represents him as prior to, distinct from, and not dependent on anything or anyone is called "transcendence." It means that God must not be confused in any way with the universe he has created because he is not part of it.

The Bible also teaches that God is transcendent because he is not contained within time. He is the one who created time and is therefore outside of, above, and beyond time. This is what the Bible means by describing God as "eternal." Applied to God, "eternal" does not signify infinite longevity; rather, it refers to the fact that, as the creator of time, God is a nontemporal or timeless being. God cannot be contained by anything he has created, including time, though he can act within time and affect history.

Likewise, God is not contained within space because he is a spiritual being who does not need to occupy a place in order to exist. He has the freedom to intervene in the physical universe and even to assume visible form without becoming a part of the material world.

Because God is a personal being, the Bible describes him as being capable of experiencing emotions, such as surprise, disappointment, indignation, pleasure, and love. God's transcendence does not prevent him from responding with true feelings to situations that develop within his creation. Despite this seeming vulnerability of God, however, the Bible maintains that God is the one absolute being. Since he is transcendent, he cannot transcend himself. In other words, God cannot grow, surpass himself, or change who he is. He is already the highest and the ultimate form of existence beyond which there can be no other. The lives of human beings are in constant process. They are born, they grow up, they grow old, and they die. God is without beginning and without end. As a matter of fact, it is his stability that provides the steady backdrop against which all the changes of history and the motions of this world acquire significance.

It is customary to express the doctrine of the transcendence of God in terms of his "omni" qualities—his omnipresence, omnipotence, and omniscience. These concepts may be helpful in a general sort of way to dramatize the infinite differences that exist between God and humans. But we must be careful not to use them rigidly because of the risk of making them say more than what the Bible teaches.

For instance, if by *omnipresence* we mean that God's energizing power permeates this whole universe because he makes all things hold together, we are biblically correct. But if by omnipresence we mean that God is actually present in all places, this is wrong. God is not present in the bottle of liquor that is slowly killing your neighbor. God is not present in the pornographic magazines that poison the minds of our children. God is not present in a sexual act that transmits AIDS or results in an abortion. God is not present in the empty can that I kick around, because I would be controlling him with my boot. Such a narrow understanding of omnipresence runs the risk of de-spiritualizing God and of identifying him with the material world. Because he is transcendent, God has the capacity to be actively present any place where he wishes to be or where he is needed and called upon. But no part of his creation can contain him or parts of him. The popular idea of omnipresence is too limited to describe adequately the magnitude of the transcendent God.

Likewise for the *omnipotence* of God. This word may be correctly used to indicate that God is all-powerful and that, by virtue of his being Creator of all things, he has ultimate mastery and sovereignty over all things and all beings. However, biblically speaking, the word *omnipotence* cannot mean that God can do everything and anything. As a matter of fact, there are some things that we humans can do that God cannot do. For example, God cannot be tempted by evil; he cannot commit sin; he cannot be untrue to himself; he cannot commit suicide; and he cannot violate his own nature.

Because of his rights as Creator, God has absolute sovereignty over everything that exists. This would seem to imply that God is omnipotent in relation to humans and that his will always prevails among them. But we all know that this is far from being the case— even in our own lives. The sad story of sin runs throughout the Bible, demonstrating that God's will is not being done on earth as it is in heaven since, by definition, sin is violation of God's will.

Again, the Genesis story provides a case in point. When God set Adam and Eve in the Garden of Eden, he gave them guidelines that spelled out his sovereign will. He told them not to eat of the forbidden tree, but he left them free to make their own decision about it. A puny god, insecure about his sovereignty, would have ruthlessly imposed his will on them by following them in the garden and whacking them every time they got close to the tree of the forbidden fruit. Or he would have manipulated their lives in such a manner as to give them the impression that they were making their own decisions when they were actually programmed to do his will alone. But when the transcendent God of the Bible endows his creatures with freedom, he does so with integrity. His sovereignty is comprehensive enough and secure enough to enable him to limit it selectively in order to make room within it for the exercise of human free will. Thus, the omnipotence of God must be defined in terms that do not violate his freedom-giving nature and that do not negate his ability to assign self-imposed boundaries to his own sovereignty.

The same caution must be used in regard to the *omniscience* of God. Indeed, the Bible teaches that God is perfect in knowledge. Being the Creator of time, God cannot be unaware of the past, the present, or the future. The maker of time is also its master. As a result, God has total perspective on the full sweep of history. At times, however, the Bible also registers God's surprise, disappointment, and even regret at the discovery of what happens on the human scene, as if he were suddenly becoming aware of it for the first time. For example, when God returned to the Garden of Eden after the Fall, the man and the woman were hiding from his presence. Looking for them, God called out, "Where are you?" (Gen. 3:9). This was obviously a straightforward inquiry—not a rhetorical question. God was not playing games with the humans by deceptively asking them a question, the answer to which he already knew. Similarly, because God had become aware of the outcry against Sodom and Gomorrah, he determined to go down and check out the report (Gen. 18:20–21).

Sometimes God discovers a state of affairs that causes him to take action (Gen. 6:5–7; 11:5–7; Ex. 3:9–10; 1 Sam. 15:11, 35; 2 Sam. 24:16; Jer. 18:9–10). At other times, he responds to pleas for deliverance or to human expressions of repentance by changing a predetermined course of action (Ex. 32:12–14; 2 Kings 20:1–6; Ps. 106:44–45; Jer. 18:7–8; 26:19; Joel 2:13; Amos 7:3,6; Jonah 3:9–10). Through all this, God's nature and purpose remain unchanged. But because he is interactively involved with his creatures, God holds humans responsible for the decisions they make.

In order to respect the integrity of human freedom and not to interfere with its exercise, God often seems to limit his awareness of their actions—as if he were surrounding them with a bubble of non-interference, sheltering them from the full scope of his omniscience. Perhaps it is not too much to expect of the transcendent God that he should be able to limit his knowledge selectively whenever he sovereignly decides to do so. God's ability to control the limits of his omnipresence, his omnipotence, and his omniscience does not minimize his sovereignty. To the contrary, this capacity enhances the infinite dimensions of his sovereignty by showing that God is sovereign even over the exercise of his own sovereignty.

The doctrine of God's transcendence emphasizes his "otherness" and his autonomy from his creation. Humans have always attempted to identify God with his created works by attributing divinity to the stars, to the sun and moon, to mountains, animals, rivers, and trees, to man-made idols, and even to themselves. But the writers of the Bible are unanimous in claiming that God may not be confused with any part of his creation because he is prior to it, above and beyond it, and distinct from it.

2. God is a Dynamic Being

The idea of God's transcendence may suggest that he is imprisoned in remote majesty as an infinite abstraction, frozen in silent immobility. The Bible teaches quite differently. It shows that God's life is an explosion of activity, both within his own being and in his actions.

a. Dynamic within himself

We do not have to go very far into the Bible to discover that God is a trinity of persons within one being.

- In Genesis 1:1, we are introduced to God as the one who conceives and designs the works of creation. Because he is the mastermind behind creation and the one who generates the universe, we recognize him as the Father of lights from whom derives every good and perfect gift (cf. James 1:17). In the first sentence of the Bible, God is presented as the Father and originator of the created world.

- In Genesis 1:2, we are introduced to God as the Spirit who watches over the works of creation in his role of protector and perfecter. In this verse, God is identified as the Spirit of God.

- In Genesis 1:3, we are introduced to the "Word" of God through whose agency God's will becomes activated. God speaks, and the Word makes it happen. This is the Word who was in the beginning, who was with God, who was God, and who was one with the Father. Through him all things were made and, eventually, he became flesh and lived among us as the Son who had come from the Father (cf. John 1:1–18). In Genesis 1:3, we are introduced to God the Son.

There is only a hint of the doctrine of the Trinity in the first three verses of the Bible. It receives fuller treatment in the rest of the Bible, especially in the New Testament, which has strong teachings on the oneness that exists between Father, Son, and Holy Spirit (Matt. 3:16–17; 28:19; John 10:30; 14:26; 15:26; Rom. 1:4; 5:5–6; 8:2–3, 9, 16–17; 14:17–18; 15:16–17, 30; 1 Cor. 12:4–6; 2 Cor. 13:14; 1 Pet. 1:2; etc.) But as sparse as the Genesis reference is, it already defines a community of three divine personalities, united in one being. This plurality in oneness points to a dynamic divine being whose mode of existence is active and interactive rather than inert and passive.

b. Dynamic in his activity

At one point during his ministry, Jesus was persecuted by the Jews because he had healed on their Sabbath, the day when they celebrated God's rest after he had finished the work of creation. In response, Jesus taught that God was always at work, even into the present. He described the Father and himself as workers (John 5:16–17).

That God is a worker is evident from our first introduction to him in the Bible. From the very beginning, we see him in action. With method and progression, he establishes the universe and, within it, an earthly cradle suitable for human life. As he completes each successive phase of his enterprise, he inspects his achievements and celebrates their conformity to his intentions by declaring them to be "good."

But God's involvement with his creation did not stop with its making. In fact, just as the universe came into being by the power of his word, it is now held together and supported by that same word of power (Col. 1:17; Heb. 1:3). Even when humans strayed away from God's creational intentions, God continued to love the world. He sought people who would turn to him; he nurtured and guided them, comforted them, and answered their prayers. Most of the historical books of the Old Testament and particularly the Psalms describe God's continued involvement with the lives of humans.

In Jesus Christ, God made himself supremely available in person among humans in order to reclaim a world that had become infiltrated with evil and death. To this day, God is at work not only in sustaining the physical world so that it will not self-destruct, but also in calling to himself people who desire to become part of the new creation that God is bringing out of the old.

The doctrine of God as a dynamic being emphasizes God's presence and involvement with his creation. The God of the Bible is not a remote and aloof divinity who disappeared into infinity after creating the universe. He is not an impersonal first cause or an unmoved mover of the universe, untouched by its plight once he gave it life. He is one who sustains his creation and abides with it in order to fulfill his purposes for it. This doctrine of the continued presence of God and of his persistent interest in and love for his creation is called the "immanence" of God.

3. God is Absolute Goodness

So far in our discussion of the doctrine of God, we have discovered that the first chapters of the Bible lay out archetypal themes, or basic ideas, that are then developed throughout the Bible. This is equally true of the concept of the goodness of God as evidenced in his holiness and in his loving nature.

a. The holiness of God

Since holiness is not a quality commonly recognizable among humans, it remains shrouded in mystery. But when we realize that God existed before any form of evil ever occurred, we get a glimpse of the awesome and radiant splendor of this aspect of the divine being as pure righteousness.

The Bible teaches that God is holy by virtue of his transcendence. Moses, singing to the Lord, asked, "O LORD, who is like you—majestic in holiness?" (Ex. 15:11 NIV). Because of their remoteness, we view the starry skies and the snow-capped mountains as domains of dazzling purity, untouched by our earthly pollutions. Likewise, the infinite "otherness" of God points to a crystalline purity that is untainted by the deceits, the diseases, and the death that blight human life. God cannot be tempted to do evil because, by nature, he cannot deny himself and become untrue to his purity. But even if he were vulnerable to evil, his transcendence would shield him from it. He has no need to resort to evil devices, for he would gain nothing by entertaining devious thoughts or committing wicked actions. Because he is transcendent, majesty, power, and glory already belong to him.

Another way to express this concept is to say that holiness is an *ontological* attribute of God. *Ontology* pertains to being or existence. Earlier we discussed the person of God as a dynamic being—first within himself, and then in his actions. The first part of that discussion could have been entitled: "God, Ontologically Dynamic." Likewise, to say that God is ontologically holy means that God is holy in his essential nature, apart from any consideration of his actions.

The Bible also shows that God's holiness is reflected in his actions and in his relations with creation. The same Hebrew word that describes God as "good" (such as David's exclamation in Ps. 34:8, "O taste and see that the LORD is good!" RSV) appears repeatedly in the Genesis creation account to describe the goodness of his created works. Because God is good, what he creates is also good, reflective of his nature and made according to his standards of holiness. God is the author of everything good, and everything that is good reflects his holiness.

The Bible also presents God as the protector of that which is good. He values the goodness of his creation and seeks to preserve it. In his perfect creation lies a threat to the goodness he instilled within it. In Genesis 2:17, two jarring words suddenly appear: "evil" and "die." The realities defined by those words were not God's creation. They were the result of the abuse of God's creation. The ground rule for the preservation of the creatures' goodness was for them to respect the transcendence and the holiness of their Creator. To reject God's sovereignty over them and to assume it for themselves would destroy their goodness as the creatures they were intended to be. God knew that any attempt on the part of humans to act as if they were God would result in the loss of their original humanity. They would become something that God had not intended them to be.

Therefore, in his goodness God gave them a protection. In the middle of the garden, he planted the tree of warning against the menace of evil and death. The "tree of the knowledge of good and evil" must not be viewed as a trap set by God in the path of Adam and Eve to lure them, test them, and make them trip. Such actions would be worthy only of an evil god. In his holiness, the God of the Bible gave the tree to the humans as a gracious warning against the twin dangers of sin and death. The tree stood as a "No Trespassing" sign, as if God were saying, "Please, respect and protect the goodness of your humanity. Don't try to play God or to become like God. Only God is immune to evil. You creatures run the risk of losing your goodness by trying to assume for yourselves the sovereignty that belongs only to your Creator. Let God be God and you remain content to be humans. If you try to usurp God's sovereignty, you will be destroyed. You will cut yourself off from God, become dehumanized, and die." For humans to live within God's sovereignty was to live according to their intended nature, for that was how they were made. To rebel against God was to act against their nature and to lose the protection of God's goodness on them. The tree was intended to be a blessing, not a curse; a warning, not a trap.

The concepts of holiness and goodness that describe the personality of God and the nature of his actions are also used to characterize his law and commandments. "The law is holy, and the commandment is holy, righteous and good" (Rom. 7:12 NIV). The reason for such continuity between the goodness of God and the goodness of the law is twofold. First, the law reflects the goodness and the holiness of its author. But even more importantly for us, the law and the commandments were given to us for our good. Like the tree of warning in the garden, their intention is to protect us against evil and death. They are not testing devices intended to make us trip. On the contrary, they are given to make us live. Repeatedly God admonishes, "Keep my commandments and live" (for example, Deut. 30:16; Prov. 4:4; 7:2). Who can deny that it would be more beneficial for individuals and society to observe the Ten Commandments and the "greatest commandment" to love God supremely and our neighbor as ourselves, than to violate them?

Finally, the holiness of God is manifested not only in his being the author and the protector of that which is good, but also in being its restorer when that goodness was lost. In biblical history, no sooner was the Fall of humans consummated than God promised a Redeemer who would defeat the evil one (Gen. 3:15). Then follows the story of God drawing a community to himself through the death and resurrection of the Redeemer, a people made holy by the sanctifying ministry of the Holy Spirit. God's holiness is not an obstacle to his love for sinners; it is in fact the source of his love. He does not have to overcome a holy disgust at human sinfulness in order to show mercy. His holiness is the very goodness that causes the Holy One to change his fierce anger into forgiving love (Hos. 11:8-9). And at last, the promise of restoration ends with the vision of all things made new, as the redeemed multitude that no one can number, from every nation and from all tribes and peoples and tongues, joins the courts of eternity to sing "Holy, holy, holy" to the only true God who is three in one.

b. The giving love of God

Attempts are sometimes made to reduce the creation story of Genesis to a mere scientific statement on the origins of the universe. This constitutes an unfortunate misreading of the text. The Genesis account is a love story that describes God acting according to his deepest desire. Most of what the Bible contains after Genesis 2 is the story of God's reaction to human needs and emergencies. But those first two chapters show what God does naturally, according to his own inclination, when there is yet nothing in existence to which to react. What he does is to give and give and give—irresistibly, profusely, and inexhaustibly. A later text declares: "God so loved the world that he gave. . . ." The Genesis creation account could be summarized with the words, "God so loved that he gave the world."

The question is often raised as to why God created the universe. The answer is to be found in the doctrine of the absolute goodness of God expressed in his loving and giving nature. Because "God is love" (1 John 4:8, 16), he is also a giver. Love yearns to give. In fact, true love cannot stop giving; it gives compulsively and irrepressibly. When God does the giving, he does it lavishly on the scale of the universe. Like the Word that brings them into existence, the worlds of creation seem to flow from the very person of God.

In ancient pagan creation mythologies, the origin of the world is attributed to chaotic stories of conflict or cavorting between confused divinities, so that creation is the result of spite, violence, or lust. Not so in the Bible. There is only one God, and with progression, precision, and deliberation he constructs a universe infinitely diverse in its parts, yet unshakably coherent as a whole.

When he creates suns and stars, he does not gingerly scatter a few here and there; he spawns billions of them, enough to form a whole galaxy of light-year magnitude. And when he makes a galaxy out of those billions of stars, he is not content with hanging a few at the four corners of immensity; he sows hundreds of billions of those galaxies into the far reaches of the expanse of the universe.

Then, with infinite patience and attention to minute detail, he establishes a shining little planet uniquely suited for life. Out of the earth, he brings plants of all shapes and colors, with fruit and seed. Out of the waters, he brings forth swarms of living creatures that teem and multiply in the seas. Birds are let loose to fly through the sky. And by the power of his word, the earth brings forth multitudes of living creatures that walk and creep on land.

Finally, after giving the world, he gives himself—he gives his image in the fashioning of a man and a woman (Gen. 1:26–27). Next to the Son and the Spirit, it was the dearest gift he could ever make. He could not have gone higher or better. He entrusts his likeness to a form of clay drawn from the dust of the ground (Gen. 2:7), and humankind becomes the supreme object of God's love, his image for whom all things were created.

So, why did God create? Because it is his nature to create and because he is love. He gives because he loves. And because he has life, he loves to give life. The biblical statement "God is love" would make a suitable title for the cover of the whole Bible. But it applies pointedly and dramatically to the first two chapters of the Bible.

c. The servant love of God

By a strange paradox, the God of creation is presented in Genesis 1 and 2 in ways that suggest imperial and majestic authority on one hand, and the role of a servant meeting human needs on the other. Again, this servant aspect of the personality of God reaches deeply within the integrity of his essence as absolute goodness.

The Genesis story states that, after the heavens and the earth were finished, God rested on the seventh day from all the work he had done in creation. To say the least, this is an astounding idea. Why did God need to rest? Did he exhaust himself in creating the world? Does God get tired? Does he run out of energy? We humans need to rest periodically. But there is something demeaning if not contradictory about the transcendent and dynamic God of creation requiring rest as humans do.

The concept of God resting is all the more surprising since he is described creating the worlds through the power of his word without any seeming exertion—by remote control, as it were. In his sovereignty, God could have produced the finished result of creation in a split second, or in one day, or in six days, or in six billion years. To a transcendent God, time and energy are immaterial. Then, why a sabbath rest on the seventh day?

Predictably, Scripture provides answers to this question, but the answers are as surprising as the concept itself. First, God rested on the seventh day in the same manner as he expected the servants of the land to do so. The law required, "Six days do your work, but on the seventh day do not work, so that your ox and your donkey may rest and the slave born in your household, and the alien as well, may be refreshed" (Ex. 23:12 NIV). The sabbath rest of God provided the model and the incentive for lowly draft animals and insignificant servants to be allowed a one-day break from their labor every seventh day. If we should wonder why the Lord of creation would be concerned about rest for workers of the land, the Scriptures inform us that the cries of oppressed harvesters reach the ears of the Lord Almighty. Anticipating their need, God identified himself with their plight by providing an example that was to be followed for the well-being of his creatures.

Another explanation for the rest of God is provided in the fourth chapter of the letter to the Hebrews. In this passage the duration of the seventh day of creation is interpreted not as a twenty-four hour period but as an extended stretch of time that reaches through the ages into the present. According to this text, God's sabbath rest on the seventh day of creation that began from the foundation of the world (vv. 3–4) was still in effect during the time of Joshua (v. 8) and, later, during the time of David (v. 7). It remains open until today for the people of God who wish to join him in his sabbath rest (vv. 9–10). According to this New Testament interpretation of the Genesis account, the seventh day of rest was established not so much to benefit God as to provide an ever-present opportunity for seekers after God to find him and to enter into the security of his saving achievements. Through the extended Sabbath, God continually makes himself available to his needy creatures. We find here again the pattern of a servant God who seeks to fulfill the needs and the best interests of humans, the focus of his self-giving love.

The same attitude of servanthood is manifest in God's response to the rebellion of humans in the garden. On discovering the horrible mess that resulted from the Fall, a haughty and prideful god would have felt disgraced and rejected. In justified anger, he could have vaporized into oblivion the now sin-polluted garden and its occupants, or simply turned away from them in disgust and abandoned them to their desolation. But instead, God searched for them. He patiently drew out of them reluctant, halting confessions, and described for them the inevitable consequences of their downfall. He gave them the promise of a "posterity" who would bring deliverance to the human race, though at the cost of becoming "bruised" (Gen. 3:15)—thus anticipating the saving ministry of the Son of God, who was to claim that he had come not to be served but to serve and to give his life as a ransom (Mark 10:45). Finally, in order to protect the humans from living forever in their sinful condition, God prevented them from taking the fruit from the other tree, the Tree of Life, so that they would not irremediably confirm themselves into a fate worse than the death they had brought upon themselves. But certainly, the one single act that epitomizes God's servant attitude in this tragic chapter is described in one short, poignant sentence, every word of which is charged with redemptive drama: 'The LORD God made garments of skin for Adam and his wife and clothed them" (Gen. 3:21).

There is a sense in which the whole Bible, not just its beginning pages, tells the story of God's servant dealings with humankind as he does his utmost to reclaim the rebellious race. And what Jesus Christ revealed supremely by exemplifying it in his own person and ministry is that it is in the very nature of God to act as servant because of his absolute goodness.

III. THE PROBLEM OF EVIL

What we have discovered in this chapter regarding the biblical teachings about God has actually set us on a spectacular collision course with the realities of evil, sin, suffering, and death. The contradiction is massive and unavoidable. Simply stated, it goes like this: If God is great and good, why did he create a world in which there are evil, pain, and sorrow? God is a transcendent and dynamic being; this suggests that he has the ability to bring into existence a world as he wants it to be. God is also the author of good and as a divine being is incapable of doing evil or creating evil. These two factors brought together should guarantee the creation of an evil-proof world.

However, God creates human beings with the capacity to defy him, to scorn his warnings, to thwart his creational purposes, to plunge themselves and their environment into chaos, and to bring forth the twin pollutions of sin and death. As a result we live in a world where the innocent perish while the wicked gloat, where drunk drivers wipe out whole families and go unrestrained, where genocides and famines destroy entire populations, where violence is accepted as a problem-solver, where oppression finds no redress and torture gets its way, where the rich die of overeating and infants die of hunger, where diseases of the mind and of the body spread unchecked, and where the flagrant violation of the laws of God is applauded as the measure of success. Anyone who, in the throes of grief or disaster, has cried out to heaven with the question "Why?" understands the magnitude of the contradiction caused by the coexistence of God and evil.

1. Some Traditional Answers

Human beings in quest of meaning for their lives have tried to find answers to the contradictions of their existence. Most religious systems are attempts made at resolving the contradictions of good and evil, of pleasure and suffering, of life and death. This process of reflection has provided a number of tentative explanations for the problem of evil. A sampling follows.

(a) "We live in a random universe where things simply happen. Events, good or bad, are simply the results of the chance interplay between blind forces." As a popular bumper-sticker puts it irreverently but succinctly, "S–t happens." Although there is some truth to this theory, it fails to account for the obvious existence of premeditated and purposeful evil, nor does it explain the presence of intentional goodness in a supposedly random universe.

(b) "There is no evil. What seems to be evil is simply the absence of goodness." This simplistic explanation fails to account for the fact that many forms of evil are much more than the absence of something. They manifest the active presence of deliberate forces bent on inflicting pain and destruction.

(c) "Evil is an illusion, an aberration of our unlearned minds. All things are perfect as they are; evil has no objective existence. Appropriate attitudes and wholesome thought habits can rid us of what we think is evil." But as anyone who is afflicted with a terminal disease or any woman who has been raped at gunpoint can testify, evil is much more than something that happens in the human mind.

(d) "The evil that happens to us is justified because it is well deserved. It is moral requital for the wrong we all commit." This explanation is the cosmic equivalent of the ancient proverb that advises, "Beat your child once a day. If you don't know why, he does." It claims to be speaking for justice, but the abundance and randomness of evil do not guarantee that those who deserve suffering most receive it most.

(e) "Evil is the mistaken result of the creational activity of a finite, limited god who cannot keep up with his runaway creation. Since he cannot be everywhere, he is busy fixing a blunder in one place when trouble develops somewhere else." Of course, the prior question should be, "How can a finite god create a universe of virtually infinite magnitude?"

(f) "Suffering and death on the human scene are the result of a gigantic spiritual battle forever waged between two deities: one good, the other evil. We as humans, caught in the crunch, catch the fallout of this cosmic face-off." One of the problems with this theory (called "theistic dualism") is the presence of the universe itself. How could two rival gods locked in a to-the-death struggle cooperate to produce a coherent universe? If the good god is alone responsible for the creation of this vast universe, the prior destruction of the bad god would have been child's play compared to the creation of an achievement as colossal as the universe.

(g) "Evil is God's will." An airliner crashes, killing everyone aboard; a little girl is accidentally shot to death in a gun battle between rival drug gangs; a young mother dies of cancer; a soldier returns home in a body-bag. The cleric officiating at the funeral intones, "We have to accept this tragedy as the will of God." Such a person should be defrocked for uttering blasphemy and for attributing to a holy and loving God what the Bible defines as the evil work of Satan or the result of human blundering.

2. Some Biblical Answers

Because it is revelation from God, the Bible is not silent on a subject as crucial to the human condition as the problem of evil. Some of the explanations it provides are as follows:

(a) Very discreetly, almost reluctantly, the Bible allows us to peer into the existence of an order of created beings prior to humans. The New Testament calls them "principalities," "powers," "world rulers of this present darkness," "spiritual hosts of wickedness in the heavenly places" (Eph. 6:12, RSV). The Bible also intimates that although they had been created good, those beings, led by the chief angel Satan, experienced a rebellion similar to that of the humans in the Garden of Eden and suffered a fall that caused their separation from God. As one who had challenged God and boasted, "I will ascend to heaven . . . I will make myself like the Most High," the evil one found himself "fallen from heaven" and "cast down to the earth," even "brought down to the grave, to the depths of the pit" (Isa. 14:12–15 NIV). As a result, he became the "prince" or "ruler of this world" (John 12:31; 16:11; Eph. 2:2). He carries out his destructive work on earth because "he was a murderer from the beginning, not holding to the truth, for there is no truth in him. When he lies, he speaks his native language, for he is a liar and the father of lies" (John 8:44 NIV). He also "holds the power of death" (Heb. 2:14).

As the self-appointed "ruler of this world," Satan challenges the authority of God and attempts to usurp it at every turn. Right from the beginning, he was present in the garden under the cover of the "serpent," undermining the work of God and prompting the first humans to strive to "become like God"—as he himself had done and failed.

Thus, to some extent the Bible explains the emergence of evil in God's beautiful world with the account of the slithering intrusion of an outside influence, originally created good but become corrupt as a result of his arrogant grasping for equality with God. Consequently, he opposes God in this world, and God's will is not being done on earth as it is in heaven.

(b) The presence of evil in the world is also explained in Scripture as the result of humans abusing the freedom granted to them by God. Because they were made in his image, the first humans exercised freedom of the will. As God's image-bearers, they reflected his autonomy in that they could make their own decisions. The only limits that God had set for them were designed to protect them from the potential loss of that very freedom, knowing that with that loss they would jeopardize their true humanity. The Tree of the Knowledge of Good and Evil was intended to make them accountable for their decisions. Following the lead of Satan, these first humans challenged the sovereignty of God, just as each one of us does when we sin. Such a challenge constitutes the very essence of evil. Like our first ancestors in the garden, we too become responsible for the existence of evil as we defy or ignore God in our decisions. Human disobedience is a major hindrance to the will of God being done on earth as it is in heaven.

This ability of humans to defy God and reject his rule inevitably raises questions about the nature of God's sovereignty. How can the Bible affirm divine sovereignty when humans violate it at will? How can divine sovereignty and human free will coexist?

Humanly defined, sovereignty means control. In order to rule, an earthly sovereign has to be the person in charge and to impose his will on his subjects. They do not have freedom. The monarch or dictator controls a tightly held system of enforcements that prevents or punishes any infraction to his rule. He tolerates no dissent.

Too often, we project on God this kind of human sovereignty, reducing him to the dimensions of an extraterrestrial tyrant. We think that in order to have his way, God must make everything go his way. So we imagine him manipulating humans from behind the scenes in order to get them to execute his predetermined agenda. According to this view, humans may think they are acting freely, but they are actually executing a sinister puppet dance, with God pulling the strings from behind his transcendence.

Such a view of divine sovereignty is demeaning to the God revealed in Scripture. God is always greater than our highest conception of him, and his sovereignty has no common measure with our human practices of sovereignty. The Bible shows God's sovereignty to be of such magnitude that it is enough for him to decree his will and, without him having to lift even a finger to make it happen, history will inexorably end up where God wants it to arrive. In other words, God sets objectives and determines the outcome. But he does not have to control the *process* in order to reach the outcome. Despite all the crazy twists and turns of human events, despite the opposition and sometimes by means of the opposition, God's intentions for the world and for those who commit themselves to him will ultimately prevail. This is full-scale, transcendental sovereignty—not a simple projection on God of our petty, hands-on, controlling instincts.

The flexibility of that process allows room for the exercise of human free will within the framework of divine determination. The fact that God does not necessarily control the processes of history does not exclude his involvement in history whenever he deems it necessary or whenever he hears the prayers of his people. That is, God remains attuned to unfolding history. He yearns to hear from his children prayers that invite him to become involved in their concerns (Luke 11:5–13; 18:1–8). The Bible teaches much about the mystery and the power of the convergence of our human wills with his divine will, even to the extent that prayer can help influence the course of events in the world and in our lives.

Some biblical illustrations may help clarify our point. After the

Israelites had been held in bondage in Egypt for four centuries, God decided that they should be released from slavery and settle in the promised land of Canaan. He decreed his will for the people to be delivered, and he determined the outcome—reaching Canaan as their destination. Had God rigidly controlled the process, he could have efficiently led them across the Sinai Peninsula in just a few days. Instead, God moved in the background and allowed the people to do it their way. This process resulted in murmurings, backslidings, unbelief, idol-worship, repeated acts of rebellion, countless detours, and forty years of wandering in the desert. But eventually, the people got into the land, just as God had said they would.

In Jesus' teaching, God is compared to a master who assigns tasks to his servants and then absents himself (Matt. 13:24–30; 21:33–43; 24:45–51; 25:14–30; etc.). A human type of sovereign would remain on location and ride herd on the servants to make them accomplish his will. Not so in Jesus' teaching. God exercises sovereign detachment so that his earthly servants can assume their share of responsibility, although he will have the last word with the final execution of his decrees. Jesus himself made it clear that the evil one is allowed a free hand during the course of history; only "at the end of the age" will God bring under his dominion "everything that causes sin and all who do evil" (Matt. 13:24–30, 36–43).

The same conclusion was reached by long-suffering Job at the end of his lengthy discussion with his friends and with God. Because he was confusing divine sovereignty with control, Job kept blaming God for everything bad that was happening in the world (Job 9:4–24; 12:13–25; etc.) and especially to him (6:4; 16:7–17; 19:6–22; etc.). In his final answer to Job, God impressed upon him the truth that he remains sovereign in this world, despite the fact that unruliness and turmoil (chaps. 40–41) occur alongside structure and order (chaps. 38–39). Finally, a subdued Job acknowledged God's sovereignty while proffering: "No plan of yours can be thwarted" (42:2). This was his way of saying to God, "I know things are not the way I would like them to be. But I also know that you will have the last word in this matter." The process may be chaotic but the outcome is secure.

(c) Although God does not cause evil, the Bible teaches that he occasionally achieves positive results through it. According to Jesus, a terrible act of group murder and a natural disaster resulting from an earthquake were reminders for each one of the necessity to repent and escape a tragic destiny (Luke 13:1–5). Likewise, hardships should be interpreted as disciplinary training that produces increased maturity and development of character in God's children (Heb. 12:3–17) through the purging power of pain (1 Pet. 4:1). Even a persistent, lifelong affliction can become the means of producing greater dependency on God and of discovering the sufficiency of his grace (2 Cor. 12:7–10). The Bible teaches that, although God abhors evil, he sometimes utilizes it for beneficial purposes.

(d) The Bible also teaches that the ultimate value of the objectives God wants to achieve through history transcends the suffering that occurs in bringing them about. In other words, the desired ends are worth the painful process. The present sufferings pale into insignificance when compared to the value of the objectives that God is achieving through them. Even if the world is now caught in a state of bondage to the power of decay, it will be set free as its cosmic labor pains bring forth the new community of the children of God (Rom. 8:18–23). The present afflictions are preparing a state of glory that is beyond all comparison (2 Cor. 4:16–5:10).

Christ himself set the pattern. He endured the cross, discounting the shame of it because of the joy of redemption made available through it (Heb. 12:2–4). As his followers consider how Christ suffered, they do not give up in the face of their own suffering but accept it as ministry to Christ in order to share his glory. To suffer according to God's will is to exhibit both an attitude of acceptance in the face of hardship and one of confidence in God's ability to act as the faithful Creator. He will achieve his eternal purposes despite the interference caused by the adversary who prowls about like a roaring lion checking who can be destroyed. In due time, God will exalt those who have suffered during what is only a little while compared to the glory that will be theirs eternally (1 Pet. 4:12–5:10).

According to Scripture, there are two dimensions to God's sovereignty in relation to this world. On the one hand, he is sovereign *within* history over those who accept his sovereignty and submit to it. On the other, God is sovereign *over* history in determining its outcomes. Unfortunately, within these parameters, rebellious humans have the freedom to bring ruin on themselves and their environments whenever they refuse to submit to God's sovereignty.

3. The Heart of the Matter

As valuable as they are, these biblical answers do not go to the heart of the problem of evil. Each one carries an element of truth, but neither separately nor together do they resolve the dilemma of a holy God creating a world vulnerable to evil. They fail to address the issue of divine responsibility for the existence of evil. Undeniably, human abuse of God-given freedom opened the way for evil to appear in a world created good. But as shocking as it may sound, since it was God who had created the world into which evil would emerge, his responsibility is also involved. Had God not created the world, there would have been no evil. The real question is: Why did God proceed with creation, knowing that it would become ravaged with evil and that countless numbers of his creatures would doom themselves to eternal death? Or, put differently: Why did God create free will, knowing that it would become self-destructive?

Many sincere people cannot believe in God or in his goodness because he knowingly created a world that held the high risk of generating evil and inflicting unspeakable suffering upon itself. Perhaps a tragic story will help illustrate why they feel this way. A certain married couple have had six children, all of them institutionalized because of near total developmental disablement. After the birth of the second child, it became obvious that they made together a defective genetic combination that resulted in severely handicapped progeny. However, they persisted in having more children because of strict adherence to the teachings of their church against birth control. One cannot help wondering about the mentality of parents who kept on procreating grievously deformed children, while being aware of the risks involved with every new pregnancy. Likewise, many sincere people are skeptical about a God who created a world vulnerable to self-destruction.

So, while acknowledging the fact that human responsibility is definitely involved in the existence of evil, we must honestly face the issue that God bears his share of the responsibility for going ahead with the creation of a world that he knew to be corruptible. Fortunately, the Bible does not sidestep and ignore this formidable challenge. Two answers drawn from its teaching and relevant to this issue are outlined below.

The first answer has to do with the reason for creation. The accusation of cosmic sadism could be justifiably leveled at God if he had whimsically created a world with built-in corruptibility. However, as we discovered above, the world did not derive from a divine caprice, as if in the course of eternity, God had suddenly come upon the idea of creation and decided to put it into effect. Rather, we found that the disposition to create pertains to the very nature of God. Because he is love, God is by nature a giving God. When he gives, he is not content with giving galaxies, mountains and lakes, rocks and plants, fish, birds, and cattle. He irresistibly invests in his creation what is most precious to him: he gives himself by giving his own image. Because God cannot go against his own giving nature, he creates human beings endowed with the capacity to make decisions.

Thus, by grounding creation in the nature of God rather than in a decision of his will, Scripture suggests the inevitability of the formation of beings made in God's image and endowed at the same time with the freedom of making decisions. This very freedom that God granted to his image-bearers so that they would reflect his likeness held the potential for rivalry with God, rebellion, sin, and death. In other words, God neither willed evil nor did he create it. But because he by nature loves freedom and gives freedom, he was compelled by the necessity of who he is to give the very freedom that would turn against him and against itself. God is neither sadistic nor whimsical. Like a compulsive lover, he is outrageously giving to the point of creating beings whom he allows to function beyond his direct control.

The book of Job is the one book of the Bible that deals exclusively with the problem of evil. The bulk of the book serves to introduce us to God's concluding statements to Job as recorded in chapters 38–41. In this final answer, God describes for Job the magnificence, the diversity, and the complexity of his creation. He claims total ownership of creation in a series of questions directed at Job, and through him at all humankind, "Where were you when I laid the earth's foundation . . . while the morning stars sang together and all the angels shouted for joy?" (38:4–7), and, "Who then is able to stand against me? Who has a claim against me that I must pay? Everything under heaven belongs to me" (41:10b–11).

Despite his rights of ownership over creation, God acknowledges the presence in it of uncontrollable elements—such as the proud and wicked man who can be mastered only in the grave (40:11–13), the metaphorical behemoth that is so untamable that his Master can only approach him with his sword (40:19), and the leviathan representing wild forces loose in creation about whom God says, "Any hope of subduing him is false" (41:9 NIV). God seems to be saying to Job, "I know you are suffering because of the evil present in the world, but so am I. We're in this together." In one of the most profound passages of Scripture, God throws a challenge to Job as he struggles in his desperate attempt to understand the reason for his suffering. God dares him to go ahead and to play God. Let Job take upon himself glory and splendor, honor and majesty. Let Job contend with the evil represented by pride, the original cause of all evil. Can Job do it better than God? If you can, God seems to be saying, you are better than I am:

45

"Then I myself will admit to you that your own right hand can save you" (40:7–14).

This story highlights a basic truth found throughout the Bible: Having created free will, God had to cope with the consequences of his creation. His loving nature compelled him to make independent life possible, with the full knowledge that it had the power to turn against him. The making of the world and of humans was not a bad decision or a miscalculation on God's part, but a necessity imposed by his creative nature. In this sense and through no desire of his own, God also bears responsibility for the emergence of evil.

The second answer provided by Scripture to the startling concept of divine responsibility in regard to the existence of evil is that God, lovingly and servant-like, accepted that responsibility and assumed it upon himself. An arrogant and unholy god could have turned his back on a rebellious and corrupted planet, forsaking it to its self-destructive plight. But the same giving love that caused God to create the world also compelled him to save it. For God so loved the world that he gave his Son. God took it upon himself to enter the world—he became flesh and lived among us, full of grace and truth. The first Adam was made in the image of God and communicated sin and death to the human race. Christ, the new Adam, manifests the glory of God and communicates righteousness and life.

The God who created the freedom that would turn against him in pride and rebellion also took it upon himself to come into the world as a baby and to grow up as a servant, perfectly subjected to the Father and submitted to humans to the point of dying at their hand. The God who created beings who chose evil and brought into the world sin, suffering, and death, also took it upon himself to defeat sin through the righteousness of the Son, to bear our suffering on the cross, and to overcome death in the victory of the resurrection. At infinite cost to himself, God initiated a redemptive program that required his own identification with humans at their lowest point. As a result, God is able to offer those who submit to him access to new personhood in Christ, inclusion in God's new community, and deliverance from the eternal consequences of evil.

4. Summary Conclusion on the Problem of Evil

Evil appeared as the result of two forces:

—God's creative activity springing from his love;
—The freedom of his creatures wrongfully used to defy him.

The problem of evil is resolved in two initiatives:

—God's redemptive involvement climaxed in the crucifixion and resurrection of Christ;
—Human submission to God in repentance and faith as a reversal of the process that led to the Fall.

IV. CURRENT VIEWS OF GOD

The foregoing discussion on the nature of God has evoked something of the mystery and infinite greatness of the divine person. Because of this, our best and loftiest definitions of God remain puny attempts at describing in human words that which eludes human understanding. The very immensity of the concept of God precludes a comprehensive definition of him. It makes it impossible for different people to think exactly the same thing about God. Therefore, the insights people have about God are infinitely varied. But as we survey different approaches, some trends appear.

First, the God-denying positions—those of atheists and agnostics. Atheists believe that there is no God. They flatly reject the idea of a supernatural being and of a supernatural world existing beyond the physical realm of this material universe. Their position is well represented by the now-deceased Soviet Cosmonaut Yuri Gagarin who, in 1961, was the first man to orbit the earth in a space flight. On his return to earth, he mockingly claimed that he had gone to heaven and that there was no God there. Although his intent was to disparage belief in God, his observation was accurate. To make their claim with integrity, atheists should travel the length and breadth of this universe, check every planet, look under every rock, search the depths of the oceans, verify the spiritual as well as the physical realms, and then return to report that, having ransacked the entire universe, they have factually established that there is no God. In other words, only an omniscient person who has, for a fact, verified the nonexistence of God throughout the universe may honestly claim to be an atheist. This means that the only being qualified to claim that there is no God is God himself! Because of the comprehensiveness of his knowledge, he is the only person who could know for sure that he does not exist.

Agnostics are somewhat different from atheists in that they believe there may be a God, but they claim that the human mind cannot know for sure. In terms of intellectual integrity, this position is not much better than the preceding one. Agnostics should speak only for themselves about their inability to know

God. By what right do they universalize their incapacity to believe and deny the ability of someone else to know God? A much more acceptable form of agnosticism is that of the person who says, "At this point, I do not know whether there is a God." This statement expresses a wholesome, open-minded form of doubt that can receive the visitation of faith. This person does not speak for anyone else and does not preclude the possibility of faith in the future. Scripture teaches that only a narrow, chronic, cynical, close-minded form of doubt displeases God. But God is willing to reward with eventual faith the honest doubtings of a Thomas and of the "I believe, help my unbelief" variety of doubt.

God-affirming views. Those who affirm the existence of God often vacillate between an overemphasis on his transcendence or on his immanence. On one side are those for whom God is completely outside of this world. He is necessary as a first cause for the creation of this universe or as a force to keep it going, but he does so from a distance and has no personal or relational connection with the world. Several religious traditions suggest a divinity who is to be worshiped and feared but who will not get involved in the affairs of this world. The general term used to define such understandings of God is "deism."

On the other side are those who emphasize God's immanence, sometimes to the extent that the universe and all that exists within it constitute together the being of God. In this tradition are the religions, often influenced by Oriental belief systems, that claim an element of divinity to be present in each individual. Obviously, the so-called New Age religions fall in this category. The theological terms used to describe such beliefs are "pantheism," which means that God is the sum total of all that exists, and "panentheism," which means that all things are within the being of God as they ascend together into a state of emergence with the fullness of divinity.

The biblical view of God. This view affirms both his transcendence and his immanence. He is transcendent because he is Creator of all things and not part of them. His glory cannot be exchanged for that of mortal humans or other created beings. But he is also immanent because he intervenes in his creation to sustain it, to care for it, and to redeem it when his creatures reject him.

RESOURCES

For further study on the doctrine of God, see the following resources:

Alan F. Johnson and Robert E. Webber. *What Christians Believe: A Biblical and Historical Summary.* Grand Rapids: Zondervan, 1989, pp. 59–102.

John Boykin. *The Gospel of Coincidence: Is God in Control?* Grand Rapids: Zondervan, 1986.

Alister McGrath. *Understanding the Trinity.* Grand Rapids: Zondervan, 1991.

J. B. Phillipps. *Your God Is Too Small.* New York: Macmillan, 1964.

Philip Yancey. *Disappointment with God.* Grand Rapids: Zondervan, 1988.

DISCUSSION QUESTIONS

1. Can God's existence be proven to unbelievers?
2. How can we be sure that our idea of God is not a projection to infinity of our humanhood?
3. Can God limit his sovereignty without incurring its loss?
4. Can God change?
5. Does God really allow evil to happen when he could stop it?

The Doctrine of Christ

Outline of Chapter Three

I. Jesus, The Person
  1. His Physical Appearance
  2. His Personality
    a. Strength
    b. Sensitivity
    c. Simplicity

II. Christ In His Preexistence
  1. Christ, the Logos—John 1:1–18
  2. Christ in Kenosis—Philippians 2:6–11
  3. Christ, the Firstborn—Colossians 15–20

III. Christ In His Humiliation
  1. The Birth of Christ
    a. His identification with humans
    b. His uniqueness as Son of God
  2. The Baptism of Christ
    a. His identification with humans
    b. His uniqueness as Son of God
  3. The Ministry of Christ
    a. His identification with humans
    b. His uniqueness as Son of God
  4. The Death of Christ
    a. His identification with humans
    b. His uniqueness as Son of God

IV. Christ In His Exaltation
  1. Christ's Resurrection
    a. Passive evidence
    b. Positive evidence
    c. Evidence from the effects of Jesus' resurrection
  2. Christ's Ascension
  3. Christ's Session

V. Current Views on Christ

The Doctrine of Christ

The humble presence of Jesus Christ towers over the jagged skyline of human history. Through the ages, visionaries have come and gone, strong men and heroes have immortalized themselves into the memory of the race, sages and seers have lifted the human spirit toward its Maker, thinkers have plumbed the depths of the mysteries of existence, crusaders and conquerors have created kingdoms and destroyed them, saints and martyrs have sacrificed their lives for noble causes, but no other man has ever accomplished so much in so little time to affect the course of the world as Jesus of Nazareth. He is at the center of human history.

In this chapter, we will attempt to discover from Scripture who this Jesus Christ is. We will survey the doctrine of Christ according to the outline provided in Philippians 2:6–11. This passage begins with references to Christ's divine status, before he came to earth (v. 6); we will call this phase of our survey "Christ's Preexistence." Then the text goes on to describe how Christ humbled himself in obedience and death (vv. 7–8); this section will be discussed as "Christ's Humiliation." Finally, the passage deals with Christ's reinstatement in glory (vv. 9–10); accordingly, we will finish with "Christ's Exaltation."

As useful and as biblical as this approach may be, it presents one major flaw. It risks reducing the wonder of who Jesus is to the dry formulations of a doctrine. While such a doctrinal study is necessary, the subject of Christ's person and mission may be treated from a purely academic perspective with little appreciation for him as the living Savior. The Bible claims that Jesus is the same yesterday, today, and forever (Heb. 13:8). Therefore, he is much more than a doctrine, and he is infinitely more definable than the fuzzy, shiny, benevolent blur suggested by some of the teaching and worship of the church today. The Bible teaches that the resurrected and glorified Lord in heaven is also the carpenter of Nazareth, an individual who had full human identity and definable personality traits. Thus, before engaging in a doctrinal study of

Christ, we will attempt to define from the historical record of the Gospels who Jesus was, what he looked like, and what he was like.

I. JESUS, THE PERSON

1. His Physical Appearance

The ancient Greeks and Romans left statues and images depicting their great leaders, but not so with the Jews, for it was against their religion. The fear of falling into idolatry prevented them from making any graphic representations of persons. Therefore, what we can know about the physical appearance of Jesus has to be gleaned from information relative to his background and activities.

Jesus was born of a peasant Jewish woman of humble origins. From the outset of his life, he was under the threat of unusual dangers. Shortly before his birth, obscure forces in faraway imperial Rome imposed an edict that drove his mother and stepfather on the dusty southern trek. When Mary's labor pains began, there were only shuttered doors, suspicious glances, and stony faces. A hastily found shelter for cattle was the only place available, and the feeder served as a crib. Amazingly, the child survived, but only to face a danger even more deadly: the blood-splattering fury of a king gone mad. In a breathless rush of anguished panic, the parents made it across the border through the shadows of the night and, suddenly, they had become Palestinian refugees in the land of Egypt.

While Jesus was still a toddler, his family returned to Galilee and settled again in the quiet mountain village of Nazareth. There he grew up among the local youths. From all evidence, he developed normally and got along well with the young people of his own age (Luke 2:40, 52). He spoke like them, played with them, went to school with them, and when he grew into a man, he was one of them. They called him "the Galilean." This easy integration into a fairly typical population suggests that he blended naturally in his social environment, not much different from the average man of his race. It would be almost impossible to know what that meant today except that some enclaves of Jewish population have survived in the Middle East until the twentieth century. These are the Oriental Jews from among the Sephardim. It may be assumed that their appearance is fairly representative of what an average Jew looked like two thousand years ago. If Jesus looked like one of them, he would have been a man of short stature by American standards, with a swarthy complexion, thick black hair, deep-set brown eyes, a sharp salient nose, and strong facial features.

By trade he was a carpenter, which in those days was essentially an outdoors job. It required physical strength and multiple skills such as masonry, stonework, timberwork, and woodwork. Undoubtedly, Jesus' hands had become thick and calloused by the use of heavy materials and rough tools. Since he was a manual worker, he probably had the physique of a laborer with broad shoulders and strong arms. His face was tanned and furrowed by exposure to sun and wind, strain and pain.

Although the Gospels contain no description of Jesus' appearance, they confirm the impression of a physically strong person. They report the responses of other people to his presence. By noting those responses we can imagine him as if he were reflected in their eyes. A few examples will illustrate this method for discovering Jesus through the impression he made on others.

At an important time during his ministry, Jesus gathered the disciples and asked them for a report on what was said about him among the people. The disciples' answers showed that he was identified in the popular mind with some of the most intense, overwhelming, and influential figures in their history—men such as Elijah, Jeremiah, and John the Baptist, prophets who had stood alone in the face of opposition when they had called the nation to repentance (Matt. 16:13–14).

On two occasions, one at the outset and the other at the end of his earthly ministry, Jesus entered the court of the temple in Jerusalem where a shameful racket of sacrifice animals and money exchange was being conducted under the guise of religion and the protection of a temple Mafia. Taking things in his own hands, Jesus boldly cleared the place, chasing the evildoers and scattering their goods without meeting any resistance. Evidently, his opponents thought it better to leave him the field than to stand in the path of his indignation (John 2:15 and Matt. 21:12).

Several times Jesus is described facing powerful opponents ready to kidnap him, arrest him, or kill him, and yet unable to do him any harm. He either intimidated them into powerlessness or simply tore himself out of their hands and walked away when they tried to subdue him (for instance, John 5:18; 6:15; 7:30, 44; 8:59; 10:31, 39). Finally, when they came after him as a mob under the cover of darkness, his enemies did not recognize him at first. Then Jesus came out of the shadows and identified himself to them. When they suddenly saw him close, they panicked, drew back from him, and fell to the ground on each other in a reverse stampede (John 18:6). Only because he knew that his hour had come and he was ready to meet his destiny as the suffering Messiah were they able to arrest him and lead him away.

Popular art, educational materials, and especially dismal portrayals in Christian films often represent Jesus as a wimpy, slow-moving, long-haired dreamer, an anorexic blond model disguised as a guru with a beard and a sad face. Obviously, Jesus was much different. He was a forceful, intense, fast-moving man of action, who commended the respect of friend or foe by the sheer strength of his presence.

2. His Personality

Much more is available in the Gospel record on the personality of Jesus than on his appearance, since it contains an abundance of reports on his words, attitudes, emotions, and responses. Three traits of character stand out, summarized under the words strength, sensitivity, and simplicity.

a. Strength

A person may have great physical strength, even be a champion weight lifter, but if he or she does not have inner strength, that person is a weakling. Everything in the Gospels indicates that Jesus was not only physically strong but also that strength of character was a significant trait of his personality.

He was a strong person because he had a solid sense of his own identity. He knew who he was and felt comfortable with it. His acceptance of himself gave him the stability and the consistency that made him a reliable person on whom others could depend. He also knew what his life-objectives were. He had obviously pondered them since his youth when, at the age of twelve, he declared his commitment to the work of his Father. Despite threats and obstacles, he never swerved from that vision. And on the eve of his death he was praying, "Not what I want, but what you want."

From his strength, others were strengthened. His vitality sufficed for his own needs and flowed over into his teaching, his discipling, his healing ministry, and his works of compassion both to individuals and to the multitudes. For three years, he was constantly under pressure to meet the needs of others with only rare opportunities to be by himself. Often, there was no time to eat or to rest. Whenever he did manage to get away and enjoy some seclusion, the crowds would search for him, find him, and relentlessly press their demands upon him.

Yet Jesus met such pressures with adequacy and even good humor. He was never depicted as being on the verge of exhaustion or exasperation because of the crowds or the amount of work. Quite to the contrary, his most serious teachings are laced with imagery and parabolic exaggerations that convey his message—often with a chuckle. He loved to use object lessons and gave many in the form of practical contradictions, if not practical jokes. Having made sure that there would be an abundant supply of wine to brighten up the festivities of a wedding, he stood back and observed the surprise on the face of the master of ceremonies, who tasted quality vintage wine where there should have been only water. To exhausted disciples who urged him to get rid of the crowds, he said probably with a twinkle in his eyes, "You give them something to eat." The same disciples caught in a violent storm watched him sleep on a cushion in the stern of the sinking boat. When he woke up and quieted the storm, thus delivering them from sure death, he seemed surprised and asked the terrified disciples, "Why are you so afraid?" One can almost see him hide a smile as he nonchalantly brushes water off his sleeve. When the tax people got after him for some money, he sent Peter fishing to find it at the end of his line. And when they returned to the tomb to finish embalming his body, it was gone.

To live out a tragic destiny as Jesus did but to face it with peace and determination, to reach out ceaselessly to the needs of others in the midst of personal opposition and murderous conspiracies, to remain true to his mission and his principles when accommodation with the opposition would have guaranteed security and worldly success, to face the hardships of a life of service and self-sacrifice with joy and good humor, to communicate trust and confidence in the midst of confusion and corruption—all of these point to the greatness, the nobility, and the strength of Jesus' inner being.

b. Sensitivity

Strong people are those who get things done and find success. But they usually are insufferable. They go through life like steam-rollers, crushing everything and everyone in their path in order to reach their goals. Not so with Jesus. His personality presents the amazing combination of strength and sensitivity. Sensitivity is the ability to perceive the feelings of others and to identify with them. Sensitive persons are kind and considerate; they go out of their way to reach out to people in situations of need and pain.

As Jesus went about announcing publicly that the time had come when God was doing something new in the world, he came across many people who were struggling in hopeless situations. They were afflicted with diseases that made them blind or rotted their skin; they were paralyzed on stretchers in courtyards and on doorsteps; they were the abandoned and the hungry who begged for food on the streets; they were the women used, abused, and thrown out like trash; they were the small, unimportant people of the earth—widows and orphans, the lame and the halt, the disadvantaged and the disabled, the whores and the homeless, the despised rich and the despairing poor, those crying out their wail to an indifferent world and those pushing down their secret pain in the dark tunnels of the soul. Jesus saw each one of them. He felt their hurt, and on behalf of their God, he reached out to them with healing, comfort, forgiveness, and love.

There seemed to be within his being a homing device that detected without fail situations of distress, locked in on them, and drove him irresistibly to meet needs. This love-activated radar once zeroed in on a symbol of scorn and rejection staring at him yearningly from the safety of a tree, and he could not go until he brought salvation to the house of the publican Zacchaeus. The sorrow of a woman terminally afflicted with a secret hemorrhage fell within his range, and he uplifted her with healing and joy. The voiceless despair of a widow burying her only son screamed her pain into his consciousness, and he gave her back what she wanted the most and expected the least—her son. And during the fateful moments when he was himself dying on a cross for the sins and the hurts of all humans, he sensed the torment of his mother and the devastation of his beloved disciple. Heaving himself beyond his pain, he spoke to give her a son and him a mother.

This sensitivity to the plight of suffering people was nothing less than the love of God become human in order to weep with the brokenhearted, to embrace the untouchables, to communicate life to dead limbs, bodies, and souls, and to gather all the brokenness to himself and funnel it forever into hell through the lightning rod of the cross.

c. Simplicity

If strong people lack sensitivity, even more so they lack simplicity. Their power often makes them arrogant and unapproachable. It is easy for them to look down with contempt on those they consider weak and to treat them as disposable conveniences. The stronger they are, the more aloof and haughty they can become. As we consider Jesus, there is no trace of such pride in him or in his conduct. His presence could have easily been overwhelming, but he came as a humble and poor person. From the time of his birth, he identified himself with the lowly. As a baby, he slept in a stable. As an adult, he was a manual worker in an unknown village of a remote province of the Roman empire. During his ministry, he had no place to call his own. And when he

died, his killers unashamedly fought over the only earthly possessions he had claimed as his own: one set of clothes.

As a result, he was accessible to anyone who wanted to see him.
He never rejected anyone, regardless of his or her insignificance.
He was just as much at ease in the presence of the rulers, the
learned, and the powerful as he was with the small, the wretched,
and the racial outcasts of the day. Once, parents wanted to bring
children for him to bless. The disciples took it upon themselves to
act as bodyguards to protect him from wasting his time on the little
pests. But Jesus gave the disciples a scathing warning, announcing
that unless they became as humble as those very children they had
disdained, they would have no part in his purposes. Then he
stooped to the children, took them in his arms, loved them, and
blessed them as if they were the most important people in the
world.

Finally, to demonstrate humility to the disciples in a way they
would never forget, Jesus—fully aware that he was God, that God
had put all things under his power, and that he had come from God
and was returning to God—left the supper table around which
they had gathered, went into the back room, and returned dressed
as a slave. Then, acting as a slave among lowly men, he stooped to
the disciples' feet with a basin, washed them one by one, and dried
them with a towel. The supreme Lord became the lowest servant.

These are only three character traits of a vital, dynamic, multi-
faceted personality. There is no one among the readers of these
lines who cannot discover more of the richness of Jesus' personality by pondering the content of the four Gospels. And there is no
reader of these lines who does not need the friendship and the
closeness of Jesus. He is the same today as he was yesterday and as
he will be forever. He is just as powerful, yet as loving and humble
with those who seek him today as he was during the days when he
rubbed shoulders on this earth with people not much different
from ourselves. And he can be closer to you than your closest
friend.

II. CHRIST IN HIS PREEXISTENCE

At first glance, the word "preexistence" looks like a contradiction. How can anything exist before it does? Yet that word has
been used by theologians to refer to two beliefs about the person of
Christ. The first is that Christ existed eternally as a person within
the triune God prior to anything else, including the created
universe. The second meaning of "preexistence" is that this

eternal Christ is the same person who came into the world as the human being Jesus of Nazareth. In other words, Christ was preexistent to Jesus. This transition from the eternal Christ to the human person Jesus is called the "Incarnation" (meaning "to provide with body"), a convenient word that we shall use again. When God in Christ assumed human form, he became incarnate. To speak of the preexistent Christ, therefore, means that he existed prior to everything else and also that he existed prior to the Incarnation.

The Bible contains many explicit teachings concerning Christ's preexistence. We shall survey briefly three "Christological" statements (that is, statements pertaining to teachings about Christ) that deal with this doctrine.

1. Christ, the Logos—John 1:1–18

The repeated use of the term "Word" in John 1:1–18 may seem unusual to us. But at the time when John used it, it came enriched with meanings from two different traditions. The first tradition was that of the Old Testament, where "the Word of God" referred to an aspect of the divine being that had a life of its own. As already noted in the creation story, it was the word God spoke that brought the worlds into existence (Gen. 1). Later, when the prophets spoke, it was because the Word came to them, often like an unexpected visitor, and compelled them to give God's message. In other words, in the Old Testament the Word is God's agent whose function was to execute God's will.

Closer to New Testament times, in the Greek culture, the concept of the "word" (the "logos") was used to define the organizing principle that holds the universe together and gives it meaning. From a religious perspective, the logos was viewed as giving unity and coherence to all that exists.

The combination of those two traditions provided a starting point for John in John 1:1–18. He incorporated them in his use of "Logos," but he also reached far beyond them to make his use of the Logos a distinctly Christian concept. Some of the highlights of this "Logos passage" include the following truths:

- Verse 1a: As far as his existence is concerned, the Logos preceded the "beginning," that is, the beginning referred to in Genesis 1:1.
- Verses 1b, 2: The Logos was *with* God, meaning that he was distinct from God the Father.
- Verse 1c: But the Logos *was* God; he and God were united in a community of oneness.

- Verse 3: The Logos was the active agent responsible to bring into existence all that was created.
- Verses 4–5: The agent of creation was also the light, which means that he was also the agent of revelation. Like the Word of the Old Testament, he brought life (creation) and light (revelation) into the world. He brought to the world knowledge from God, like light in darkness.
- Verse 12: The agent of creation and of revelation also became the agent of redemption as he enabled believers to relate to God as their Father.
- Verse 14: Most significantly, the eternal Logos became flesh, taking upon himself the human condition. This transition or incarnation was the decisive moment of salvation history. The Logos became human and lived among humans as the only Son from the Father. The Logos and the Son are the same.
- Verse 17b: The Logos is Jesus Christ, the only source of grace (redemption) and of truth (revelation).
- Verses 12, 18: He is the only one who could bring us close to God and God close to us.

2. Christ in Kenosis—Philippians 2:6–11

The apostle Paul was writing to the Philippian Christians to encourage them to realize a community of oneness in their relationships by being humble and submitting to each other. In order to illustrate this teaching about mutual servanthood, he decided to cite Christ as the model. The sentence structure and the word cadence of this passage suggest that Paul was quoting the lyrics of an ancient Christian hymn that may have been used in the worship of the early churches. This text is called the "kenosis passage" (from the Greek word *kenosis*, meaning "empty"). In the Greek text, this word appears at the beginning of verse 7. The teachings of this text begin with references to Christ's preexistence and include the following truths:

- Verse 6a: Before coming in human form, Christ was "in the form of God" (NRSV), which in Greek meant that he was of the same essence or being as God.
- Verse 6b: He was equal with God. There were no differences of rank, power, or glory between the preexistent Son and God the Father (cf. John 5:18b).
- Verses 6b–8: In his preexistence, Christ was one with God the Father, enjoying the privileges derived from his equality with God. But he did not regard that equality as "something to be exploited" (verse 6c, NRSV) or "to be grasped" (NIV); that

is, he did not hold on to his equality with God. Because he was in the form of God and because it is in the nature of God to be servant, he emptied ("kenosised") himself. He did not lose his divine nature but he gave up the advantages of being divine; he stripped himself of the awesome manifestations of his divine nature. This kenosis or downward mobility took him through a series of "demotions" from the highest to the lowest:

- He let go of his equality with God
  - He emptied himself (the Kenosis)
    - He took the condition of a slave
      - He took human likeness (the Incarnation)
        - He became a real human being
          - He humbled himself
            - He became obedient
              - He became obedient to the point of death
                - He became obedient to the point of death on
                  a cross

With his death on the cross, Jesus died as a sentenced criminal, reaching the very bottom of the human condition. But because of his obedience to his redemptive task and because the Crucified One was God and equal with God, once his earthly mission was accomplished, he was reinstated in the glory of the preexistent state that he held prior to the descent in his Kenosis. His journey went from preexistent equality with God, all the way down to the cross and upward again, to share once more in full equality with God the name "Lord," that name that is above every name. The story of the exaltation of the glorified Christ is to be read from the bottom up:

                    - to the glory of God the Father
                  - that Jesus Christ is Lord
                - and every tongue confess
              - in heaven, on the earth and under the earth
            - every knee should bow
          - so that at the name of Jesus
        - that is above every name
      - and given him the name
    - God has highly exalted him

God the Father exalts the Son to the utmost and, in return, the Son's exaltation glorifies the Father supremely.

3. Christ, the Firstborn—Colossians 1:15–20

The thrust of this passage is to show that Christ is first in everything because he is the beginning of everything and the source for the existence of everything. He has chronological primacy over everything that exists, except for the Father, since the Son is the image of the invisible God. He is even the source for the existence of the invisible powers that were created to exist in a state of goodness (verse 16b and 2:10, where Christ is "head of," meaning "fountainhead of" rather than "head over," as in NIV), though they eventually revolted against him to become the satanic opposition that had to be conquered through the cross (2:15).

He is the "firstborn of," a title of dignity like "inheritor of" (1:15). But he is also the "firstborn from," a chronological indication of him as the beginning, the initiator, the first of the line (v. 18). To him belongs the double advantage of being "firstborn"—both as the heir and the owner of all things, and as the beginner of all things. He is also the final destination of all things. In other words, he is the beginning and the end, the Alpha and the Omega (cf. Rev. 1:8; 22:13). All things were created by him and for him (v. 16b).

The most obvious affirmation made in this beautiful statement of worship and praise to Christ is that since Christ is the beginning of all things, he has preexistence over all things. In everything, he holds "first place" (v. 18c NRSV). And yet, this preexistent Christ is also Jesus, the human being in whom the fullness of God lives (2:9) and who made peace through the blood of his cross (1:19–20). He is the source of our redemption and of the forgiveness of our sins (v. 14) because:

- Verses 15, 16b: He is the firstborn of all creation and is its rightful owner, since creation was made by him and for him.
- Verse 16: He is the source for the existence of all things.
- Verse 17: He is before all things and sustains everything.
- Verse 18: He supplies life to the body as the fountainhead of the church's existence (the same function of "head" as in 2:19).
- Verse 18b: He is the firstborn from the dead; that is, he began the resurrection process.
- Verse 18c: He is the one who has "first place in everything" (NRSV, rather than "supremacy" as in NIV).
- Verse 20: He is the one who reconciled all things to God through the blood of the cross.

The main emphasis of this text is the preexistence of Christ to everything because he is the source of everything.

III. CHRIST IN HIS HUMILIATION

Christ's humiliation is the process by which he, the creative source of all things, became human through his birth as a baby, eventually to die on the cross as the victim of his own creation. This process was described above as the Incarnation and Kenosis of Christ. In this section, it will be surveyed in the following order: Christ's birth, baptism, ministry, and death.

1. The Birth of Christ

Except for the accounts at the beginning of Matthew and Luke, the rest of the New Testament makes no explicit references to the miraculous birth of Christ. Of course, the great Christological statements surveyed in the previous section imply that an exceptional occurrence took place when the preexistent Word came in the likeness of a human being (Phil. 2:7) so that the fullness of God dwelt in him (Col. 1:19), but they do not refer to the *virgin birth* of Christ. Another veiled statement describes God as "head" of Christ, meaning the source of the life of the incarnate Son of God, just as Christ as creator of all things is the source of the life of man and through Adam's body is himself the source of woman's life (1 Cor. 11:3). At the most, those references suggest that when the time had fully come, God sent forth his preexistent Son to be born of a woman (Gal. 4:4), but they fall short of mentioning the miraculous nature of the birth of Christ.

Likewise, the Gospels of Mark and John make it clear that their authors assume knowledge of the story of Christ's birth on the part of their readers. The most reliable manuscripts of Mark begin with the affirmation that Jesus Christ is the Son of God (Mark 1:1). He was also insultingly called "the son of Mary" by people who took offense at him and wanted to call attention to the uncertainty of the identity of his earthly father (6:3). A similar parallel exists in the Gospel of John, where the Word become flesh manifested himself as the only Son from the Father (John 1:14), but where opponents of Jesus accused him of having been born of fornication like a Samaritan (8:41, 48). Obviously, the story of the miraculous birth of Jesus was widely known, despite its being surrounded with discretion in all the writings of the New Testament except for Matthew and Luke.

The fact that other events of Jesus' life, especially his death and resurrection, are mentioned numerous times makes it appear all the more strange that references to his birth are so scant. Critics of biblical Christianity have had a field day arguing that the sparseness of New Testament references to the virgin birth proves it to be a legend added to a growing body of mythical traditions about Jesus.

It is important to note, however, that the two Gospels that do carry the story of the virgin birth are explicit and clear and, although presented from different perspectives, they agree about its central affirmation that the conception of the child Jesus in the womb of the virgin Mary occurred through the miraculous intervention of the Holy Spirit. According to Matthew, the angel revealed to Joseph that his fiancée, the young virgin Mary, was found to be with child through the Holy Spirit: "that which is conceived in her is from the Holy Spirit" (Matt. 1:18, 20 RSV). According to Luke, the news was broken to Mary in similar terms when she remarked that she was still a virgin: "The Holy Spirit will come upon you, and the power of the Most High will overshadow you; therefore the child to be born will be called holy, the Son of God" (1:35 RSV).

The significance of the virgin birth (or, more accurately, the virginal conception) of Christ is twofold. It demonstrates Christ's complete identification with the human race and his uniqueness as the Son of God.

a. His identification with humans

When the preexistent Christ took on human form, he did not become two persons in one being; he remained an undivided person. But, having already the divine nature, he also assumed a human nature. The evidence for his full participation in humanity reaches back even before the time of his birth to his ancestral roots. Both Gospels with birth narratives contain a family tree (or genealogy) of Jesus through his birth by Mary as well as through the lineage of his adoptive stepfather Joseph.

The genealogy in Matthew is a perfectly structured family tree in the best tradition of the time—except for one detail. In an otherwise all-male listing, it makes reference to four women of Old Testament times—all of them considered Gentiles and burdened with a doubtful past or victims of male injustice (Tamar, Rahab, Ruth, Bathsheba). Matthew's inclusion of these four Gentile women shows Christ's complete identification, even before his birth, with all sinners, men and women, Jews and Gentiles, to whom he came to offer salvation. Whereas the genealogy in Matthew goes back to Abraham, the father of the Jewish race, the genealogy in Luke traces Jesus' ancestry all the way back through

Abraham to Adam, the father of the whole human race to which he came to minister. In both Gospels, the structure of the genealogies of Jesus is intended to show that, although Jesus was born a Jew, he came into the world to minister to the whole human race and that as Savior he belongs to anyone who responds to him in faith.

The conception of the child Jesus was exceptional in that it occurred miraculously without the agency of male impregnation. But the pregnancy and the actual birth were no different than for any other human. Although he was the Son of God, the baby made his way into the world through the birth canal of a woman in labor. And when he came into the world, his life was as vulnerable to danger as that of any other baby. He had to be bundled up in swaddling bands, according to the custom of the day. He was nursed by his mother and had to be protected from the evil designs of the king of the land by his stepfather Joseph (Matt. 2). He came among humans as one of them, sharing totally in their human condition from the very beginning of his earthly life.

b. His uniqueness as Son of God

While he was a participant in the fullness of humanity, there was also another dimension to Jesus' personhood. Because he had been conceived miraculously by the activity of the Spirit of God, the preexistent second person of the Trinity (the Son of God) was fully present in Jesus. When both God and man were joined together in Jesus, God was finally able to break into the human scene for the purpose of redemption. It is difficult to imagine how else God could have brought divinity into the world without destroying the world or without defacing divinity.

Because of the supernatural dimensions of Christ's birth, there were supernatural manifestations that accompanied it. Several angelic visitations prepared for and announced the birth; there was the star in the sky, the angel's celebration and the announcement to the shepherds, the visit of the wise men from the East with their royal offerings, the prophecies of Simeon and Anna, and the divine warnings about the evil designs of Herod the Great. This explosion of divine activity signaled the turning of history, when the divine Redeemer made his humble entrance among humans as a human.

The main teaching conveyed by the virgin birth of Christ is that he was both truly divine and truly human. There were not two separate persons in him, like a case of multiple personalities. Nor were the divine and the human natures combined in a fifty/fifty arrangement, as if he were half-divine and half-human. He integrated both the human and the divine in such a way as to be *fully* human and *fully* divine. Anything less would have made it impossible for God to identify himself with humans in order to save them from their sinful condition. He partook of our nature in order to minister to our greatest need (Heb. 2:14–15).

2. The Baptism of Christ

The boy Jesus grew up in Nazareth of Galilee, a city that, due to its geographic location, was a multicultural environment. Although the population of the area was mostly Jewish, there were also Gentiles living among them. Roman soldiers were stationed in Galilee since its people were prone to revolt against them. Jesus lived among all those people, surrounded by brothers and sisters (Mark 6:3) and working at his trade until he became thirty years old. At that age, he left Nazareth and came to the Jordan River to be baptized by John (Mark 1:9).

John the Baptist was an old-style prophet who preached like a revivalist. The gist of his message was that the people of Israel had strayed so far from God's purposes that they had become like Gentiles and could claim no racial privilege (Luke 3:7–9). In order to have a part in the coming kingdom, they would have to repent and receive baptism, just like any Gentile who wanted to convert to Judaism. Since John's baptism was obviously for sinners, why did Jesus want to receive it? Our model of identification and uniqueness provides the answer to this question.

a. His identification with humans

Jesus needed neither repentance nor baptism as a sign of his readiness for the coming of the kingdom. He was the one who was bringing the kingdom, God's decisive solution for the problem of evil. But by being baptized with sinners, he declared that he was casting his lot with them; he was taking his place among them in order to minister to them. This public identification of Jesus with sinners at the outset of his ministry was a foreshadowing of the cross when, at the close of his ministry, that identification would become total. In this sense, Christ's baptism was a preview of his crucifixion. Jesus himself understood the relation between his baptism and his death in this manner. Several times after his baptism, he referred to his expected death as another baptism (Mark 10:38–39; Luke 12:50).

b. His uniqueness as Son of God

Jesus' baptism also provided the occasion to make it clear that he was no ordinary sinner seeking forgiveness. Two incidents took place that revealed the uniqueness of Christ.

When Jesus presented himself to John as a candidate for

baptism, John flatly refused to administer baptism to him (Matt. 3:14–15). John correctly perceived that Jesus was different from the rest of his followers and recognized him as the future sin-bearer for all humankind by calling him "the Lamb of God who takes away the sin of the world" (John 1:29). John finally consented to baptize him only after Jesus convinced him that this was the way to accomplish God's will.

Then, as Jesus was being baptized, God, in the fullness of the Trinity, became perceptive to human senses. A voice as of the Father's recognized Jesus as his Son, while the Holy Spirit came upon him in the manner of a dove. Thus, at the beginning of his ministry of humiliation, Jesus received approval of himself and his ministry from the Father. At the same time, John the Baptist and the people who witnessed the baptism received an impressive confirmation of the divine nature and uniqueness of Jesus.

3. The Ministry of Christ

One might expect that the Son of God coming into a sinful world would accuse and condemn it. Instead, he came to serve and to save. During three years, he ceaselessly dispensed the love of God. He taught the disciples and shaped them into the nucleus of a group of followers who would eventually become the new community. He also prepared them for the climactic outcome of his ministry—his death and resurrection. The eternal Word who had given the world to God in creation was now giving himself to the world in redemption on behalf of God.

a. His identification with humans

Not only did Christ assume human nature but he also became a servant among humans. He devoted himself to meet the needs of others—precisely what a servant does. In his own words, bor-rowed from the predictions of the ancient prophet, he described himself as preaching good news to the poor, releasing captives, giving sight to the blind, setting free the oppressed, and proclaim-ing God's acceptance of sinners (Luke 4:18–19). Even more pointedly, he declared that he had come into this world not to be served, which would have been his legitimate right, but to serve and to give his life for many (Mark 10:45). Some years later, the apostle Paul affirmed that Christ became a servant to the people, thus expressing the true nature of God (Rom. 15:8).

The Incarnation also required that Jesus Christ be servant to the Father. While performing the task of redemption, Jesus became obedient (Rom. 5:19; Phil. 2:8; Heb. 5:8 summarize this theme). He sought to do not his will but the Father's will (Matt. 26:39; John

4:34; 6:38; 10:18). He did nothing on his own authority but spoke as the Father had taught him (John 8:28). And as a human being during the time of his humiliation, Jesus acknowledged that the Father was greater than he was (John 14:28).

The tasks of the incarnate Son of God required him to be subject to the Father from the time of his birth until the end of all things. The last task the Son will accomplish as Redeemer is delivering the kingdom to the Father (1 Cor. 15:24). Even in so doing, Christ will be acting as servant to the very end. As he subjects all things to God, Christ will also subject himself to God one last time in order to achieve the goal of redemption for God to be all in all and thus to give ultimate oneness to his redeemed creation (1 Cor. 15:28).

In summary, therefore, Christ was servant to both God and humans without being subordinate to either God or humans. He was servant to God, but equal with him; he was servant to humans, but Lord over them.

b. His uniqueness as Son of God

Christ's servant disposition was not just an expression of his humanity. It is in the very nature of God to be servant. God is love. Biblically defined, love is not emotions or feelings but self-giving deeds and acts of servanthood. Therefore, it was inevitable for the Son of God to minister as servant. The miracles he performed were the expression of divine transcendence at the service of human need. The Gospels report numerous miraculous interventions of Jesus when, in order to bring divine deliverance to desperate situations, he reversed, suspended, or accelerated the laws of nature and caused God's power to bear directly on human needs.

According to the Gospels, Christ's miracles were motivated by compassion in the presence of human need. But even more importantly, the miracles demonstrated the Father's unique commitment to the Son. If the Son acted as servant to humans and to God, the Father likewise acted as servant to the Son, making himself available to the Son. In deference to the Son, the Father had committed all things to him (Matt. 11:27), so that all authority in heaven and on earth belonged to the Son (28:18) As a result, when Jesus was performing miracles, it was the "finger of God" that was working at his behest (Luke 11:20).

According to the Gospel of John, because the Father loves the Son, he has given all things into his hands (3:35; 13:3), so that all that belongs to the Father belongs also to the Son (16:15), including the people whom the Father had given him (17:6). Just as the Father has life in himself, he also granted the Son to have life in himself (5:26). The Father does not judge; he has given to the Son the authority to judge (5:22, 27). The Son glorifies the Father and the Father glorifies the Son (17:1). There is, in other words, perfect reciprocity between Father and Son. The relationship between them is one of mutual giving and servanthood.

During Christ's ministry, it became obvious that despite his ministry of humiliation, Jesus was the only human being to enjoy a relationship of perfect mutuality between God and himself. Out of love, Jesus gave of himself without measure. Likewise out of love, the Father gave of himself without measure. The servant ministry of Christ cost both the Father and the Son dearly. They were in the work of redemption together, united through mutual servanthood within their community of oneness (John 10:30).

4. The Death of Christ

Death is a monstrous intruder in God's world, a savage contradiction of God's works, the ultimate violation of his creation. Because humans were made in the image of God, they should normally have been immortal just as God is. Even if death possibly existed in the Garden of Eden in relation to the ecological food chain, it should have never put its foul grip on human life. God's image should have remained as invulnerable to death as God himself is.

But even more tragically, the work of redemption required the death of the Son of God, the only one who did not deserve to die. His death was inevitable, having been predicted numerous times by the prophets of old; the Gospels make it clear that the death of Jesus was the expected climax of his whole ministry. Again the identification/uniqueness model will help us delve into some dimensions of the impenetrable mystery of the death of the God-man Jesus.

a. His identification with humans

From the outset of Jesus' ministry, it became clear to the people in power that he was too outspoken and too popular to go unchallenged. In the face of divine love and righteousness, an evil world system conspired to silence him. There were four power groups whose interaction with Jesus resulted in his death.

The *Pharisees* were members of a religious sect that represented the religious establishment of the land, official Judaism. They were the people of the Law. They believed that the salvation of Israel would come as the result of their perfect observance of the Law of the Old Testament. They were so eager to achieve perfect obedience to the Law that they kept adding to it a multitude of man-made rules intended to cover every aspect of human behavior. Eventually, all this man-made legislation became to them even more important than the God-authored Law of the Bible. Jesus mercilessly denounced the sham of this religion of forms and rituals (Matt. 23; Mark 7:1–8), and he rejected their attempts to control him (Mark 8:11–13). His refusal to go along with the Pharisees and their program made them decide to kill him. Jesus anticipated their move and predicted that they would rule themselves out of God's purposes so that the kingdom would be open to the new chosen people of God, the church (Matt. 21:33–46). Jesus identified himself with this new chosen people without reservation (Matt. 16:18–19; Luke 12:32).

The *Sadducees* were a political party that represented the interests of the priests, the officers, and the guardians of the temple. Because they were friendly with the Roman occupants of the land, they were influential and wealthy. Their power base among the people was derived from their control of the temple of Jerusalem, the central shrine for worship and for offering sacrifices. Throughout his ministry, Jesus maintained a negative attitude toward the temple system and the people of the temple. At the outset of his ministry, he raided the temple to chase away the racketeers who had turned religion into a business (John 2:13–17). He declared that the temple would become useless because his death would replace all the sacrifices that were offered there (John 2:19–22); worship in the temple would be replaced by a new approach to God (John 4:20–24). He also predicted that the temple would be terminally destroyed (Matt. 24:1–2). A few days before his crucifixion, Jesus entered the temple courtyard again and cleared it once more, declaring that it was being misused as the monopoly of one people although it had been intended to be "a house of prayer for all nations." As a result, the guardians of the temple decided that he should be destroyed (Mark 11:15–18). On his part, Jesus announced that both Jerusalem and the temple would be destroyed instead (Matt. 23:37–24:2). Jesus refused to identify himself with the temple because he identified himself with the whole world through his own death as the real sacrificial "Lamb of God" (John 1:29).

The *Zealots* were a secret guerrilla group of anti-Roman freedom fighters. They believed that by getting the people to start a revolt, they would force God to intervene and send them a warrior-king Messiah, who would chase the Romans from the land and establish his universal rule. Early in his ministry when he was tempted in the desert for forty days, Jesus faced the Zealot program as an alternative to his suffering servant Messiahship and he rejected it, because he considered it a satanic idea (Matt. 4:1–11). He knew that his mission required him to be a suffering servant rather than a conquering ruler. Therefore, he insisted that the kingdom of God would be a spiritual reality (Luke 17:20–21), not a kingdom of this world (John 18:36).

But the temptation for Jesus to achieve the kingdom according to the Zealot program was pressed upon him throughout his ministry (John 6:15). In the aftermath of the resurrection of Lazarus, the populace organized a noisy ticker-tape parade to acclaim his grand entrance into the capital city. In order to defuse any triumphalist expectations, Jesus carefully prepared his arrival and appeared riding a lowly donkey, like a humble man of peace (Luke 19:28–40).

It is possible that Judas Iscariot was a Zealot agent among the twelve disciples, stealing for the cause. Having become disillusioned by the pacifism of Jesus, he decided to take matters in his own hands and to place Jesus in a position where he would have to fight back and thus start the long-awaited revolt. Instead, when Jesus chose to obey his destiny as a suffering Messiah, Judas realized the extent of his miscalculation, threw the betrayal money in the temple, and killed himself (Matt. 26:47–56; 27:3–6). Jesus consistently refused to identify himself with the strong and the violent. Instead, he called the weary and the exhausted and identified with them and with their hurt, for he was gentle and humble in heart (Matt. 11:28–29).

The *Romans* were the rulers of the world of which Jesus was a part. For the people who lived in Palestine, the presence and the rule of the Romans were intolerable. But Jesus was careful not to appear anti-Roman. He acknowledged the presence of the Roman government and recognized their rights within the limits of their governmental function. But he also reminded the people that Rome could not take over that which belonged to God (Matt. 22:15–22). Jesus' acceptance of the Romans was not politically motivated. It had to do with the nature of his redemptive ministry. In historical sequence, salvation had first come to the Jews because they had received God's revelation before the Gentiles (John 4:22). But from the Jews, salvation was to spread to the whole world (John 4:42). When Jesus predicted his own death, he explained that through it he would draw all humans to himself (John 12:32–33). It was a bitter irony that a Roman official made the final decision to have him crucified (Matt. 27:22–26) and that another Roman recognized him as Son of God at the moment of his death (27:54).

While commending a Roman officer for his faith, Jesus taught that the new chosen people of God would be gathered not on the basis of race but of grace (Matt. 8:10–12). Unbelieving Jews would exclude themselves from the purposes of God while believing Gentiles would be brought in (11:20–24; 12:41–42). As a result, issues of race would become irrelevant in God's kingdom (Col. 3:11), and the members of the new community would all be the true children of Abraham regardless of their racial background (John 8:39–47; Gal. 3:6–9, 29; 4:21–31).

b. His uniqueness as Son of God

Had Jesus been an ordinary human being, the memory of his death would have been long forgotten. But his crucifixion is viewed as the turning point in history because of the divine identity of the One who was crucified. Both Jesus during his ministry and his followers after his resurrection interpreted his death in two ways: as a sacrifice and as a victory.

Sacrifices of several kinds were offered to God in old covenant times to secure his favor, forgiveness, or fellowship. The offering of the Passover lamb on the eve of Israel's escape from the bondage of Egypt had left its mark in the memory of the people as the symbol of their deliverance (Ex. 12:1–28). To the prophet Isaiah was revealed the idea of one sacrifice as the divine remedy for all sins. He predicted that God would provide an all-sufficient sacrifice in the person of God's righteous servant who would be led to the slaughter like a docile lamb in order to bear the sins of the guilty (Isa. 53).

At the outset of his ministry, Jesus was identified by John the Baptist as "the Lamb of God who takes away the sin of the world" (John 1:29). This statement predicted the purpose for the death of Christ by combining the two images from the Old Testament: the Passover lamb killed for the deliverance of the people (significantly, the decision to execute Jesus was made at the very moment when the slaughtering of the Passover lambs began in the Jerusalem temple; see John 19:14) and Isaiah's suffering servant who takes upon himself the sins of the people and bears them up like an innocent lamb.

As he pursued his ministry, Jesus was fully aware that it would be short and that it would end tragically. On three important occasions, he predicted his death as a victim of violence (Mark 8:31–32; 9:30–32; 10:32–34). He even explained the meaning of his death as the natural outcome of a ministry of servanthood: he would give his life as a ransom for the deliverance of many (Mark 10:45). He described himself as the Good Shepherd who lays down his life for his sheep (John 10:11). Evil men motivated by murderous designs would have no power over him since he could easily summon twelve legions of angels to fight and protect him (Matt. 26:53). But he had chosen to lay down his life of his own accord (John 10:17–18). Just as the blood of the Passover lamb had been the sign of salvation for the people of the old covenant, his blood, poured out for the forgiveness of sins, would be the sign of the new covenant for the new chosen people of God (Matt. 26:27–29).

This was precisely how the new community of his followers understood Jesus' death. They claimed that Christ, their Passover Lamb, had been sacrificed (1 Cor. 5:7), because he had died for their sins in accordance with Scripture (15:3). They compared the power of the blood of Christ that obtained eternal redemption for the people of the new covenant to the blood of bulls and goats that could not ultimately take away sins in the old covenant (Heb. 9:11–14; 10:4–9). They rejoiced in the fact that they were ransomed from the destructive effects of sin by "the precious blood of Christ, like that of a lamb without defect or blemish" (1 Pet. 1:18–19 NRSV). And they saw the Lamb who had been slaughtered now enthroned at the pinnacle of God's glory (Rev. 5:6, 9, 12).

The death of Christ is also defined in the New Testament as a preliminary victory over Satan in the agelong battle between God and evil, between life and death. During the time of his ministry, Christ had described his forthcoming death as an elevation, a "lifting up" that would enable him to become the giver of eternal life (John 3:14–15). His death would cause the "ruler of this world" to be conquered and all people to be drawn to him (12:31–33). In this light, Christ's death was the moment of his glorification (12:23–24; 13:31–32), a decisive battle in the confrontation between God and Satan. God in Christ entered Satan's territory and fought him with his own weapons. In Christ's mighty hands, the cross became a sword that he thrust in the vitals of the evil one (Col. 2:15), inflicting a wound that became mortal at his resurrection and that will have its terminal effect at his second coming. At the moment of his death, the temple desecrated itself when the curtain was torn from top to bottom, as it were by the finger of God, thus permitting direct human access to his presence. The earth shook and the rocks split under the impact of the clash between life and death. And energized by the victory of Christ in grappling with death, the bodies of his followers who had died during the time of his ministry came back to life at the moment of his death and, three days later, celebrated the resurrection of Christ with their own (Matt. 27:50–53).

This insight into the nature of Christ's death as a victory over death itself is explained in a deeply moving section of the letter to the Hebrews (2:10–18). In this passage, Jesus is presented as the point-man ("pioneer," "author") of human salvation. In order to achieve their salvation, he identified with humans by becoming one of them, even to the extent of calling them his brothers. Christ shared with them the human reality of being flesh and blood. Having himself suffered hardship, he became able to rescue them in their own suffering. He became human in every respect, even in that he tasted death for everyone. But because of his unique dignity as Son (1:2–3), his death accomplished a secret mission: through his death, he destroyed the devil who has the power of death and released all those who were held captive in the devil's stronghold through the fear of death. In a cosmic "capture the flag" commando-like operation, Jesus entered the territory of death, released the prisoners, and at the cost of his own life, destroyed the power of death. This was the end purpose of the humiliation of the Son of God.

IV. CHRIST IN HIS EXALTATION

From all evidence, the death of Jesus marked the end of his redemptive task; he had paid the penalty for human sin and accomplished his mission by crying out from the cross, "It is finished" (John 19:30). His body lay in the tomb but his spirit was in Paradise with the Father (Luke 23:43, 46). For all intents and purposes, the burial of Jesus could have signaled the end of the story of redemption.

Certainly, for us humans, death has become a normal component of life. As popular wisdom has it, "In this world, nothing is certain but death and taxes." Because we know that death is inevitable, we accept the horror of it—even joke about it. But for a sovereign and holy God, death is the supreme evil, the ultimate enemy. It is unacceptable and must be destroyed (1 Cor. 15:26). Because God abhors death, it was impossible for Christ to be held in its power (Acts 2:24).

During his ministry, Jesus could not allow death to remain unchecked. Every time he was confronted with death in its preliminary forms of disease or disablement, he was irresistibly attracted to the dreadful mess. In every instance, he demonstrated the supremacy of life over death by providing healing. He shivered and wept in the presence of death, returned to life a little girl and a young man who had just died, and even raised a man who had been dead for four days. His presence put death on the run.

As noted above, his redemptive mission required that he too

experience death. Death took a spectacular revenge on him. He lay in the tomb still and lifeless. It was the Sabbath. Nothing ever happened on the Sabbath; it was the day of a dying covenant. But early on the next day, the Lord's Day, in a mighty heave of life energized by the same power that had crackled the worlds into existence, he rose from the dead. The death of his Son had been unacceptable to God the Father. He could not tolerate it one more hour. On the first Easter Sunday, Jesus burst out of the tomb before sunrise.

However, the resurrection was not his final destination. He would yet ascend and be reinstated in the glory of his preexistence, "seated at the right hand of God." Therefore, in this section on the doctrine of Christ's exaltation we will survey his *resurrection, ascension,* and *session.*

1. Christ's Resurrection

Although the fact of the resurrection is well established in history, modern people find it difficult to believe. Because we live in a world where dead men don't rise, they think that commitment to belief in Christ's resurrection requires them to discard their brains. The event seems too extraordinary to be accepted as fact. Thus, they either reject it as unhistorical or attempt to explain it in spiritual terms only. They claim that Jesus' body did not return from the dead but that his spirit continued to be active in his community even after the tragic end of his life. According to this view, his followers misinterpreted his continued spiritual presence with them as a physical resurrection.

However, it is appropriate to ask who that person is who claims to have been raised from the dead. If the employees of the local grocery store announced that their produce man, who had just died and been buried, had come back to life after three days and was back on the job, the news might be received with skepticism. But Jesus was no ordinary person. He was the eternal Logos, the incarnate Son, the Author of life who had made it his personal mission to grapple with the powers of death and to conquer them. Given who Jesus was, it would have been astounding if something special had not occurred in connection with his death. As a matter of fact, his resurrection was only the beginning of a chain of supernatural events that took him to supreme glory. During his mission on earth, Jesus had predicted his death and resurrection on several occasions. It is unthinkable that his ministry could have ended in a grave. The resurrection was the natural outcome of his ministry and the appropriate expression of who he really was. Any obituary written on him was bound to become irrelevant by the time it went into print.

Another obstacle to faith in the resurrection is caused by the accounts of it. There are essentially five reports on Christ's resurrection and his post-resurrection appearances in the New Testament, one in each of the four Gospels and the other in 1 Corinthians 15. On the basis of the contents of those accounts it is difficult to outline in orderly fashion the details of the circumstances that surrounded that event. Who came to the tomb first? Who saw the risen Christ and in what sequence? How many angels were present? Where were they? What did they say? The differences in the accounts make it difficult to answer such questions to everyone's satisfaction. It would be too easy to shut our Bibles over those differences in the reports of the resurrection of Christ and to dismiss them. However, intellectual integrity requires that we probe further and raise the deeper questions.

On the basis of the Gospel record, it is undeniable that an explosive reversal took place on the first Easter morning. The smothering silence that insulates the domain of the dead from the world of the living was suddenly shattered. The resounding news that life had erupted among the dead threw the followers of Jesus into a delirium of hope. It is important to enter into their state of mind and to identify with their response as they were first confronted with the earth-shaking reality that Jesus was alive. The intensity of their experience must have made that morning pass before their eyes like a dazzling blur. The very differences that are pointed out in the reports of the resurrection reveal a state of euphoric upheaval among those followers. Overwhelmed by the powerful impact of an intensely emotional experience, they reported their involvement in subjective terms that are different from, but not necessarily contradictory to, each other. As a matter of fact, the very existence of those differences in the resurrection accounts vouches for their integrity. Had the resurrection been a made-up story, care would undoubtedly have been taken by its authors to check their versions with each other so as to say the same thing and not risk losing credibility.

Finally, it must be noted that all the accounts are emphatic in their agreement on the central fact of the resurrection of Jesus. Without hesitancy, they affirm this main truth: the same Jesus who had died on a cross came out of a grave and resumed his ministry among the disciples and other followers. They offer a massive amount of evidence that cannot be lightly dismissed. We shall survey briefly this evidence under the following categories.

a. Passive evidence

Passive evidence consists of the witness of lifeless objects. The body of Jesus was verified as dead by his executors. Since death was their business, it is unreasonable to theorize that Jesus was not really dead but that what was believed to be a resurrection was in reality a recovery from a comatose state.

The tomb was verified as being empty and no one, friend or foe, was ever able to locate a dead body for Jesus in order to disprove reports of his resurrection.

Ancient burial practices also strongly substantiate what we find in the Gospel of John. The body of Jesus had been wrapped, mummy-like, in burial bands, except for the head that had been temporarily covered with a simple piece of cloth. When Peter and an anonymous disciple, presumably John himself, rushed to the tomb, Peter went in and found the piece of cloth neatly folded and set apart while the rest of the wrappings lay undisturbed (John 20:6–7). Then the other disciple also went into the cave-like tomb, and what he saw produced instant faith in the resurrection (vv. 8–9). The text gives away the compelling evidence: John saw the cocoon-like wrappings that had contained the body of Jesus but with nothing in them, as if the body had vaporized through the shell. He knew immediately that only a supernatural power could have freed the body of Jesus from the burial bands without having torn them apart and scattered them on the floor of the tomb.

b. Positive evidence

Positive evidence has to do with the fact that Jesus appeared alive after his resurrection in a variety of circumstances—often unexpectedly, indoors as well as outdoors, morning and evening, to individuals, to small groups of people, to the Twelve, and sometimes to very large crowds during a limited period of forty days. These appearances provided eyewitnesses with ample opportunities to verify that they were dealing with the same Jesus. They recognized his wounds, his voice, and his touch. Some three decades after the resurrection, there was still a large number of people who could testify that they had seen Jesus alive after his resurrection (1 Cor. 15:6).

c. Evidence from the effects of Jesus' resurrection

Several profound changes were brought about by Jesus' resurrection that remain inexplicable without it. The first was the disciples' belief in the resurrection itself. At the death of Jesus, the disciples had scattered in a flurry of panic. Not only were they in no frame of mind to fabricate a resurrection story, but when Christ appeared alive among them for the first time, they were reluctant to accept the obvious evidence (Luke 24:36–43). Only the historical fact of the resurrection can explain the disciples' sudden belief in the resurrection.

The disciples also displayed a sudden about-face in their behavior. After the death of Jesus, they had resigned themselves to failure and had given up the dream that had been ignited among them by him. But upon rediscovering him alive, their hearts burned within them and they were ready to take on the world.

The disciples and other followers of Jesus quickly gathered in a new community, the church. It became a mighty movement of witness to his resurrection. Apart from an actual resurrection, there is no adequate explanation for the irresistible dynamic that resulted in the establishment and rapid growth of the community of the new chosen people of God.

Transformed beliefs and practices also vouch for the factuality of Jesus' resurrection. Religious traditions are among the most difficult to change. Yet the weekly observance of the Sabbath that had been held for centuries on the last day of the week as a kind of sacrament of the old covenant gave way to the weekly celebration of the resurrection on the first day of the week. Since Jesus had risen on the first day of the week (John 20:1, 19), Christians took the habit of gathering for worship on the same day (Acts 20:7; 1 Cor. 16:20). For this reason, the first day of the week came to be known as "the Lord's Day" (Rev. 1:10). However, Christians did not surround one particular day of the week with idolatrous exceptions as the Pharisees did for the Jewish Sabbath. It is not one special day that causes Christians to be worshipful, but rather what they do when they assemble for worship on any day set aside for that purpose (Rom. 14:5; Gal. 4:8–11; Col. 2:16–17).

As momentous as the event of Christ's resurrection was, its theological meaning is even more important for the Christian faith. First, the resurrection provides a brilliant confirmation of Jesus' teachings and of his claims. Because of it, the apostle Peter could stand in a public place just a few days after the resurrection and boldly declare, "This Jesus God raised up, and of that all of us are witnesses. . . . Therefore let the entire house of Israel know with certainty that God has made him both Lord and Messiah, this Jesus whom you crucified" (Acts 2:32, 36 NRSV). Jesus' resurrection proved that he was right in everything he had said and done during his earthly ministry.

Second, Christ's resurrection is the dynamic principle that makes available to believers the benefits of the redemption achieved on the cross. In other words, it released a new kind of life into the world. By dying on the cross, Christ obtained the forgiveness of sins; by returning to life, he became a "life-giving" agent (1 Cor. 15:45). Just as he was raised to new life from the dead, his followers may now walk in newness of life also (Rom. 6:4). God makes us alive in Christ through his resurrection (Eph. 2:5–6). The divine power that sparked new life in Jesus at the resurrection is exactly the same immense energy and limitless might of God that are at work in the lives of believers (1:19–20). So the resurrection is also a means of redemption. The new life that energized the dead body of Christ is also the power that energizes the dead souls of sinners who come to faith in him.

Finally, the resurrection of Christ is the first evidence of a victory that will become complete in the last day when those who have died in Christ will also rise to be gathered into the eternal community (John 5:25–29). In this light, his resurrection is to be considered a preview of the final resurrection (1 Cor. 15:20–23). It gives us a peek into the mystery of a mode of existence where life has permanently conquered death. After he assumed his resurrection body, Christ's range of action was not limited to this physical world. He had acquired properties that enabled him to move in and out of the spiritual world as well. He could be in a room with the disciples one moment and disappear into transcendence the next, while the doors were shut (Luke 24:31, 36; John 20:19, 26). The resurrection had done much more than bring his body to life; it had also caused a transformation that made his body relevant to the spiritual realm of God's existence. The Scripture teaches that he thus laid the pattern for our own resurrection state in eternity. Our bodies die "physical" but they will be raised "spiritual" (1 Cor. 15:44). This suggests that the final resurrection will involve more than dead bodies coming to life. The body connection will guarantee continuity between what we are now and what we shall be. But the final resurrection will also be a re-creation of who we are now into a new form of life suited for God's spiritual kingdom, a transformation of mortal "flesh and blood" into life eternal (1 Cor. 15:50).

2. Christ's Ascension

The resurrection of Christ should have marked the end of his earthly ministry. However, the record indicates that Jesus remained forty days longer among his followers (Acts 1:1–8). There were compelling reasons for Jesus to extend his ministry in this manner. Through several appearances, he confirmed the historical fact of his resurrection. He also used that time to do some follow-up teaching to prepare the disciples for the coming of the Holy Spirit and to commission them to their task of world outreach. At the end of this period of forty days, he led them to the place where he would depart from them (Luke 24:50–51).

The account of that departure is brief (Acts 1:1–11). Three features stand out in it. First, we are told that Jesus was lifted up from among the disciples. The one who had come from above to identify himself with humans was being elevated to his rightful position. His self-imposed Kenosis had caused him to descend into the most degrading humiliation. By a reverse process, he was now being exalted to the utmost glory.

Next, we read that a cloud took him out of their sight. Both in the Old and New Testaments, the cloud is often a theophanic element, that is, a sensory manifestation of the presence of God (for example, Ex. 13:21–22; Matt. 17:3). In this case, the Christ of the Incarnation was being formally reunited with the God of transcendence. His ascension was not some kind of space travel that transferred the physical body of Jesus from this earth to some remote extraterrestrial location; rather, it was the visible sign of Jesus' exaltation and return to the Godhead.

Finally, the promise of Christ's return given by divine messengers at the moment of his ascension was a reminder that his departure was not the end of the story of redemption. He would come again to give history its final consummation and to deliver the redeemed creation to the Father. His second coming will also be on the clouds of heaven, but this time with power and great glory (Matt. 24:30).

3. Christ's Session

The authors of the New Testament were convinced that the ascended Christ continued his redemptive ministry from his position of recovered glory. To describe this phase of the activity of Christ between his ascension and his second coming, they went back to the Old Testament and applied to Christ a concept that had first been expressed by King David in Psalm 110, the psalm most often quoted in the New Testament. This psalm begins with an invitation extended by God for the Messiah-King to sit on his throne in victory: "Sit at my right hand until I make your enemies a footstool for your feet" (Ps. 110:1 NIV). Early Christians read into this text an invitation extended by God to Christ to sit down at his right hand, that is, to the place of supreme preeminence. Theologians call this phase of the ministry of Christ the *session*, from a Latin word that means "to sit," or more specifically, "to sit for the purpose of conducting business" (as in, "This class is now in session.").

During his ministry, Jesus had used the same text messianically, that is, to show that the text applied to him as the Messiah (Matt. 22:41–46; 26:64). Therefore, after he ascended, it was natural for the disciples to use the same text in the same manner. Beginning with Peter's Pentecost sermon, Psalm 110:1 was used frequently to describe the present status of Christ (Acts 2:33–34; 1 Cor. 15:25; Eph. 1:20; Heb. 1:3, 13). The early Christians understood perfectly that God, being Spirit, does not have a right hand and that in transcendence, Christ does not need to sit down on anything. But the imagery was meaningful to them; their Savior was now supremely preeminent right next to the Father and he was victorious over evil, as if the enemy had been made to squirm under his foot.

The New Testament defines Christ's ministry during his session in terms of three functions. First, Christ is achieving cosmic victory by subduing all hostile forces in the universe (Eph. 1:20–21; Phil. 2:10; 1 Pet. 3:22). According to 1 Corinthians 15:24–28, this process of bringing all things under subjection will be completed only at the end of time, with the final resurrection. Although Christ is at the right hand of God, the completion of his redemptive work requires that he continue to remain subject as Son until the purpose of the Incarnation is thoroughly accomplished, God becomes all in all, and the ultimate oneness of redeemed creation is finalized (v. 28).

Second, during his session, Christ continues to function as mediator between God and humans. The same Christ who is qualified to be the go-between because he gave himself as a ransom for all (1 Tim. 2:5–6) is also the one who "is able for all time to save those who approach God through him, since he always lives to make intercession for them" (Heb. 7:25 NRSV). Fortunately, Christ's mediatorial ministry extends beyond saving the lost. He is also concerned with the need for continuing forgiveness of the ones already forgiven. He "is at God's right hand, and indeed pleads our cause" (Rom. 8:34 NEB), so that when we sin, "we have one who speaks to the Father in our defense—Jesus Christ, the Righteous One" (1 John 2:1 NIV).

Finally, and most importantly in terms of God's ultimate purposes, Christ now functions as "head" in regard to the church, God's eternal community. The word *head* is not used to indicate Christ's rulership in these contexts, since they emphasize Christ's servanthood to the church rather than his lordship over it. In his headship to the church, Christ gives it growth, cohesion, and fullness. "Primarily" or "above everything else," God has made Christ head to the church (Eph. 1:22), which means that, since the church is his body, the head supplies the body with the very fullness of God (Eph. 1:23; 4:15–16; Col. 2:19). Christ's motivation in this ministry of servanthood is that he wants "to present the church to himself in splendor, without a spot or wrinkle or anything of the kind" (Eph. 5:27 NRSV). He wants the church, his supreme and dearest achievement, to be perfect for eternity.

As committed as he was to his redemptive mission during his time on earth, Jesus yearned for his exaltation. Close to the time of his death, he prayed to the Father, "Glorify me in your own presence with the glory that I had in your presence before the world existed" (John 17:5 NRSV). During the time of his humiliation, the preexistent Christ was looking forward with joyful anticipation to his exaltation. "Therefore God exalted him to the highest place and gave him the name that is above every name, that at the name of Jesus every knee should bow, in heaven and on earth and under the earth, and every tongue confess that Jesus Christ is Lord, to the glory of God the Father" (Phil. 2:9–11 NIV).

V. CURRENT VIEWS ON CHRIST

No serious student of history denies the fact that the man Jesus lived in Palestine at the beginning of the first century of our era, that he incurred the opposition of the religious and political establishments of his day, and that he was put to death as a troublemaker after leaving a legacy of teachings that impacted deeply the community of followers that survived him.

Of course, Christians who accept the spiritual as well as the historical validity of the New Testament record find such a summary highly inadequate. For them, Christ was fully human as described in the preceding paragraph, but he also was fully God as proposed in the discussions of this chapter. The relationship between the divine and human natures of Christ poses a considerable problem of logic that Christians have been debating since the early centuries of the church. The present understanding of the relationship between the Father and the Son within the Trinity, as well as the connection between the two natures of Christ, were defined in a series of general gatherings of the church, of which the first four were the most significant.

- The Council of Nicea in A.D. 325 produced the Nicene Creed, affirming the essential oneness between the Father and the Son.

81

- The Council of Constantinople in 381 confirmed the Nicene Creed and clarified the relationship of the Holy Spirit to the Father and to the Son.
- The Council of Ephesus in 431 defined the unity of the two natures in Christ.
- The Council of Chalcedon in 451 produced the Chalcedonian Creed that defended the integrity of the two natures of Christ against teachings that would have minimized the human nature.

The work of those councils, and the Nicene and Chalcedonian Creeds in particular, have provided the basis for the traditional Roman Catholic and the classic Reformation Protestant doctrine of Christ. But in modern times, the view that Jesus was anything more than a man has been challenged. It was inevitable that a God-denying age would also deny the divinity of Christ. As a result, there are many people who believe that Jesus was an exceptional man, even an original visionary who set the course for new ways of thinking about life and about human relations. But they would consider any claim of Christ as having a divine nature a myth that was invented by the early church in order to explain supernaturally his impact on his contemporaries.

Other theologians have proposed the view that Christ was an exceptionally righteous man, a holy prophet uniquely sensitive to God's will. As a result, he was able to put humans in touch with God. According to this view, while the teachings of Jesus should be followed, he cannot himself be considered divine. At best, he spoke on behalf of God and showed us how to relate to him. On this basis, all kinds of movements have claimed Jesus as their instigator, many of them trying to identify Jesus as the champion of their cause, but with little concern for the broader ministry and saving significance of the life of Christ.

More subtle approaches try to maintain the uniqueness of Christ while denying the fullness of his divinity. This treatment of the doctrine of Christ is most characteristic in sects and cults. They would claim that God was active in Christ without Christ being fully God. He was God's first creation, or he was a mere mortal who was adopted as Son by God. But his humanity overshadows whatever element of divinity that may be recognized in him.

Such beliefs are not really new. They are revivals of ancient teachings that were designated as *subordinationism*, for they emphasized the difference between God and Christ rather than their equality. Today, some evangelical theologians claim that Christ was equal to the Father in his essential being, but that he is in functional subjection to him. While this distinction is valid in relation to Christ functioning on behalf of the Father as creator Logos and incarnate Redeemer, it cannot be applied to the eternal relationship between God and the preexistent Christ, since these functions began with Creation and will cease with the final consummation. Christ will remain in the subjection of a servant through the very end of his redemptive ministry (1 Cor. 15:28). It is true that during the creation/consummation interval Christ acts as servant to the Father. But he also acts as servant to humans (Mark 10:45; Rom. 15:8). In no way does this ministry of servanthood mean that Christ remains in subjection to humans or that he is in eternal subjection to the Father. Christ will maintain his servant function to God even after submitting the kingdom of God to the Father, until the ultimate goal of creation and redemption is achieved, when God becomes "all in all" (1 Cor. 15:24, 28). The principle of downward mobility is a dominant feature of the kingdom, where greatness is achieved through servanthood. It finds its origin in God's practice of it among the three persons of the Trinity.

Any teaching that minimizes Christ's dignity or his status of equality with the Father poses a threat to the very foundations of the Christian faith, since Christianity rests squarely on the premise that the salvation of the human race required that the Redeemer be nothing less than fully divine in every respect. The one sentence summary of the Evangelical Theological Society accurately declares, "God is a Trinity, Father, Son and Holy Spirit, each an uncreated person, one in essence, equal in power and glory."

RESOURCES

For further study on the doctrine of Christ, see the following resources:

Alan F. Johnson and Robert E. Webber. *What Christians Believe: A Biblical and Historical Summary.* Grand Rapids: Zondervan, 1989, pp. 103–47.

George E. Ladd. *I Believe in the Resurrection.* Grand Rapids: Eerdmans, 1975.

I. Howard Marshall. *I Believe in the Historical Jesus.* Grand Rapids, Eerdmans, 1977.

Alister McGrath. *Understanding Jesus.* Grand Rapids: Zondervan, 1990.

John R. W. Stott. *The Cross of Christ.* Downers Grove, Ill.: InterVarsity, 1986.

The Doctrine of the Holy Spirit

Outline of Chapter Four

I. The Coming of the Holy Spirit
   1. The Expectation of the Old Covenant
   2. The Fulfillment in the New Covenant
      a. Preparation for Pentecost
      b. The event of Pentecost
      c. The three extensions of Pentecost

II. The Ministries of the Holy Spirit
   1. The Ministry of the Holy Spirit to the World
      a. Convicts of sin
      b. Convicts of righteousness
      c. Convicts of judgment
   2. The Ministry of the Holy Spirit to the Church
      a. The teaching
      b. The fellowship
      c. The stewardship
   3. The Ministry of the Holy Spirit to the Individual
      a. Salvation
      b. Sanctification
      c. Service

III. Current Views on the Holy Spirit

The Doctrine of the Holy Spirit

When Dr. Dennis F. Kinlaw, president of Asbury College, was a young pastor in upstate New York, a successful businessman became a Christian under his ministry. Although the man's Christian experience was genuine, he had no knowledge of religious language, having come out of a completely secular background. As they were riding together one day, the man kept referring to "the Spook." The Spook had showed him this, and impressed him thus, and guided him that way. At first, Dr. Kinlaw was at a loss to understand what his friend was talking about. Finally, it dawned on him that this rock-hewn pagan now become Christian was referring in his stammering, unsophisticated ways to his experience of the Holy Spirit. Having committed his life to Christ, he had become aware of an indwelling presence that was reconstructing him from within. Not knowing the proper terminology, he was calling this presence "the Spook." Close enough!

This man's experience was really not much different from that of the first Christians. Before they had met Jesus, they already knew God. They had been instructed in the Scriptures, prayed regularly, and trusted God to meet their needs. When they became acquainted with Jesus, they were surprised to discover how much Jesus was like the God they already knew. The more closely they got to know Jesus, the more they felt compelled to identify him with God, until they became fully convinced that God and Christ were really one (John 20:28). After Jesus' departure, they felt his continuing presence within and among them in the form of the Holy Spirit. And the more they experienced the Holy Spirit, the more they became convinced that the Holy Spirit was like the God and Christ they already knew; consequently, they had no choice but to identify the Holy Spirit with God and Christ. The final result was a full conviction that God, Christ, and the Holy Spirit were truly one (see, for example, Rom. 15:30; 2 Cor. 13:14). They knew that the Son who had commissioned them was with them and that the Holy Spirit within them was as close to Christ as his own breath (John 20:21–22).

Nowhere in the Bible is there to be found a formal description of the Holy Spirit that would be equivalent to the great Christological texts that we surveyed in John 1, Philippians 2, and Colossians 1. This lack of formal definition does not mean that the Holy Spirit is to be viewed as an impersonal force or a mystical influence devoid of personality. On the contrary, the Holy Spirit is very much presented in Scripture as a personal being endowed with all the qualities of deity. But Scripture is generally reluctant to call attention to the person of the Holy Spirit apart from his work in performing ministry. Although references to him abound, especially in the New Testament, the Holy Spirit is never glorified as are the Father and the Son.

The reason for such restraint may be twofold. First, the Holy Spirit was the inspiring agent in the writing of Scripture (2 Pet. 1:21). As the divine author of Scripture, he may have been reticent to call undue attention to himself. Second and more importantly, the coming of the Holy Spirit represented the last phase of a process of increasing personalization of the Godhead to humans. The God of the old covenant made himself known essentially through the law and the prophets. Then, he became incarnate in the person of Jesus Christ; in him, God drew close to humans as he lived among them as one of them. But with the advent of the Holy Spirit, he came even closer as the indwelling presence of God within the community of believers and within the intimacy of their individual lives. Thus, the subjective nature of the experience of the Holy Spirit in human life may have hindered the formulation in Scripture of a detached, analytical description of the person of the Holy Spirit. In other words, the authors of the New Testament may have been too involved in their own experience of the Holy Spirit to be able to describe it objectively. For this reason, we shall conduct our analysis of the doctrine of the Holy Spirit by analyzing first the historical process of his coming and then the experience of the community of faith in his ministries.

I. THE COMING OF THE HOLY SPIRIT

1. The Expectation of the Old Covenant

At the very beginning of the Bible is a reference to the activity of the Spirit of God (Gen. 1:2). The Holy Spirit, however, was not at the forefront of the action during the time of the old covenant. He intervened sporadically and temporarily to enable select individuals to perform specific tasks, such as prophecy (Num. 11:24–30), craftsmanship (Ex. 31:2–3), and leadership (Judg. 3:10; 6:34; 11:29). Such visitations were functional, selective, and limited. There was no sense of the Spirit's continued residency among the people.

There was enough involvement of the Spirit in the old covenant, however, to create in the people's hearts a deep yearning for intimacy with God. The Old Testament contains various expressions of God's people aspiring for an intimate relationship with him that eluded them. Occasionally they had intimations of what personal relationship with deity would be like but not the fullness of it. Note King David's lament: "As a deer longs for flowing streams, so my soul longs for you, O God. My soul thirsts for God, for the living God. When shall I come and behold the face of God?" (Ps. 42:1–2 NRSV).

Peering into the future, the prophet Isaiah anticipated the coming of the Spirit in connection with that of the Messiah (Isa. 11:1–2; 42:1) and described the Spirit's visitation as a pouring out from heaven upon the people (32:15). The prophet Ezekiel compared the spiritual state of the people to a valley covered with scattered human bones. But he anticipated that the Spirit of God would come and raise the dead back to life: "I will put my Spirit in you and you will live" (Ezek. 37:14). And Zechariah reminded his people that God's designs were accomplished not by might nor by power but by his Spirit (Zech. 4:6). Such cries of yearning for the presence of the Spirit found their most dramatic expression in the exclamation of Isaiah, "O that you would tear open the heavens and come down" (Isa. 64:1 NRSV).

The decisive answer to the agelong plea for the bestowal of the Holy Spirit was finally given in a climactic prediction made by the prophet Joel when he solemnly promised on behalf of God:

> And afterward,
>   I will pour out my Spirit on all people.
> Your sons and daughters will prophesy,
>   your old men will dream dreams,
>   your young men will see visions.
> Even on my servants, both men and women,
>   I will pour out my Spirit in those days.
>
> (Joel 2:28–29 NIV)

At last God's people were assured that the Holy Spirit would be available, not selectively and fleetingly but abundantly and permanently, as if heaven's floodgates were to open and the Spirit were to flow inexhaustibly. When that occurred, the Spirit would be available to all people—not to just a few privileged leaders, not even to a privileged race, not to men only, but to all. And as a sign of the reality of the presence of the Spirit, both men and women would have access to the highest expression of ministry on behalf of God: they would prophesy. Both the old and the young would receive divine revelation, not just the patriarchs. The sheer comprehensiveness of the promise must have set Joel and his people dreaming about a reality they could not begin to imagine. Only its fulfillment at Pentecost would demonstrate the staggering dimensions of the visitation of the Spirit on all flesh.

2. The Fulfillment in the New Covenant

The prophet Joel uttered his momentous prediction, but nothing happened. He died. Even the children who had heard him grew old and died. The centuries rolled on, and still nothing happened. The expectation of the great outpouring lay dormant.

Then suddenly, some quiet stirrings. In a village of Galilee, the Spirit activated the womb of a virgin. Her cousin Elizabeth was filled with the Holy Spirit and called the virgin blessed. Zechariah the priest was filled with the Holy Spirit and prophesied. Then, as the miraculous infant was brought to the temple, the prophet Simeon, inspired by the Holy Spirit, took him in his arms and blessed God; at the very same hour the woman prophet Anna gave thanks for him who, one day, would stand in Nazareth and boldly proclaim, "The Spirit of the Lord is upon me." The floodgates of heaven were beginning to shake for the great outpouring of the Spirit.

a. Preparation for Pentecost

John the Baptizer appeared by the Jordan River preaching a baptism of repentance for the forgiveness of sins. As the multitudes came to him expecting a fulfillment from him, he pointed to Jesus and declared him to be the fulfiller: "I have baptized you with water; but he will baptize you with the Holy Spirit" (Mark 1:8 NRSV).

Joel had predicted the great outpouring of the Holy Spirit. John borrowed from Joel the imagery of fluidity, abundance, and outflow to describe the expected release of the Spirit in human life as a spiritual washing in the waters of the river. The predicted great *outpouring* of the Spirit was now defined as the great *baptism* of the Holy Spirit that would be released by Jesus, the Son of God.

As if to prove him right, Jesus came to be baptized a few days later. As he was coming out of the water, the Spirit alighted on him in the manner of a dove (Mark 1:10). In preparation for the great outpouring, the Holy Spirit had finally found a point of entry in the world. Like the dove in Noah's time (Gen. 8:8–12), the Spirit found in him a resting place from where he would soon pour out his newness into the world. John had recognized in Jesus the one designated by God to throw open the floodgates of the Spirit.

At a critical turn during his ministry, Jesus went down from Galilee to Jerusalem during the week when the Jews celebrated the Feast of Tabernacles, a feast that commemorated God's continued care for his people in the desert journey to the promised land of Canaan. On the last and culminating day of the weeklong celebration, a ritual of water-offering was taking place in the temple. At that very moment, Jesus stood among the people in the temple and proclaimed that he was the one who made available "rivers of living water." This he said about the Holy Spirit who would be received through the great outpouring (or baptism) by all those who believed in him (John 7:37–39).

As the time drew close, Jesus became more explicit about the forthcoming event. During the last phase of his teaching ministry, just prior to his ascension, Jesus gave the disciples detailed instructions for the coming of the Holy Spirit (Acts 1:4–5).

- For the first time in his teaching, Jesus referred to the coming of the Spirit as the "baptism with the Holy Spirit," thus using the same descriptive term that had been coined by John the Baptist (Mark 1:8), who had himself adapted the imagery from Joel's prediction of the Spirit's outpouring (Joel 2:28–29).
- Jesus declared to the disciples that the baptism of the Holy Spirit would be a specific event in time.
- He gave them an indication of the place where it would happen: in Jerusalem, where the great redemptive events of his crucifixion and resurrection had already taken place.
- He gave them an indication of the time when it would happen: in a few days, during which the disciples were to wait without leaving Jerusalem.
- He also gave them a history of the three predictions that had been made to announce the baptism of the Spirit. (1) The Father had promised the gift of the Holy Spirit; this was an obvious reference to God's commitment through the words of Joel, "I will pour out my Spirit" (Joel 2:28–29). (2) John the Baptist had baptized with water in the Jordan and had made of his water baptism an illustration of the greater baptism that would occur when Christ released the flood of the Holy Spirit (Mark 1:8). (3) The disciples had also heard Jesus speak

91

about the coming of the Holy Spirit, most notably as reported in the Gospel of John (7:37–39; 14:16–18, 25–26; 16:7, 13–15). Jesus had even given them an object lesson when he had breathed on them to illustrate the complete identity that existed between himself and the Holy Spirit they were about to receive (20:22).

● He promised that they would *all* receive the Holy Spirit. It would not be a selective experience that would affect some and leave others out. In this connection, it must be noted that the expression "baptism of the Holy Spirit" (or its equivalents "baptism by," "baptism in," or "baptism with the Holy Spirit") is always used in Scripture to designate the one corporate event of the day of Pentecost. It is never applied in the Bible to individual, subjective experiences with the Holy Spirit. This is not to deny the validity of personal encounters with the Holy Spirit, such as "being filled with the Holy Spirit." But the terminology of the "baptism of the Holy Spirit" pertains to all believers, not just to some. According to Scripture, whoever becomes a member of the body of Christ is, at the same time, baptized by the Spirit into the body (1 Cor. 12:12–13; Eph. 1:13–14). At Pentecost, the baptism of the Spirit was given, once for all, to all Christians present and future. By becoming a Christian, one becomes inducted into the body as a partaker in the baptism of the Holy Spirit at Pentecost. Jesus died once for all to give redemption to all believers. In the same manner, Jesus poured out the Spirit once for all to give Spirit baptism to all believers. Regarding individual, post-conversion experiences with the Holy Spirit, we should use biblical terminology by describing the experience in terms other than the "baptism of the Holy Spirit." For instance, one might properly say, "When I became a believer, I was baptized with the Holy Spirit as all Christians are, but since then, I have also experienced being filled with the Holy Spirit." This suggestion does not invalidate the legitimacy of deep experiences with the Holy Spirit. It is simply an appeal for the proper use of biblical terminology.

b. The event of Pentecost

Fifty days after the Passover during which Jesus had been killed and ten days after his ascension, large crowds of people had come to Jerusalem from many other countries for the annual celebration of the Jewish Pentecost, also called the Feast of Weeks. This was a joyful occasion when the people remembered the giving of the Law on Mount Sinai as well as celebrated the harvest season. On this day of thanksgiving for God's revelation and for his physical provision the ascended Christ chose to "pour out" his ultimate gift, the Holy Spirit (Acts 2:33).

The account of what happened on the day of the "baptism of the Holy Spirit" is brief, but every detail it contains is significant (Acts 2:1–13).

- On the day of Pentecost, about one hundred and twenty followers of Jesus (cf. 1:13) were gathered in one place. The Greek text literally states, "They were all together together," thus emphasizing the collective nature of the event (2:1). The form of community was beginning to appear.

- Suddenly, a hurricane sound came down from heaven. The word that refers to the "wind" also means "breath." It was as if the breath or Spirit of God had broken out of transcendence and was sweeping over all of them—the sound filled the entire building where they were gathered (v. 2). Again, we read about the corporate nature of the experience. The baptism of the Holy Spirit was bringing forth the new community.

- The people in the room saw what appeared to be a bunch of flames coming down, splitting, and resting over each person like tongues of fire (v. 3). Obviously this was not the fire of judgment, since no one got burned. It was the soft, purging, glowing fire of revelation that illumines without consuming, similar to the fire of the burning bush where God had made himself known to Moses (Ex. 3:1–14).

- As a result of the baptism of the Holy Spirit, they were all filled with or energized by the Holy Spirit (v. 4). Once the Holy Spirit became universally available at Pentecost, such experiences of "being filled with the Holy Spirit" recurred as needed (for example, Acts 4:8, 31; Eph. 5:18).

- Enabled by the Spirit, the believers started speaking in tongues other than their own (v. 4). This was not the speaking in tongues that required interpretation (as in 1 Cor. 14:27–28); rather, they were preaching in specific foreign languages, about twelve of them, that were directly understood by the people who heard them (vv. 6, 8, 11). Thousands of years before Pentecost, when the human race had been scattered from Babel, both the unity of the race and the unity of its language had been lost. As the human community became fragmented under the effect of sin, so did its means of communication. They could no longer understand each other (Gen. 11:1–9). When the Holy Spirit came, the first thing that happened was the restoration of the oneness of the human community. People could now understand each other again because the Holy Spirit was baptizing them into one body. The speaking in other languages was positive proof that "all flesh," men and women from all races and cultures, were called to become the new chosen people of God. Christ's command to take the gospel to the ends of the earth was beginning to be fulfilled right there in Jerusalem (Acts 1:8).

Obviously, this momentous event required explanation. It was Peter who spoke on behalf of the new community (Acts 2:14–40). His analysis of what had just happened was clear and bold. He solemnly declared, "This is what was spoken by the prophet Joel." He then proceeded to quote in its entirety Joel's prediction of the outpouring of the Holy Spirit on all flesh, of sons and daughters prophesying, of old men and young men receiving revelation, of servants (both menservants and womenservants) receiving the Holy Spirit. And he added that Jesus was the one who had fulfilled this ancient promise: "Exalted to the right hand of God, he has received from the Father the promised Holy Spirit and has poured out what you now see and hear" (v. 33 NIV).

With those words, Peter was not only announcing the historical realization of the outpouring/baptism of the Holy Spirit on the day of Pentecost, but he was also defining in the prophet's words the shape of the new community being created by the Holy Spirit—a community where differences of *race* would become irrelevant since the Spirit was being poured out on all people; where differences of *gender* would become irrelevant since both men and women now had access to one of the highest forms of ministry (that of prophecy); where differences of *rank* would become irrelevant since both young men and elderly patriarchs could receive revelation; and where differences of *class* would become irrelevant since servants were receiving the Holy Spirit. The Holy Spirit had finally brought about the community of oneness.

And to show the finality of this form of community, Peter also quoted Joel's perspective on the closing day of history, the Day of the Lord (vv. 19–21). Pentecost marked the beginning of the last phase of history, the age of the church. What began at Pentecost would endure until the end when the universe would disintegrate and the Day of the Lord would finally usher salvation into God's eternity.

c. The three extensions of Pentecost

As wonderful as the event of Pentecost was, it fell short of fulfilling completely its promise that the recipients of the outpouring of the Spirit would be "all people" or "all flesh." Because the cultural framework of Jesus' ministry had been essentially a Jewish environment, the people who received the original baptism of the Holy Spirit were all Jews. In that harshly racially segregated society, the belief grew that the baptism of the Holy Spirit was a Jewish privilege, denied to other peoples. So strong was this belief that in flagrant disobedience to the command of Christ for the disciples to take the gospel from Jerusalem to Judea, to Samaria, and to the ends of the earth (Acts 1:8), the church remained for a long time landlocked in Jerusalem. The city of Jerusalem was being filled with the teaching of the gospel (Acts 5:28), but the apostles made no attempt to break away and share it with other people.

But eventually persecution drove the church out of Jerusalem. Where self-contented complacency had prevented them from obeying the command of Christ, persecution was now forcing them to comply. It took a "great" persecution against the church in Jerusalem for believers to be scattered from there throughout Judea and Samaria, so that those who were scattered preached the gospel wherever they went (Acts 8:1, 4). Ironically, this forced outreach followed the same geographic sequence as that which had been ordained by Christ (1:8): the extension of Pentecost to the Samaritans, to the Gentiles, and also to the sectarians.

The *Samaritans* responded to the preaching of the gospel enthusiastically, and great numbers of them believed. But amazingly, none of them received the Holy Spirit, despite the fact that the baptism of the Spirit had been promised for all peoples, including the Samaritans (Acts 8:6, 16). At last and after the fact, the mother church at Jerusalem became aware of its responsibility and sent to Samaria their foremost representatives, the apostles Peter and John. It was only when they, as the original believers, laid their hands upon the new believers as a sign of acceptance, identification, and oneness that the Samaritans received the Holy Spirit as a group that represented all Samaritans (Acts 8:14–17). The racial barrier had come down and the demonstrated oneness of the body had made it possible for all believing Samaritans to be henceforth included in the outpouring-baptism of Pentecost.

By this time, the church had expanded from Jerusalem to Judea and Samaria (Acts 9:31), but it had not yet reached the *Gentiles*. Another racial barrier needed to come down. The man whom God chose to break it down was the most typical Gentile imaginable: a Roman officer, the commander of a crack unit of the imperial legions stationed in the headquarters city of Caesarea by the Sea (Acts 10:1–48). Through special guidance, the apostle Peter was brought, reluctantly, to the house of this Gentile.

In a rather cold greeting, Peter started to tell Cornelius how wrong it was for a Jew like him to enter a Gentile household, but that God had forced him to come. Peter then uttered one of the most astounding statements that has ever been spoken in history. Here was Christ's commissioned apostle, the rock on whom Christ would build his church (Matt. 16:18), who had been trained by Christ for three years for this very task, who had been ordered by him to preach the gospel to all the nations, and who was now standing in front of a group of receptive Gentiles inquiring, "May I ask why you sent for me?" So strong was the racial barrier that it did not occur to Peter that he had been sent to those Gentiles in order to preach the gospel to them and so bring them into the faith. Scandalously, it was the pagan Cornelius who gently reminded the apostle of his Christ-ordained responsibility to tell them the good news: "We are all here in the presence of God to listen to everything the Lord has commanded you to tell us" (Acts 10:33 NIV).

Finally, it dawned on Peter that it was proper to preach to the Gentiles because God was not racist and showed no partiality (10:34). As Peter, the representative of the original church, accepted these Gentiles and was now preaching up a storm, the Holy Spirit fell on them and they became integrated by baptism into the body of Christ. As a group, Cornelius and his believing household opened the way to the baptism of the Holy Spirit for all believing Gentiles. The Gentile racial barrier of hostility was coming down in order to make believing Jews and Gentiles one community in Jesus Christ; only through him do we have access in one Spirit to the Father (Eph. 2:11–22).

The level of racial prejudice was so high that the Jewish Christians accompanying Peter were amazed that the Holy Spirit had been poured out "even" on the Gentiles—as if the Gentiles were a subhuman species (Acts 10:45). When Peter returned to Jerusalem, some Jews in his own church hotly criticized him for having had anything to do with Gentiles (11:2–3). They were silenced only when Peter told them his complete story, explaining that the Spirit baptism received by the Gentile converts was exactly the same Spirit baptism as the Jerusalem Christians had received at Pentecost (11:15–17). Another racial barrier had come down and the Gentiles were now included in the community of oneness. Never again was there the need for Gentiles to receive the Holy Spirit apart from their reception of him at conversion.

In the course of his missionary travels the apostle Paul arrived in the city of Ephesus and came across a small *sect* of disciples. He noticed that something was different about them (Acts 19:1–7), so he asked them if they had received the Holy Spirit when they had believed. Paul could not understand that they would be converted apart from receiving the Holy Spirit. But those people had not even heard of the Holy Spirit. At this point, Paul knew that something was radically wrong. Upon further questioning, he discovered that they were not Christians but belonged to the sect of John the Baptist. John had been dead for a long time (Mark 6:17–29), but some of his followers regarded him as the real Messiah and never made the shift to the Christian faith. They were a small sect who had come out of the old covenant with John, but had never made it into the new covenant with Jesus. The sect survives to this day in the few Mandaean communities scattered in the Middle East.

Paul therefore preached the gospel to them and they believed. When he laid his hands upon them as the consecrated sign of acceptance and identification, the Holy Spirit came on them. They were brought from their spiritual no-man's land into the oneness of the body of Christ. The conversion of those sectarians vividly demonstrated to the church that its outreach included not only the Samaritans and the Gentiles but also those who had erected a religious barrier between themselves and the gospel.

Apart from those three groups separated from the church by walls of discrimination and prejudice, the Scriptures mention nowhere else a special intervention for converts to receive the Holy Spirit. Now that those three segregated groups had been representatively included in the body, any human who became a believer was automatically included in the great outpouring-baptism of the Holy Spirit that had taken place on the day of Pentecost.

II. THE MINISTRIES OF THE HOLY SPIRIT

In the Gospel of John, Jesus teaches that he would send a successor to continue his ministries after his departure. He designated this successor with a beautiful name, the *Paraclete*. Unfortunately, this term for the Holy Spirit is difficult to translate because of the richness of its meaning. Various translations render it as Counselor, Advocate, Comforter, or Helper. These translations are not wrong, but each one of them describes only one aspect of the meaning of Paraclete. Perhaps Bible translators would do better to leave the term "Paraclete" in the text and thus allow the readers to discover from the use of the word in the gospel itself the breadth of its meaning.

The Paraclete is the Spirit of truth (John 15:26), who will be with believers forever (14:16) to guide them into all truth (16:13), to teach them (14:26), and to take what is Christ's and make it available to them (16:15). The Spirit is really "another Paraclete" like Christ himself, also sent from the Father (14:16, 26). In this sense, it may be said that the Paraclete is Christ's substitute, one who would continue to perform Christ's ministries after his ascension. During his time on earth, Christ ministered to the world, to his disciples, and to individuals. Since the task of the new Paraclete is to expand Christ's ministries, it is therefore appropriate to consider his ministry in relation to the world, to the church, and to the individual believer.

1. The Ministry of the Holy Spirit to the World

This aspect of the work of the Holy Spirit could be very difficult to define because of its scope. Fortunately, the Gospel of John contains a convenient summary that describes three dimensions of the ministry of the Spirit to the world (John 16:8–11).

a. When the Paraclete comes, he will convict the world of sin.

The presence of Christ in the world was proof that God had not abandoned it to its sinful condition. An unbelieving world needed the ministry of Christ. After his departure, Jesus promises that the Holy Spirit will see to it that the ministry of the gospel continues because sin will continue to thrive. Consequently, the Holy Spirit will energize efforts that present an alternative to unbelief. In other words, the evangelistic outreach of the church will be sustained by the power of the Holy Spirit (v. 9).

b. When the Paraclete comes, he will convict the world of righteousness.

With the advent of Christ, the supreme expression of the will of God had become incarnate in him. Christ represented the right-eousness of God both in his person and in his teaching. He was the Christ of the Beatitudes (Matt. 5:3–11), of the Sermon on the Mount (chaps. 5–7), of the Golden Rule (7:12), and of the two great commandments (22:37–40). Would all this revelation cease after his ascension (John 16:10)? The answer was an emphatic NO, because the Paraclete would continue Christ's work. He sees to it that there remains in the world a common grace that causes the same standards of righteousness to be upheld despite Christ's absence. The world will be abandoned neither to sin nor to unrighteousness, for the Paraclete will see to it that a witness for righteousness is present. Whenever the church is sensitive to the Spirit, it refuses to be conformed to the values of the world and presents radical alternatives to the unrighteousness of pagan cultures.

c. When the Paraclete comes, he will convict the world of judgment.

For that part of the world that refuses to respond to the Spirit's conviction against sin and for righteousness, there remains the prospect of judgment. Jesus had warned the rebellious and the indifferent of the danger of judgment. Yet he had not come to judge the world but to deliver it from judgment (John 3:17–20). The very presence of the Spirit is now a sign of the defeat of Satan and an indication that the final phase of history has begun and the end is sure. The presence of the Holy Spirit himself signals that we are in the last days (Acts 2:16–20) when the judgment of the ruler of this world, begun at the cross, becomes final. In the meantime, the mission of the Holy Spirit is to convince the world of the judgment to come. He does this through the ministry of the church as it proclaims the message of salvation and of the judgment of the ruler of the present world (John 16:11).

Jesus was aware that the range of his ministry to the world was limited by his physical, human nature. Through his death and resurrection, he would achieve redemption for the whole world, but he could not as a person take that redemption throughout the world. So, in his stead, the Holy Spirit is ministering redemptively by convincing the world of sin, righteousness, and judgment. The Spirit is not localized; his range of influence is universal. To entrust this ministry to the Paraclete was to secure its progress throughout the world.

2. The Ministry of the Holy Spirit to the Church

Jesus had handpicked the twelve disciples at the outset of his ministry. During three years, he attempted to band them together into a nucleus of what would become the church. But the Gospels describe mercilessly the failure of the disciples to respond to Jesus' efforts. As he was teaching them the necessity of his sufferings and death because of the servant nature of his messiahship, the disciples were arguing among themselves behind his back about which one of them was the greatest (Mark 9:33–37). When they were all travelling for the last time toward Jerusalem,

Jesus explicitly revealed to them the full extent of the humiliation that was awaiting him in the city. At that very moment, two of his closest disciples approached him with a power-play scheme intended to secure their dominance over the other ten. Jesus severely denounced their craving for authority and defined Christian leadership as acceptance of the self-humiliation that he was exemplifying all the way to the cross (Mark 10:32–45). It seemed that the only thing Jesus could do for the disciples to become a real community was to pray the Father that they would become one (John 17:11, 21–22) and to give final instructions through the Holy Spirit to those whom he had chosen (Acts 1:2). The rest was up to the Holy Spirit.

The prayer of Jesus for his followers to become a community received spectacular vindication at Pentecost. Overnight, a group of distraught and shiftless disciples became a bold, motivated, organized, and united movement energized by God's power. This remarkable transformation is given in a brief summary of the life of the church at its very beginnings, in Acts 2:42–47. This passage describes the changes that occurred among the disciples under the impact of the Holy Spirit at Pentecost. It provides us with a unique source of information on the ministry of the Holy Spirit to the church. Three elements characterize this ministry: the teaching, the fellowship, and the stewardship that emerged as new dimensions of the activity of the Spirit in the community.

a. The teaching

Three thousand people were baptized into the church as a result of Pentecost. The first thing that is reported about them is that "they devoted themselves to the apostles' teaching" (Acts 2:42 RSV). This means that the teaching function of the word of God was as foundational to the establishment of the church as it is now to its survival.

What was the content of this teaching? Jesus had prepared the disciples for the ministry of teaching, training them for three years and patiently committing to them his teaching with a variety of pedagogical methods to make sure that it would remain fixed in their minds. He had promised that the Holy Spirit whom he would send would bring to their remembrance all that he had taught them (John 14:26). Prior to his ascension, he had commissioned them to teach future believers to observe all that he had commanded (Matt. 28:20). Obviously, what the disciples taught after Pentecost was no different from what Christ had taught them. This explains the success of the teaching ministry of the disciples; it reflected the vigor, the newness, the radicalness, the authority, and the finality

100

of Jesus' own teaching. At the core of Jesus' teaching was God's self-giving love for the world. In response, his followers were to heed the divine agenda that summarized all prior revelation: communion with God and community among themselves (22:36–40).

A measure of the profound change that the Holy Spirit brought overnight to the thinking of the disciples is illustrated by an incident that took place a few days before Pentecost. As Jesus was teaching them about the kingdom of God and the forthcoming baptism of the Holy Spirit, the disciples incongruously asked him if that would be the time when he would restore the kingdom to Israel. Their question shows that they were still struggling with the narrow, nationalistic ideas of the kingdom that were current in their day. In his answer, Jesus taught them that the scope of his program was not confined to one nation but that it was universal; the disciples would have to reach the whole world (Acts 1:6–8).

Pentecost caused the thinking of the disciples to shift completely. When Peter spoke about the kingdom in his first sermon, he explained that the prophecy about the Son of David sitting on his throne was fulfilled not in an earthly kingdom to Israel but in the resurrection of Christ (Acts 2:30–31). The promises of the kingdom made to Israel were now being fulfilled in Christ and in the church (Acts 3:24), as "all the families of the earth" were being blessed, beginning with the family of Israel (Acts 3:25–26). As a result, Peter announced that the fulfillment of the promise was both for the Jews "and to all who are far off," referring to the Gentile world (Acts 2:39). Under the impact of the Holy Spirit, the thinking of the disciples had begun to expand from the narrow racist categories prevalent in their day to Christ's vision of God's love for the whole world.

b. The fellowship

The second sign of new life generated by the Holy Spirit at Pentecost was the fellowship (*koinonia*, v. 42). The believers had come to know God in a new way through the apostles' preaching; now they came to know each other in a new way through the quality of communal life that resulted from Pentecost.

According to the summary in Acts 2:42–47, the corporate life of the church had two main components: worship and communal involvement.

(1) Worship. The Christians met to "break bread" (meaning the Lord's Supper), to pray together, and to praise God together (vv. 42, 47). They recognized that the vitality of the church was directly

related to the quality of its worship, since worship is the loving recognition of the reality and the centrality of God in human life.

Their worship took place in two locations. They met together as a large group in a section of the huge courtyard that surrounded the temple. This was their central and formal place for gathering. But they also met in homes where they celebrated the Lord's Supper (v. 46). The home meetings functioned as decentralized, informal micro-churches. They served as neighborhood centers for worship, for body-life, and for outreach. Thus the Holy Spirit brought to the believers new forms of worship that enabled them to establish a more intimate relationship with God.

(2) Communal Life. The Holy Spirit also brought the believers into an intimate relationship with each other. According to the summary, they could not stay away from one another. They loved to come together and they did it often (vv. 44, 46).

People who enjoy each other like to eat their meals together. This was the case for the early Christians. Their homes were open to each other and they shared their food with joyful and sincere hearts (v. 44); they were "one in heart and mind" (4:32). The Holy Spirit had transformed people who had acted as strangers if not enemies into one large family, where they were set free to know, to enjoy, and to love one another. Only the Holy Spirit can create such an open environment where mutual edification, mutual caring, and mutual accountability make it possible for the strong to help the weak survive in a hostile world and for all to attain mature oneness in Christ (Eph. 4:13).

c. The stewardship

The Holy Spirit had helped the first Christians discover a shared faith through the apostles' teaching, a shared communal life in their fellowship, and also a shared task. After Pentecost, they were suddenly able to care and serve in a new way.

During his ministry, Jesus had performed many "wonders and signs" to help the needy, the broken, the diseased, and the desperate (Acts 2:22). Now, because the Holy Spirit was continuing Christ's ministry through the apostles, it was their turn to minister with "many wonders and miraculous signs" that were done through them (v. 43, see 3:6–8, 16 as an example).

But the most startling aspect of their new stewardship was the decision of the believers to have "everything in common" (v. 44). The purpose of this sharing was to make sure that no one in the Christian community was in "need" while the others had enough or too much (v. 45). They recognized that experiencing need is Satan's work and that God's children may not remain indifferent to it. God is the great Giver who lavishes his bounty on his creation; Satan is the one who takes away, destroys, and creates pain and want. Just as the "wonders and signs" were performed to undo the work of Satan by bringing the power of God to bear on extreme situations, the stewardship of possessions was intended to thwart the evil work of Satan by making the resources of the community available to those in need.

Early Christians rightly recognized that none of the things they possessed was really their own (4:32). Everything they had, including their bodies, their goods, their lives, and their breath, belonged to God. In Job's words, we come naked into this world and we go naked into eternity (Job 1:21). Whatever we own is a gift of God, intended to be used in stewardship in order to counter needs with the sufficiency of God. The early Christians understood this principle. Therefore, of their own free will, those among them who could afford to do so without becoming themselves welfare cases sold their surplus property and made the proceeds available to the community (v. 45; 4:34–35). The Holy Spirit had shown them that the privilege of stewardship took precedence over the right of ownership.

This availability of private possessions for the common good should not be regarded as a wild-eyed idealistic venture that was quickly outgrown by the church. The principle of the strong helping the weak sacrificially derives from the very nature of God (2 Cor. 8:9) and is an integral part of Christian life (8:14–15). The church continued to practice this form of benevolence not only within local bodies (Eph. 4:28), but also from church to church among Christians who had never laid eyes on each other (Acts 11:27–30; 1 Cor. 16:1–4; 2 Cor. 8–9). They knew that it was a disgrace to Jesus for some in the Christian family to have too much when others were in dire need.

These three marks of the presence of the Holy Spirit in the church are valid for all churches at all times. Their absence is an indication that the Holy Spirit has been grieved (Eph. 4:29) and that there is a need for repentance and renewal. We live in a world that relentlessly destroys community by creating and emphasizing differences and inequalities. The rich flourish while the poor perish. The strong oppress the weak. Power is misused to harass and abuse. The church is God's answer to the community-shattering forces loose in the world. It is called to establish and to model community by minimizing differences and by striving for equality among its participants (2 Cor. 8:13–15).

It may seem strange that evangelistic outreach is not listed as one of the new elements brought into the life of the church by the Holy Spirit. The text explains that the Lord added daily to their numbers those who were being saved (Acts 2:47). It should be noted that evangelism is described in this passage as the inevitable by-product of an authentically Spirit-energized church (cf. 1:8). It was the Lord who utilized the teaching, the fellowship, and the stewardship to bring in those who were being saved. Evangelism is too important a ministry to be carried out randomly. Its methods and approaches need to be carefully strategized and contextualized to local situations. But the most important part of the strategy for evangelism is for the church to be a true community by pursuing Spirit-sustained excellence in its teaching, intensity and openness in its fellowship, and responsibility in its stewardship.

3. The Ministry of the Holy Spirit to the Individual

Shortly before his death, Jesus was talking to his disciples about his approaching departure from them. Their hearts were filled with sorrow (John 16:6). In order to comfort them Jesus told them, "It is for your good that I am going away" (v. 7 NIV).

Those words must have thrown the disciples into a state of shock. One can easily imagine the apostle Peter protesting that Jesus was absolutely wrong. Jesus' departure would be the ultimate disaster. He was all that the disciples had. He had delivered them from religious confusion and spiritual darkness. He had taken them on a thrilling journey of hope. He was to them the way, the truth, and the life. He was their Good Shepherd. Without him life wouldn't be worth living—"Lord, how can you say that it is good for us that you should go away?"

So Jesus explained, "If I do not go away, the Advocate [Paraclete] will not come to you; but if I go, I will send him to you" (John 16:7 NRSV). Jesus was telling the disciples plainly that they would be better off with the Holy Spirit than they presently were with him. At the time, this made no sense to them. Therefore, Jesus explained further that the Holy Spirit would carry forward Christ's ministry to them but with an added plus. As long as Jesus was with the disciples, he was next to them. Despite their closeness, he remained another person, exterior to them. However, when the Holy Spirit came, he would take residency *within* them. He would indwell their beings and enter into their hearts in an intimate way that was not possible now. Since the Holy Spirit was really Christ's own Spirit, they had nothing to lose in the exchange. Jesus in the form of the Spirit would still be with them, but also within them. In this manner, the Holy Spirit would act on Jesus' behalf as his secret agent, doing an inside job within his followers.

Later, as the apostle Paul reflected on the ministry of the Holy Spirit in the lives of believers, he acknowledged the inwardness of God's activity through the Spirit within the privacy of their beings (1 Cor. 2:9–13). In words that show the complete interchangeability between the terms Holy Spirit, the Spirit of God, and the Spirit of Jesus, he described the indwelling of the Holy Spirit as a matter of life and death (Rom. 8:9–11). Seen in this light, it is no wonder that Jesus promised the disciples that they would get to know him more closely through the Spirit within them than they could with his own presence among them. The biblical definitions of the ministry of the Holy Spirit with individual persons may be summarized under three concepts: salvation, sanctification, and service.

a. Salvation

The Scriptures present the Holy Spirit as the member of the Trinity who relates the benefits of the salvation achieved by Christ to the needs of individual persons. We have already discovered that the purpose of the Spirit's ministry to the world is to influence people in preparing them to receive the Gospel. By convicting them of sin, righteousness, and judgment, the Holy Spirit opens minds and hearts to the urgent need of humans to receive the salvation made available through the ministry of Jesus.

But the ministry of the Holy Spirit does not stop with bringing conviction to the human conscience. The ensuing process of salvation is dependent on the Spirit's activity. The Scriptures often describe salvation as a new birth (1 Pet. 1:3, 23; 1 John 2:29; 3:9; 4:7). When the learned teacher Nicodemus came to Jesus to receive instruction from him, Jesus explained the new birth to him by using the imagery of water and Spirit, just as Joel and John the Baptist had done before him. He made it clear that there can be no new birth apart from the work of the Spirit (John 3:3–5). The Holy Spirit's role in bringing forth a new Christian into the world is like that of an expectant mother in bringing a new baby into the world. The Holy Spirit produces a new Christian at the time of his or her new birth (v. 6). And probably in anticipation of the hurricane sound of Pentecost, Jesus explained that the impact of the Holy Spirit is like the wind sweeping over a valley of deadness to bring new life in its wake. Christians are people who were formerly spiritually dead but are now "born of the Spirit" (vv. 7–8).

b. Sanctification

The work of the Holy Spirit in the lives of believers is not supposed to stop with their receiving God's salvation. The new birth is exactly that—only a beginning. New Christians are like babies who must grow into maturity. The Scriptures call this process of growth *sanctification,* an activity defined in Scriptures as one of the works of the Holy Spirit (for example, Rom. 15:16; 1 Pet. 1:2).

One of the consequences of the Fall in Eden was that the image of God in humans became radically disrupted by sin. It remained present in them but in a marred and distorted state. Sanctification is intended to restore God's image by reproducing God's character in his children. It is the assignment of the Holy Spirit to produce this Christlikeness within believers.

Obviously, there are many aspects to this process of restoration (see Rom. 8:5–16, 26–27). But its effects are clearly defined as *the fruit of the Spirit.* The Holy Spirit helps believers come out of the fallen human condition (described in Gal. 5:16–21) into a Spirit-produced maturity described as the "fruit" or the product of the Holy Spirit (5:22–23). The characteristics and relational behaviors listed in this last passage derive from the very nature of God. "love, joy, peace, patience, kindness, goodness, faithfulness, gentleness and self-control" (NIV). The laws of God and the rules of decency condemn the works of the flesh, but there is no reasonable prohibition against the fruit of the Spirit (v. 23b). As a matter of fact, the absence of the fruit of the Spirit in a person's life indicates that the sanctification process has been stunted and that the Holy Spirit has been spurned (Eph. 4:30–32).

It should be sadly noted that our pagan, secular culture often wrongly despises as "feminine" the traits described as the fruit of the Spirit. It exalts their exact opposites as the condition for worldly success and acceptance. Real men are supposed to be tough, hard, competitive, expeditious, assertive, aggressive, self-promoting, self-seeking, and self-indulgent. Yet Christ was a real man, and he exemplified to perfection the fruit of the Spirit; thus the Spirit's ministry of sanctification places a special challenge before Christian men. Their choice is either to conform to the demands of a pagan culture and to adopt its values and standards or to reject the pressures of conformity and dare to be obedient to God's expectations. It ultimately comes down to a choice between the Lord God and the god of this world (Matt. 6:24).

c. Service

Since it is in the nature of God to love, to give, to serve, and to sacrifice, it is predictable that the indwelling Holy Spirit will inculcate the same ideals into believers. Scripture requires Christians to be servants to one another through love (Gal. 5:13) and to contribute to the common good by the enablement of the Spirit (1 Cor. 12:7). Qualities such as love, patience, kindness, goodness, and gentleness—elements of the fruit of the Spirit—form Christians who are caring, considerate, and compassionate. Such people inevitably act as servants toward others.

According to Scriptures, the Holy Spirit also assigns gifts to believers in order to provide for their active participation in the ministries of their churches. These enablements are called "spiritual gifts" or the "gifts of the Spirit." (The Greek word in the Bible for "gift" is *charisma; charismata* in the plural.) They are talents and abilities that are energized by the Holy Spirit so that they can be used for spiritual purposes under the guidance of the local church community. According to the New Testament, every believer has at least one spiritual gift to be used for ministry. In this sense, every church member is a minister.

There are four lists of gifts in the New Testament, two of them in the same letter (Rom. 12:3-8; 1 Cor. 12:8–11, 28–30; Eph. 4:11–12; see also 1 Pet. 4:10–11). Since these lists are not the same, it follows that the mix of spiritual gifts varies from church to church. Therefore, those lists should not be regarded as exhaustive but as open-ended. Any individual involvement that contributes to the ministry of the church and to the common good is a spiritual gift. Because of the variety of needs, the apostle Paul encouraged individual initiative in seeking and developing gifts (1 Cor. 12:31). The church also has a responsibility to detect, develop, and deploy the talents of its members. Importantly, individual believers must understand that spiritual gifts have not been made available to them for their own benefit and enjoyment but for ministry to the entire community (1 Cor. 12:7).

This survey of the ministries of the Holy Spirit suggests the breadth of his operations: creative involvement in the world, in the church, and in individual persons. But the Holy Spirit ministers quietly, without calling attention to himself and always acting as servant. In this regard, he is really no different from God the Father and God the Son. While the functions of the members of the divine Trinity—namely, God the Father as Creator, Christ the Son as Redeemer, and the Holy Spirit as Paraclete—demonstrate their differentiation, their shared passion for servanthood points to their essential oneness.

For this reason, when Christians approach God in worship, in singing, and in prayer, they are instructed in Scripture to address themselves to the Father, in the name of Christ, and through the active support of the Holy Spirit. There is no model in Scripture for offering prayer to the Son or to the Holy Spirit. Moreover, according to the New Testament, the Holy Spirit is not the object of Christian worship; the Father and the Son certainly are. But it is the indwelling Spirit who guides and assists believers in worshiping the Father and Son properly. As believers approach God, the Holy Spirit assists them in relating to the Father in the name of or through the mediation of the Son. Even when the church rises to worship its God and its Redeemer, the self-effacing Spirit acts as servant both to the church and to the other members of the Trinity. God is obviously too gracious to reject theologically incorrect forms of worship. But the consistent violation of biblically sound patterns of worship may lead to distorted understandings of our relationship with each of the three persons of the Trinity.

IV. CURRENT VIEWS ON THE HOLY SPIRIT

Some versions of the Bible refer to the Holy Spirit as the Holy Ghost. For too many people, the Spirit is just that, a benevolent super-ghost, a shadowy, elusive, indefinable absence that will not cause harm but cannot do much good either, the lingering trace of a God who would rather forget the world but cannot quite bring himself to let go of it. So, out of nostalgia, he sticks around, like the spirit of the long-dead owner of a medieval castle who still haunts the place.

In keeping with this ghastly view of the Holy Spirit, some theologies reduce his ministry to a subtle influence at work in the world at large, endeavoring against all odds to uphold some semblance of morality, goodness, and beauty among humans. Acccording to such thinking, the Spirit is a symbol for the best expressions of human creativity, the promoter of aesthetic and philosophical change, the inspirer of movements of economic and political liberation. While the protective influence of the Holy Spirit over the nobler aspects of culture cannot be discounted, such definitions of the work of the Spirit ignore the biblical data and reduce to mere social, ethical, and aesthetic concerns the redemptive ministries of the Spirit as described in this chapter.

Other people take the biblical teaching on the Holy Spirit more seriously. They analyze the Bible on the subject, systematize their findings, and express them in beautifully worded statements of faith. Such statements are held in high regard, and assent to them is often required as a condition for church membership. So far, so good. But unfortunately, recognition of the Holy Spirit stops at this point. He is reduced to an item of doctrine and is left imprisoned in the books. At times, these people may give him lip-service, but very gingerly for fear that he could suddenly become a troublesome intruder in their lives. Better not take a chance but keep him at the safe distance of theological abstractions, unconnected with real life. Being practically shut out of the lives of Christians and of their churches, the Holy Spirit does not force his way into them. Every instance of the intervention of the Holy Spirit reported in the New Testament indicates that he cooperates actively in situations where he is expected and wanted.

Where there is no Spirit, however, there is no life. Lack of Christian growth and vitality are reliable indicators of the need for openness to the quiet but powerful impact of the Spirit on human life. A typical prayer for help may go like this, "Heavenly Father, I surrender this situation to you and ask for your Holy Spirit to help me with it. I acknowledge the need for the influence of the Holy Spirit in my life and in the life of my church and family. I am willing to be open to his assistance and to cooperate with him in this matter. In the name of Jesus, Amen" (see Luke 11:13).

If the first position described above may be called *humanistic* or *immanentist*, and the second *scholastic*, there remains another view that must be surveyed. It is the *Pentecostal/charismatic* view of the Holy Spirit. At their beginnings, the Pentecostal and charismatic movements were, to some extent, reactions against what was perceived as a complete neglect of the Holy Spirit in many churches and denominations. Both movements emphasize the role of the Holy Spirit in Christian life, teaching that the Spirit is received apart from and later than conversion and that one of the signs of receiving him is the capacity to speak in tongues.

The Pentecostal movement started on the West Coast at the beginning of the twentieth century and quickly spread through established churches and mainline denominations. The people who identified with it usually left their churches and formed new Pentecostal congregations.

The charismatic movement was an offshoot of the older Pentecostal church but developed independently from it. It started after World War II in mainline churches and spread rapidly from denomination to denomination, and from North America to other continents. But in this case, the Christians who were influenced by the charismatic experience generally remained in their churches and identified with each other in small local groups or in large rallies that gathered them periodically without regard for denominational distinctives.

The charismatic movement has made several positive contributions to contemporary Christianity. In many sectors of the church that had succumbed to the deadness of nominalism (where people were Christians in name only), it brought spiritual renewal through the recovery of personal faith. Through their experience of the Spirit, many who had been indifferent to spiritual things were able to establish a meaningful personal relationship with God. The movement also challenged the deadness of formalism (the mindless participation in religious rituals and ceremonies) through the recovery of active worship, of community life, and of personal involvement often expressed in small group participation. Christians who discovered their gifts (*charismata*) became eager to use them in the service of their communities.

As a result, the charismatic movement also challenged the deadness of theological indifference. Through their experience of the Holy Spirit, many charismatic Christians discovered the Bible and its importance for personal faith. They found that they could grow in understanding their faith without being dependent on priests or pastors. Finally, the charismatic movement contributed to the recovery of personal evangelism. Motivated by their fresh experience of the Holy Spirit, many of those Christians burned with a desire to share their discovery of God with relatives, friends, neighbors, co-workers, and fellow church members. As a result of their witnessing, large segments of society that had been counted as a loss by the established churches were reclaimed. They were able to penetrate successfully with the gospel into areas where traditional churches had failed and retreated.

Along with such positive gains, however, are some tendencies within the Pentecostal/charismatic tradition that threaten to limit its effectiveness. Three of these will be mentioned. One is the tendency to reduce the process of sanctification to the one-time experience of the filling of the Holy Spirit, erroneously called "baptism of the Holy Spirit" (see above). This experience is too often viewed as a shortcut to spirituality and as proof of spiritual attainment. As a result, there is often a discrepancy between the claims of having received the Holy Spirit because of that one-time experience and the absence of the fruit of the Spirit, the latter being the only scripturally valid test of the presence of the Holy Spirit in a Christian's life.

Second, some adherents of the charismatic movement have a tendency to spiritual *totalitarianism* in that they press the pattern of their own experience as normative for all Christians. Having had a meaningful experience of the fullness of the Spirit associated with speaking in tongues, they eagerly expect all Christians to go through the same mold. They insist on the necessity that one particular form of piety be adopted by all, instead of allowing the

110

Spirit to deal creatively with each individual on the basis of the infinite versatility of his resources.

Finally, some segments of the Pentecostal/charismatic movement show a disposition to go beyond Scripture, especially in regard to public expressions of their religious experience. Most conspicuous among such expressions is the practice of speaking in tongues (the New Testament Greek word for it is *glossolalia*). Because this matter is dealt with at length in Scripture, we can analyze this teaching and draw some implications. In the early church, the practice of glossolalia had caused questions to be raised in the lively congregation at Corinth. Responding to this situation, the apostle Paul wrote precise definitions and laid down specific regulations for its practice (see 1 Cor. 12–14). Since Paul derived those definitions and rules from principles that pertain to the very nature of the church, their range of application is universal and permanent. A survey of Paul's argument follows.

In 1 Corinthians 12, the apostle establishes the legitimacy of the diversity of spiritual gifts and emphasizes the common good or edification as the purpose for their use. In doing so, he provides two lists of gifts (vv. 7–11 and 28), the latter arranged by order of decreasing importance on the basis of their comparative usefulness for the common good. Accordingly, the first three gifts (apostleship, prophecy, and teaching) are the "higher gifts." These three gifts require the use of intelligible speech communication as a means of serving the common good. Paul goes on to rank the gift of prophecy as the most desirable of all gifts (14:1, 39), carefully defining it in terms that make it virtually equivalent to today's ministry of preaching (v. 3). Moreover, to make sure that his readers understand what he means by prophecy as a higher gift, he actually demonstrates for them an excellent use of that gift (12:31b) by quoting one of his own preachings on the topic of love (chap. 13).

The relation of 1 Corinthians 13 to Paul's discussion on spiritual gifts has often been debated. Love is not itself a spiritual gift but one of the character traits produced by the Holy Spirit as his fruit (Gal. 5:22). It seems, therefore, that this chapter is intended to provide a sample of Paul's exercise of his own gift of prophecy to serve as a model for his readers to imitate in their own prophecy/preaching ministry. The chapter looks like the last point of a three-point sermon on faith, hope, and love. In quoting it, Paul seems to be saying, "If you want a spiritual gift, speak like this and you'll really be doing ministry." In Corinth, there were formally authorized prophet/preachers (12:10, 28), but every believer could also aspire to contribute in this manner from time to time (14:1, 5, 31).

Against this background, Paul then discusses the relative value and the practice of glossolalia (chap. 14). He begins with a definition of this practice. Glossolalia is not speaking foreign languages; no one understands what is said by one who speaks in a tongue because it is unintelligible speech (vv. 2, 9). Note that the communication phenomenon on Pentecost was different; it consisted of specific foreign languages, not unintelligible sounds.

Furthermore, glossolalia is not an exclusively Christian practice. Indeed, speaking in tongues was a sign for pagan unbelievers, not for Christians (v. 22). Several pagan religions of Paul's day used glossolalia as a sign of the activity of their gods among their worshipers. Today as well, glossolalia is widely used among ecstatic and illuminist non-Christian religions. Paul states that when glossolalia occurs in the Christian community, it has an entirely different meaning and value than it has in the religious practices of unbelievers.

The Holy Spirit can use glossolalia in the life of believers, but primarily as a private devotional practice. One who speaks in a tongue does so not to other humans but to God (v. 2) and edifies himself or herself alone (v. 4); one who prays in tongues worships in isolation without usefulness to others (vv. 16–17). Paul reveals, under some duress, that he practices glossolalia in his private worship but never in public (vv. 18–19). If tongues are not interpreted for public edification in corporate worship, they should be exclusively relegated to private use (v. 28).

In these definitions, Paul establishes the personal value of glossolalia as a private method of individual worship. Apart from this passage, it would be impossible to determine, either from Acts or his letters, whether Paul ever practiced glossolalia. Only reluctantly does he reveal his secret to the Corinthians in order to illustrate a point. Paul's discretion in this regard should be recognized and emulated. No one has any business inquiring of another Christian whether he or she uses glossolalia in private worship, and no one has the right to boast about the use of glossolalia. According to Paul, it is something between God and an individual, a matter that pertains to one's prayer closet, the door of which is to be kept tightly shut. Jesus had the same concern about the need for humility in one's devotional exercises, although he made no reference to glossolalia (Matt. 6:6).

Paul admits that all believers may speak in tongues, but only in the context of private devotional practices (1 Cor. 14:5). He prefers for them to prophesy, because he considers speaking clearly "to other people for their upbuilding and encouragement and consolation" to be of greater value than tongues (vv. 3, 5). As legitimate as it may be, glossolalia is self-serving, while preaching is a servant ministry that contributes to the good of the whole community (v. 4).

Paul recognized that glossolalia could be practiced in public under certain conditions. When used publicly, glossolalia becomes a spiritual gift since it contributes to the common good. (Note, therefore, that the private use of glossolalia is not a spiritual gift, for by definition, a spiritual gift must serve the common good; 12:7.) Private glossolalia benefits only the individual practicing it (14:4, 17). But when glossolalia is interpreted, it becomes prophecy and can contribute to the edification of the congregation. Paul establishes this equation (vv. 29–31):

public glossolalia + interpretation = prophecy.

However, for this to happen properly and genuinely, Paul lays down a number of controls (1 Cor. 14:26–33).

Rule 1 All things that are done when Christians come together should be done for mutual edification (1 Cor. 14:26). The dominant concern in the use of spiritual gifts is the common good (12:7; 14:4, 5, 6, 12, 17, 18, 26, 31). Subjective glossolalia edifies or helps the speaker but is not intelligible to others; therefore, it has no place in public worship but belongs in the prayer closet.

Rule 2 "If any one speaks in a tongue. . ." (14:27). The "if" indicates that glossolalia is not an indispensable component of public worship. It may or may not be included.

Rule 3 If glossolalia is available and needed when Christians come together for worship, there should be one, two, or three at the maximum who speak in tongues (v. 27). The Scripture places a strict limit on the number of people who may speak in tongues per meeting.

Rule 4 They should each speak in turn, never all together (v. 27). When they all speak in tongues together, they create a scandalous stumbling block for the gospel (v. 23).

Rule 5 An interpretation should follow after a person speaks in a tongue (v. 27). This is not a process of translation of one language into another, since Paul already stated that tongues were not languages (v. 2). Interpretation is the rendering, under the guidance of the Spirit and for the benefit of the congregation, of the experience of the person who spoke in tongues. It might be noted here that rules 3, 4, and 5 are the ones most often broken in meetings where a lot of people go on speaking in tongues at the same time with no concern for interpretation and for mutual comprehension.

Rule 6 The person intending to speak in tongues must secure the interpreter in advance (v. 28). If his or her preparation for the worship service has not made an interpreter available, then the person must keep quiet. He or she does the glossolalia privately, where no one else can hear it. No interpreter, no speaking in tongues.

Apparently, many people in Corinth liked to speak in tongues because it brought the focus of attention upon them and because they thought it demonstrated their spirituality. But few were found to do the more routine interpretation into the current language. Speaking straight was not as glamorous as speaking in tongues. So Paul asks the ones speaking in tongues to pray instead for the gift of interpretation (v. 13). As indicated in 12:10, speaking in tongues and interpreting are two distinct gifts.

Rule 7 Once the speaking in tongues has been interpreted, it becomes intelligible prophecy that must be evaluated (v. 29). Individual presentations of the word of God are subject to review by the congregation (1 Thess. 5:20–21), among whom are those especially qualified for this ministry with the spiritual gift of discernment (1 Cor. 12:10). Since the New Testament documents were not yet available as the benchmark for Christian truth, there was need for general vigilance to be exercised over the preaching and teaching functions of the church.

Rule 8 Opportunity for ministry should be shared (14:30). No one person, regardless of rank, position, or authority, has the right to monopolize ministry when others have a valid contribution to make.

Rule 9 Broad participation in ministry is beneficial to the church (v. 31). Paul had limited the number of those who could speak in tongues to a maximum of three. However, if they prophesy in intelligible speech that provides learning and encouragement, they may "all" take part, as long as they do it in turn, "one by one." This form of ministry, not speaking in tongues, is the genuine demonstration of the activity of God within the congregation. Thus utilized, prophecy even has the power to bring unbelievers to obedience to God (vv. 24–25).

Rule 10 People who participate in worship, especially in ecstatic expressions such as glossolalia, are responsible to control their behavior (v. 32). No genuine prophet will go against the rules or engage in rude and inconsiderate actions with the excuse that the Spirit made her or him do it. Self-control and accurate teaching distinguish genuine prophecy from pagan religious practices (12:2–3). The God of Christians delights in peace—not in the confusion created by mindless ecstatic outbursts (14:33).

We may wonder why the Scriptures set so many stringent rules for the public practice of glossolalia, making it almost prohibitive, while they place no restrictions on the practice of secret or closet glossolalia. The reason should be obvious. God places a priority on the common good and on mutual edification. Where the direct, intelligible word is available, it is more profitable to the common good than the circuitous and potentially confusing process of glossolalia, which has to be interpreted and evaluated in order to result in beneficial ministry. Therefore, prophecy takes precedence and is listed as a higher gift, whereas glossolalia appears at the bottom of the list (12:28). Especially now that the final word of God is available in the canon of the New Testament, recourse to roundabout and therefore fallible ways of obtaining Christian truth through the convoluted glossolalia/interpretation/prophecy/evaluation process may become justified only in exceptional circumstances. The clear, distinct sound of a harmony is infinitely preferable to a garbled performance (14:7–9), and hearing speech in a language that one understands is infinitely preferable to hearing it in an alien language (vv. 10–11).

In conclusion, it would seem that there are two errors to be avoided in regard to glossolalia. One is to deny its validity and to condemn its use as demonic or carnal because it is allegedly rendered obsolete by Scripture (1 Cor. 13:8–10). However, the same Scripture also claims that knowledge "will pass away"–but, for most people, it has not. Paul categorically commands to "not forbid speaking in tongues" (14:39). The opposite error is to require glossolalia as an evidence of the activity of the Holy Spirit in the experience of believers and to display it as a badge of spirituality. The only genuine test of the work of the Spirit in the life of a believer is the production of the fruit of the Spirit in change of character and conduct (Gal. 5:22). However, should glossolalia be present, its exercise should not be forbidden as long as it is conducted according to the biblical requirements, "decently and in order" (v. 40 NRSV).

RESOURCES

For further study on the doctrine of the Holy Spirit, see the following resources:

Alan F. Johnson and Robert E. Webber. *What Christians Believe: A Biblical and Historical Summary*. Grand Rapids: Zondervan, 1989, pp. 148–86.

David Ewert. *The Holy Spirit in the New Testament*. Scottdale, Pa.: Herald Press, 1983.

Michael Green. *I Believe in the Holy Spirit*. Grand Rapids: Eerdmans, 1975.

DISCUSSION QUESTIONS

1. Is it biblically appropriate to pray to the Holy Spirit and to worship him?
2. What were the differences in the ministry of the Holy Spirit during the time of the old covenant and the new covenant?
3. Who are the recipients of the baptism of the Holy Spirit?
4. What was the connection between Pentecost and Cornelius' receiving the Holy Spirit?
5. What is the purpose of the spiritual gifts according the Scripture?

The Doctrine of Human Beings

Outline of Chapter Five

I. Humans as God's Image
  1. The Image of Transcendence
  2. The Image of a Dynamic Being
  3. The Image of Absolute Goodness

II. The Limits of the Image
  1. Human Dependency
    a. Human need for food
    b. Human need for shelter
    c. Human need for others
  2. Human Mortality
  3. Human Corruptibility

III. The Fall

IV. The Consequences of the Fall
  1. Disruption of the Image of God
  2. Disruption of Communion with God
  3. Disruption of the Community of Oneness
  4. Disruption of the Physical Environment
  5. Disruption of the Social Environment

V. Current Views on Human Beings

The Doctrine of Human Beings

Our discussion of the doctrines of God, Christ, and the Holy Spirit has suggested something of the infinite mystery and complexity of the being of God. To catch but a glimpse of the immensity of God feels like standing at the edge of a chasm and peering briefly through a hole in the fog at a vast unreachable world made for giants.

As we prepare to define theologically the entity traditionally called "man," we may hope to find relief from complexity and paradox. Unfortunately, this is not to be. Humans are not less baffling and mysterious than God himself. Once, as King David was reflecting on the majesty of God and contemplating the infinite vastness of the heavens, he exclaimed, "What is man?" (Ps. 8:4). This remains a good question. On one hand, humans are very much part of the created order. Their bodies have the properties of animal life and are subject to the same biological functions. But on the other hand, humans are the only beings that have the capacity to control rationally the course of their lives and to determine their destinies. As David put it, humans are only a bit lower than God, and they have mastery over the rest of the created world (vv. 5–8).

How humans are defined can make a lot of difference on how they behave and treat each other. If they are viewed as being no different than animals, they risk living like animals and being treated like animals. However, should they be recognized as possessing a dignity that sets them apart from the rest of creation, they acquire an intrinsic worth that should make their lives and their rights inviolable.

I. HUMANS AS GOD'S IMAGE

The most important truth revealed about humans in Scripture is that they are made in the image of God: "God created man in his own image, in the image of God he created him; male and female he created them" (Gen. 1:27 NIV). In the Garden of Eden, they were the crowning achievement of God's creative works. All other created things supported their existence and made it secure (see pages 34–35).

The definition of the image of God in humans has been a subject of endless discussions among theologians. It seems obvious that God's image should not be sought in the human body since God is a spiritual being and does not have a physical form to be copied (John 4:24). If not in the body, then where is the image to be found?

Fortunately, our previous discussion of the doctrine of God provides a model that enables us to define accurately the image of God. We discovered that Scripture presents God as a being who has the qualities of transcendence, dynamism, and absolute goodness (pages 26–37). If being made in God's image implies a resemblance or a likeness between humans and God, we should find each one of those divine traits reflected in his human counterparts. This being the case, the discussion in this chapter will focus on the archetypal texts of the creation story (Gen. 1–2), where the purest expression of God's original purposes for humankind is found.

1. The Image of Transcendence

Divine transcendence was defined as God's otherness and his autonomy from the created world; therefore, humans cannot be said to be transcendent beings. However, the manner in which they were created and their relation to the rest of creation indicates that they are different from it and above it. Those facts reflect a scaled-down human analogy to divine transcendence.

God's creation of humans sets them apart not only because they are the climax of God's creational achievements, but especially because God formed them in such a careful manner. The Genesis account gives no specific details about the formation of other parts of creation. God said the word and the reality came into existence. But when the time came for the creation of humans, the procedure is carefully reported (Gen. 2). God made Adam out of the dust of the ground (v. 7); in this, the man was not different from the vegetation and the living creatures that had also come out of the ground (1:12, 24). But in order to cause him to become human, God put the breath of life in him so that he became a responsive and responsible "living being"; this means that he became endowed with personhood (2:7).

To make sure that Adam understood that the woman was no less human than he was, God cloned her body from his body rather than taking her out of the dust of the ground, and he made her into a woman, bone of his bones and flesh of his flesh (2:22–23). She became another human being like him. Adam celebrated her sameness while recognizing her womanhood. He adopted for her the designation of "woman" (v. 22). Only after the Fall would Adam give her a name of his own choosing by calling her "Eve," because in a world conquered by death she became the mother of all living (3:20). Adam and Eve came out of the "hands" of God as acts of special creation, one out of the ground and the other from existing humanity—but both uniquely set apart from the rest of creation as bearers of God's image.

The most obvious distinction conferred upon the first humans by the Creator as a result of the image was their rulership over all other living beings (1:26–28). The creation account refers to only one line of authority among all created beings: the Creator ordering man and woman together to have dominion over all living creatures and to use vegetation to meet their own needs (1:29). In this sense, their rulership set them apart from the rest of created things and reflected, however remotely, something of the "otherness" and transcendence of God.

2. The Image of a Dynamic Being

We also defined God as a dynamic being, both within himself as a Tri-unity of persons (ontologically) and in his activity.

Since humans were made in God's image, it was inevitable that the plurality within his being would be reflected in a plurality of human persons. God in community created humans in community. As God set himself ready to create the human species he said, "Let us (plural) make man (singular, as 'humankind') in our (plural) image" (Gen. 1:26). Because God is a plurality of persons, when the moment of creation of humans arrived, they also came as a plurality of persons: male and female. God is three in one, but the human being is not God; thus man (or humankind) came as two in one (5:2; cf. 2:24).

The second chapter of Genesis dramatizes the necessity for the male/female duality. Adam was created first, but he was alone, undoubtedly lonely. In a world created good, God declared Adam's situation "not good" (2:18). His life was yearning for the other without whom he could not form the community of oneness. He could not, after all, be one with God since God was above him. Even less could he be one with nature since the natural world was not his equal but only the support for his life. So God created a female counterpart from Adam's body. God reached in his chest, right next to the man's heart, and took part of him to make another one like him. He split the one in two. Then he declared them one again (v. 24). Two complementary facets of God's image were now in existence.

The fact that God's image in human life came as male and female does not mean that God is male or female, or even both at the same time. God is a spirit; he is not bound by the physical properties that determine sexual identity. A spiritual being does not have sexual organs. In his transcendence, God is above and beyond sexuality. His image in humans came as male and female because both are contained within the infinitely diverse resources of his being. To say that God is either male or female is to make him in our image—in fact, in just half of the image—and to confuse the Creator with the human creature.

Most of the biblical designations for God appear in the masculine gender in the Bible ("he, him, his, Father") because the alternative would have been offensive in the idolatry-conscious, male-dominant Hebrew culture within which revelation was given in history. For similar reasons, both male and female are designated as "man" in the creation account, not because there were differences of rank between them but because no word exists in Hebrew for "humans" or "humankind." The inclusive term "living beings" was available, but it was unsuitable to designate humans distinctly since it was also used for animals (2:7,19). Their concept of "humanity" was expressed by the term "man" without implications of male leadership. The same holds true in our own culture. The Declaration of Independence states, "We hold these truths to be self-evident that all men are created equal. . ." Replacing "men" by "women" in this sentence turns it into nonsense; "men" is used to declare both men and women as equal per creation. Note too that the significance of the Incarnation is not that the pre-existent Christ was incarnated in a male, but only that in Jesus the Word became flesh.

God's dynamic nature is also evident in his creational and sustaining activities. This aspect of his being is reflected in human life in two ways: reproduction and production. God endowed humans with the power to reproduce his image by having children (Gen. 1:28). Obviously, procreation (or having babies) is not just a biological function; it is an awesome responsibility for which humans are accountable to God. A sense of the overwhelming wonder and dignity of perpetuating God's image was expressed by Eve when she held her firstborn in her arms and exclaimed, "I have produced a man with the help of the Lord" (4:1 NRSV). The ability to bring forth life made in the image of God appeared to her as a miracle in which God had participated. It seems obvious that the divine order for the original couple to multiply and to fill the earth implied also the responsible management of procreation to prevent it from going uncontrolled and becoming self-destructive. To fill the earth was not the mandate, but to fill it and to care for it at the same time.

The second responsibility that was entrusted to humans as God's image-bearers had to do with the stewardship of the earth. Because God is a worker, humans are workers. On behalf of God, they exercise dominion over living creatures and subdue the earth (1:26, 28). When Adam was alone in the garden, he was instructed to till it and keep it (2:15), though the first humans were not dependent on their work for food and survival (1:29). God directed Adam to cultivate the garden because productive activity reflects the dynamic nature of God. This is yet another trait that differentiates humans from animals—the humans' call to vocation.

3. The Image of Absolute Goodness

The holiness of God is closely associated with his transcendence. Of course, it is impossible for humans to duplicate perfectly the holiness of God, since they do not have his transcendence. However, by virtue of the goodness of God's creation, humans have a share in that goodness. God had declared practically every phase of his creative work as being "good" (Gen. 1:4, 10, 12, 18, 21, 25), suggesting that what resulted from God's creative endeavors was consistent with his purposes and reflected his nature. Moreover, as a result of the creation of humans, God declared his works not just "good" but "very good" (v. 31). God was "very" satisfied with the integrity and the righteous innocence of his image as he perceived it in humans.

However, because of the possibility of the entrance of evil in his new creation, God provided the humans with a protection in the form of the tree of the choice of good or evil (2:17). The tree served as a signpost, warning against the possible loss of their goodness (see page 33). This means that the humans were endowed with the capacity to make their own moral choices. Not only had they the freedom to choose, but God had given them the potential to choose the good wisely, just as he would.

The giver-servant aspect of God's goodness is likewise reflected in the relational dimension of God's image in the man and the woman. After creating the woman and identifying her as Adam's equal, God declared them to be one flesh as husband and wife (2:24). There can be no oneness unless there is complete mutuality. There can be a unity of sorts in a relationship of subordination, such as may exist between officer and foot soldier in a military unit or between boss and employee in an educational or business institution. But such relationships do not constitute oneness in the biblical sense. Biblical oneness can occur only where there is a relationship of mutual submission, not one-sided submission (see, for example, Phil. 2:2–3). God's giving love was defined earlier as servant love (pages 35–37). From the evidence of God's plan of oneness for the human couple, God expected the servant posture to prevail on both sides of their relationship. Only in this way would God's goodness be mirrored in human life.

II. THE LIMITS OF THE IMAGE

As lofty and noble as humans are by virtue of their creation in God's image, they remain finite creatures, limited and vulnerable. If the image reveals points of correspondence between qualities of God and human attributes, the same image also reveals radical differences. Those differences can be surveyed with the aid of the same models of transcendence, dynamism, and goodness that served us before, only this time considering the opposites of those qualities: human dependency, mortality, and corruptibility.

1. Human Dependency

God is transcendent in that he existed before creation as an autonomous, self-sufficient being, in no way needing anything that creation could provide for his well-being. Creatures made in his image cannot make such claims. Their very createdness makes them dependent on the resources of their Creator. Among all the resources that he has provided for their welfare, three stand out in the Genesis creation account.

a. Human need for food

God gave humans every plant, seed, and fruit for food to sustain their lives (Gen. 1:29). In this, they were no different from the animals, who were also given every green plant for food (v. 30). The humans were like God, but they were not God. In their dependency on the resources of the environment for mere survival, humans are more akin in the physical sphere to the animal kingdom than they are to God.

b. Human need for shelter

The transcendent God who created the universe took care to place within it a luminous planet that would be home to the human race, and within a privileged area of this planet he planted a garden that would be home to the first couple. In this garden, they had trees, pleasant to the sight and good for food, waterways, mounds of gold and precious stones, and every beast of the field and bird of the air (2:9–14, 19). God himself does not need a home since he created everything and every place; but the image-bearers needed a habitat, and God provided it for them.

c. Human need for others

According to Scripture, God is perfectly self-sufficient within the grandeur of his transcendence. He did not create humans in order to give himself companionship. Quite the opposite: He gave life out of love. He created beings other than himself for their own sakes, not his own. His creation will ultimately glorify him, but God was not and is not dependent on such satisfactions for his well-being. He is complete with or without creation.

However, since transcendence is, by definition, not a quality that can be passed on, beings made in God's image cannot survive alone as he can. They need others like themselves. In a created world judged by God to have been "very good," there was one jarring note. God also saw something that was "not good" (2:18)— it was not good that the man should be alone. In the magnificent, freshly created world in which Adam lived, there was no one or nothing else Adam could relate to as an equal because there was no one else made in God's image. No suitable companion was found for him until God made the woman.

This story does not mean that the solution to human need is romantic love or marriage and that unless people are married they are hopelessly condemned to be lonely. In fact, the Bible teaches that God calls many people to remain single while enabling them to lead fulfilled lives. Jesus taught that God wants some to remain single for the sake of service to the kingdom (Matt. 19:11–12), and in an extensive explanation, the apostle Paul laid down the principle that any Christian should first consider the option of singleness in case he or she has the capacity to remain single and can be more effective in serving God and others (1 Cor. 7:7–8, 25–35).

God's declaration that "it is not good for the man to be alone" means that humans are social beings. They cannot develop and become whole persons in isolation. They need to be in community to survive, to establish their identities as individuals, and to fulfill their vocation as humans and find contentment. Stories have been told of abandoned infants raised by wild animals, who were later discovered as undomesticated beings with no trace of human behavior or personhood in them. One such tragic case was documented in Oklahoma in 1990, where a four-year-old boy had been raised with dogs in a large dirt-floor pen. When he was discovered by the Department of Human Services, the child acted like a dog. He barked, howled, drooled, grabbed things in his mouth, and ran on all fours. To a great extent, the history of our relationships makes us who we are. Because in his triune nature the Creator is community, creatures made in his image cannot reflect that image apart from living in community.

God set about to provide Adam with what he needed the most, a "helper suitable for him" (Gen. 2:18 NIV). None of the animals was suitable for Adam since they were not created in God's image. They could not help him preserve the image. Therefore, God custom-designed Adam's female equivalent, in whom Adam immediately recognized another one like himself (v. 23). The word *helper* used to describe the woman's place in relation to Adam is significant. Recent biblical scholarship has observed that this Hebrew word for "helper" is used in the Bible as a designation for someone who rescues or saves from difficult situations rather than for a subordinate assistant, as the word suggests in English. Numerous times and almost exclusively, this word is used to designate God himself as our "helper" (Ex. 18:4; Deut. 33:7; Ps. 33:20; 70:5, etc.). In this light, the part played by the woman in Adam's life becomes clear. She was the God-appointed rescuer who would help preserve the divine image in human life. Adam acknowledged her function as the preserver and perpetuator of the divine image. He named her Eve, which means "life," because she was the mother of all living (Gen. 3:20). God did not need to make another god to maintain his deity, but Adam needed to be in community in order to fulfill his humanity.

2. Human Mortality

God is a dynamic being in that he is Creator. He is the source of life, and death can have no hold on him. Death pertains to the created world. Since, in his transcendence, God is distinct from and beyond the created world, his being cannot be affected by death.

Unfortunately, this was not the case with his image-bearers. Unlike God, they were vulnerable to death. Because of that very fact, God placed in the center of the garden the warning tree, telling Adam that he should never try to eat of the tree because the day he would eat its fruit he would die. God knew that as good a replica of his own being as was the image, its bearer could not have God's own immunity to death. In order to stay alive, the image would have to maintain its connection with God. Just as a light fades away when the switch connecting it to the source of power is turned off, so human life would fade away if and when communion with God would be broken. The tree was a warning against rebellion and the death that would ensue.

3. Human Corruptibility

God is absolute goodness; but because the image is only image and not the reality, there is nothing absolute about humans. God had endowed humans with goodness (Gen. 1:31), but that goodness was not absolute. It was vulnerable to evil and subject to corruption, the corruption called "death." Because he knew it could happen, God explained to the man that there was good and evil, that both could be part of his experience, and that the knowledge of evil was undesirable because it would lead to death (2:17). Later, when God's worst fear was realized, he held Adam personally accountable for having disdained the warning. He asked, "Have you eaten of the tree of which I commanded you not to eat?" (3:11 RSV). The "you" pronouns in this sentence are both in singular form. The prohibition had been given individually to Adam. He had knowingly and willfully violated it. As a result, he was the one who introduced the twin corruptions of evil and death into the world (Rom. 5:12–14; 1 Cor. 15:22).

To recognize human dependency, mortality, and corruptibility does not mean that God had created an imperfect world. It only means that a vast difference exists between the Creator and the image-bearers. As long as the image-bearers respected that difference, they protected the goodness invested by God in creation. But should the image-bearers deny the difference and act as if they were creator, they would take upon themselves the dreadful responsibility of triggering a chain reaction of disruptions that would devastate the goodness of creation. How this happened at the Fall and what resulted from it will be surveyed in the rest of this chapter. An examination of Genesis 3 will provide the best insights for the understanding of human sinfulness and of the results of the Fall on humans and on their environment. Indeed, the remainder of the Bible after this chapter is a commentary on the negative results of the Fall and a description of God's redemptive efforts to overcome them and to fulfill his original purposes in creation.

III. THE FALL

The boundary that God had set for humans to preserve their goodness was to remain in communion with him as they recognized his sovereignty over them and their own need for God. The issues were so clear that no misunderstanding was possible. God had given Adam the warning, and the tree in the middle of the garden served as a safeguard against anything going wrong. Had those precautions been respected, the Bible would have been a very short book: Genesis 1–2 as the story of Paradise on earth. But unfortunately, Genesis 3 happened—the Fall of humankind—and because of it, all the remaining books of the Bible follow, where the story is told of God's undoing of the effects of the Fall.

Without the intruder coming into the garden, it is unlikely that the Fall would have taken place. But the enemy, bent on destroying what was dearest to God, found a familiar disguise to slither his way into the garden and to cause the human race to suffer the same downfall that he had himself experienced (see pages 39–40).

The very first words uttered by the tempter to the woman reveal the reason for his choice of her as his point of attack. He asked her whether God had indeed prohibited them from eating of the tree (Gen. 3:1). He was testing the extent of her knowledge of the prohibition. Apparently, the tempter knew that God had given the prohibition to Adam when Eve was not yet in existence (2:16–17). Since she was the newcomer in the garden and the less informed of the two, he hoped to find her more vulnerable. Had the tempter addressed the same question to Adam, it would have sounded ludicrous, "Adam, we know that God told you not to eat of the tree, but did God tell you not to eat of any tree?" But addressed to the woman, the question made sense, "Are you really sure that God said you shall not eat of any tree in the garden?" Underlying this question seems to be another one, "How can you be sure of what God said since you weren't there?" The answer of the woman misquotes God's prohibition on several counts, but it shows that she had received a general knowledge of it (compare 2:17 and 3:3).

Having sown the seeds of doubt in the woman's mind, Satan pressed his advantage and challenged God's truthfulness. God had warned Adam that he would die if he ate of the tree. Satan, the liar, tried to make God a liar, "Of course, you won't die" (3:4). The author of death promised immortality.

The third line of the tempter's attack offered God-likeness to the humans, "You shall be like God" (v. 5). Since Adam and Eve had been made in God's image, they were already like God; but Satan suggested they could have more, that God was holding them down in order to control their lives and was depriving them of the knowledge that he possessed. They could shake the yoke of divine oppression, declare their independence, and play God. The devil's challenge for the humans to press for self-transcendence set them on a quest for upward mobility. The tempter did not suggest to Eve that they should rise up and seek to be equal with nature, for they already had dominion over it. He could not offer equality with living creatures since the humans already ruled over the animals. Neither did he suggest to Eve that she seek equality with Adam, for she already was one with him and enjoyed full parity with him. The only authority structure available for either Adam or Eve, or for both together, to challenge was God's sovereignty over them. Satan was going for the jugular. He himself had tried to be equal with God and failed. He was now telling the humans, "It's your turn. Try to be equal with God." Satan was luring them into the very essence of sin: to reject God's sovereignty over human life and to declare oneself sovereign; to dismiss God and to make oneself one's own god. They were proclaiming their declaration of independence from God—which is exactly what happens every time we commit sin. At its root, sin is telling God to move over so that we can take over.

Then the woman acted out her fantasy of liberation from God. She made herself the judge of the matter. She knew that God had said not to eat, but she dismissed the order and took the matter into her own hands. She decided that the tree was good, delightful, and desirable (v. 6). She ate of the fruit and gave some to her husband, and he also ate of it.

The passivity of the husband during this drama may seem strange. After all, he was the one who had received the command about the tree directly from God, person to person. God reminded him of this later, as if it had placed a special burden of responsibility upon him. Twice God told Adam after the Fall that the prohibition had been given to him personally, "I commanded you" (the "you" is in singular form in 3:11, 17). He alone had benefited from several experiences with God that Eve had not shared. He had seen God plant a garden and give it to him. God had spoken to him when he gave him all the trees except the one in the middle of the garden. God had created the animals and brought them to him. Finally, God had formed the woman and brought her to be joined with him (2:8–23).

Adam had enjoyed a long relationship with God that should have compelled him to stop the tempter's efforts and to dismiss him from the garden. Being the better informed member of the pair, he could have acted as their protector. Instead, he quickly ate of the fruit without raising any objection, as if he had been waiting for that very moment all along. This strange behavior and the readiness with which he ate of the fruit suggest that Adam also entertained liberation fantasies. But because of his long friendship with God, he let his wife act these fantasies out while hiding behind her skirts, as it were. Adam acted as if he had been watching Eve eat of the tree to verify whether she would die as God had warned, "When you eat of it you will surely die" (2:17). This way, should something go wrong, he could always shift the blame to her—which is precisely what happened (3:12). But God was not fooled by the stratagem. He held Adam responsible for having listened to his wife instead of to his command (v. 17). Consequently, when the predicted sentence of death fell, it fell on Adam (v. 19).

Sometimes, the harsher punishment of Adam is explained with the theory that he was the "federal head" of the human race. But no such teaching is found in the Genesis creation account, nor is Adam ever so described in Scripture. It is also alleged that Adam was more severely punished because he was the "spiritual head" of Eve in the garden. But the words "federal head" and "spiritual head" are found neither in Genesis nor in the rest of Scripture, and there is no teaching about Adam's "headship" over Eve or about him being her leader in the first two chapters of Genesis. It was a result of the Fall, not any part of God's original plan or purposes, that Adam became ruler over Eve (v. 15).

However, the New Testament draws a distinction between Adam and Eve at the time of the temptation. It teaches that Eve was deceived by the tempter's cunning and became a transgressor (2 Cor. 11:3; 1 Tim. 2:14), but Adam sinned and brought death into the world (Rom. 5:12–14; 1 Cor 15:22). There is no mention of Adam being deceived as Eve was. When Adam was still alone, God had made him keeper of the garden and keeper of the commandment (Gen. 2:14, 17). In making her decision, Eve had two sets of data to choose from; she had received one set of information from Adam, the other from Satan. Eve rejected Adam's information to follow Satan. And in making his decision, Adam also had two sets of data to choose from: one set from God, the other from Satan. Adam rejected God to follow Satan. By not keeping the commandment, he also lost the garden. "From everyone who has been given much, much will be demanded; and from the one who has been entrusted with much, much more will be asked" (Luke 12:48 NIV).

IV. THE CONSEQUENCES OF THE FALL

The sin of rebellion in the garden was the triumph of Satan. Human beings, God's pride and joy and his reason for creation, had rejected him and allowed the enemy to infiltrate the world and become its illegitimate ruler, "the prince of this world" (John 12:31; 14:30; 16:11). In the solemn words of familiar hymns, "the guilty pair, bowed down with care," had fallen victim to "the prince of darkness grim"; and "still our ancient foe doth seek to work us woe." The sin in Eden set off an unending chain reaction of disruptions that affected every aspect of human life and threatened to thwart God's purposes for history.

1. Disruption of the Image of God

The immediate consequence of sin was the opening of the humans' eyes to realize that they were naked (Gen. 3:7) and to be ashamed of it. Nakedness and shame are associated in the Old Testament with weakness and defeat. Before their downfall, the humans' nobility as God's image-bearers shielded them from the frailty of their humanity. Once the protection was removed, their eyes were opened to each other's exposure in weakness, one miserable sinner gazing at the misery of another sinner. The pain of exposure was so intolerable that they sought the pitiful cover of fig leaves as a substitute for the glory of the innocence that had clothed them.

Adam and Eve looked at each other and saw strangers. Where once the image of God had been dominant, their failed humanity now showed through. As a cracked mirror reflects a distorted picture, so the disrupted image they saw in each other reflected a new reality, that of sinners alienated from God.

After the Fall, man and woman were still made in the image of God, which continued to distinguish them from the animal kingdom. Sin could not take that image away from them. However, with their connection of communion with God broken, the image became distorted and dim. It would need to be revitalized by God's Spirit and restored through sanctification. Satan had managed to disconnect the humans from their source of power, and the light of God's image flickered out. But the circuits remained, to be rekindled some day by the Savior.

2. Disruption of Communion with God

The second result of the Fall was that sinful Adam and Eve felt the need to hide themselves from the presence of God. Leaves were enough for them to hide from each other, but with God, they needed the whole tree. They had been friends with God. The garden, given to them as a place of communion with God and as a testimony to his goodness, now became a place of terror. They knew that they were accountable to God. Indeed, God called on each one of them separately, in order to draw from them an explanation for the alienation. The man blamed God who had given him a wife who gave him the fruit (3:12). The woman blamed the tempter and admitted having been deceived by him (v. 13).

God defined for them the new situation they faced as a result of having broken their relationship with him. They were now on their own, as they had chosen to be. The woman would fall under the dominance of her husband, while the husband would struggle under the dominance of a cursed environment that would eventually overcome him and pull him back into the ground from where he had been taken (vv. 16, 19). Previously, the source and sustenance of their lives had been God. Having cut themselves off from God, they now became subject to death. They had aspired to become like God; instead, they were returning to dust, to physical nothingness.

Having been spurned, God could have abandoned the humans to their tragic fate. But to do so would have been against his nature as a loving servant God. Consequently, he extended himself to them in three gestures of mercy. First, he promised the ultimate defeat of Satan through Christ, the posterity of the woman. Satan had won the initial battle, but he would eventually be crushed (v. 15). Second, God gave the alienated wanderers the protection of animal skins. As distorted as the image may have become, humans were still its bearers. They still had a dignity as humans that placed them above the animals (v. 21). Thirdly, God put them out of the garden to prevent them from eating of the tree of life and living forever in their miserable sinful condition (vv. 22–24). They could not work out their own redemption; it would have to be provided for them. The ravages brought about by the Fall had been too damaging for humans to be able to save themselves. Only a Redeemer could now rescue them.

3. Disruption of the Community of Oneness

God had created man and woman to be one flesh, to be bonded together in a community of intimacy and acceptance where the deep human yearning to know and to be known would be satisfied in the joyful freedom of mutual love (Gen. 2:24–25). Because the oneness between the humans was an image of the oneness that exists between the three persons within the Godhead, its security was dependent on their relationship with God. Once their rebellion separated them from God, it also separated them from each other. The intimacy of Eden was lost; they were wearing coverings to hide from each other. God had given them to each other because it was not good for man to be alone. But now they were alone, like two strangers in a park. Worse than being alone are two persons sharing lives of loneliness side by side.

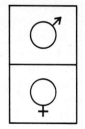 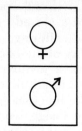

This is not oneness. Neither is this.

Even this is not oneness.

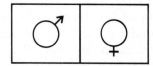

But this is certainly oneness.

For Eve, the breakdown of the relationship with God meant that she became dependent on Adam, from whom she had been made. Her desire would be for the intimacy and oneness they had known before the Fall, but now he would rule over her (3:16). Before the Fall, she was one with Adam. Now he would have dominion over her.

The loss of the community of oneness was one of the prices that Adam and Eve had to pay for their tragic mistake. But the time would come when the Redeemer would announce a new day for the restoration of the same community of oneness, just as it was in the beginning, before the Fall. At that time, husband and wife would again become one because their individual relationship with God would be restored through the cross (Matt. 19:4–8).

4. Disruption of the Physical Environment

The first two chapters of Genesis describe how God had set up the world and how it should have remained. They contain not one negative word denoting pain, hardship, or suffering, except for the warning about the possibility of evil and death (2:9, 17). But the account of the Fall (Gen. 3) bristles with terms denoting brokenness, evil, and death. It tells the story of our lives as they are contained in a closed cycle of pain. Life begins with suffering, continues in suffering, and ends through suffering.

In the story of the beginning, the prospect of reproduction was presented as a joyful challenge for humans to be fruitful, to multiply, and to fill the earth (1:28). The Fall changes that. In the most Godlike function entrusted to humans, the capacity to make beings in his image, woman was now on her own. The miracle of childbearing would continue as predicted by God before the Fall, but now it would be surrounded with pain. The woman would experience that pain (3:16). Then as the child of pain grew into a man, his days would be plagued with the need to toil and eke out a living from the ground (v. 17). The ground itself was cursed. Having become the domain of Satan, the earth that had been created "good" by God now bore the same curse that had fallen on Satan (v. 17; see v. 14). As a result, the environment became harsh and inhospitable. The luxuriant garden, adorned with "every tree that is pleasant to the sight and good for food" (2:9), gave way to arid dust that responds to man's efforts to make it productive by growing thorns and thistles in his face, wet with sweat (3:18).

Before the Fall, the plants yielded seed and fruit easily and in sufficient abundance to provide food for both humans and animals (1:29–30). The man was to till and keep the garden, but not for the purpose of survival (2:15). The ground provided naturally a cornucopia of health foods. The activity of the man was more like the hobby of a wealthy gentleman-farmer who keeps a garden not for income or out of need, but for pride and pleasure. After the Fall, survival becomes dependent on hard labor, and in the sweat of his face man eats his bitter bread (3:19). Originally, work was pleasurable activity that imaged God's dynamic nature, and humans had dominion over the earth (1:26). The environment now turned hostile, having dominion over humans and causing them to work with wearying toil. And finally, the cursed ground reclaims man's worn-out being and reduces it to nothingness (3:19).

In this dismal tale of woes one ray of hope shines through. As the man is told that he is dust and to dust he will return, he decides to call his wife with a name that evokes the hope of continuing life—*Eve*, the mother of all living (v. 20). The Fall is the story of the victory of death. But the sovereign purposes of God cannot be ultimately defeated, so life will go on.

5. Disruption of the Social Environment

The pattern of social organization established by God for the human community was the oneness that imaged the harmonious relationships that prevail within his own being. The Fall destroyed not only the oneness of the couple but also the social fabric of the human race. The instruments used for its destruction were violence and sex. Indeed, there is nothing new under the sun.

It took only one generation after the first couple exited from the garden for the first murder to be committed. The occasion was trivial: one of the differences that occur at every turn in the give-and-take of daily life and that can be resolved beneficially when approached creatively and in good will. The sacrificial offering of one of Adam and Eve's two sons was accepted and the other's rejected, presumably because of an unresolved sinful condition in his life (Gen. 4:5–6; cf. 1 John 3:12). There may have been a dozen methods to resolve the difficulty. Instead, Cain chose recourse to the most stupid of all, the use of violence. As a result, a disastrous precedent was set for recourse to violence as a problem-solver (Gen. 4:8–14). Knowing that the use of violence unavoidably escalates its recurrence, God made a special provision for Cain in order to stop the chain reaction of murderous madness. He declared a sevenfold punishment on any avenger of Abel (v. 15). But a foolish man called Lamech completely misunderstood the protective intent of God's decree. He interpreted it as a license to kill sevenfold in order to prove one's manliness. He actually bragged about avenging himself not just sevenfold but seventy-seven times (v. 24).

After Abel's murder, violence became a way of life, a regrettable but unavoidable evil, finding its way even into the legislations of the old covenant. The Law attempted to curb its escalation with the legislation of the talion that required retribution not to exceed inflicted harm, "life for life, eye for eye, tooth for tooth" (Deut. 19:21). But only when Jesus taught the way of forgiveness and love for the enemy did an alternative to violence finally become available. Jesus' concern was for community. He knew that violence destroys community. He also knew that, in order to defuse the cycle of violence and prevent its escalation, someone had to absorb it sacrificially at some point by refraining from returning it (Matt. 26:52). Therefore, he commanded his followers to bear witness to him, to his gospel, and to the values of his kingdom by refusing to participate in violence in a world ruled by the right of might. Whenever someone would insultingly slap a believer on the right cheek, the believer was to turn his left cheek for the aggressor to strike with his open hand or fist rather than respond in kind (Matt. 5:38–39; Luke 6:27–36). And because Jesus was willing to exemplify this teaching all the way to the cross, he was able to bring salvation to a world addicted to violence (1 Pet. 2:21–23).

The same Lamech also contributed to the disruption of God's ordinance for the family. Through God's order, the human family began with one man joining himself to one woman in order to form a married couple (Gen. 2:24). Lamech, however, took two wives (4:19). Not content with having degraded his first wife by taking an additional one, he gathered both and staged a concert before them, flexing his macho muscles and bragging of his murderous exploits as the neighborhood bully (vv. 23–24). This was only the beginning of a long history of polygamy that continued through the old covenant with Abraham and his descendants, kings and common men. The Fall had destroyed the oneness of the couple and replaced it with the ruler/subject relation. It was the inequality between husband and wife resulting from the Fall that made it lawful for a ruler-husband to have several subject-wives (see Deut. 21:15–17).

The disruption of the family ordinance was also reflected in the laws that governed divorce and adultery. The ruler-husband could divorce his subject-wife at will, but the wife had no such right regardless of the treatment or abuse that she suffered (Deut. 24:1–4). Likewise for adultery, the ruler-husband could not commit adultery against his wife even if he slept with all the women in town. Adultery occurred only if he violated another man's rights by consorting with his wife or betrothed. As a result, a married man could engage in sexual relations with unattached women without being punished. However, if his subject-wife did likewise with anyone other than her husband, she was put to death (22:13–30). Such were the privileges of the ruler and the devastation brought upon the relationship of oneness at the Fall. When Jesus restored marriage to the original model that had prevailed in pre-fall creation, he replaced rulership with oneness and abolished in one stroke the rulers' right to polygamy, divorce, and adultery (Matt. 19:3–9). In order to establish the new community, Jesus dealt head-on with society's addiction to the twin evils of violence and misused sex, replacing it with his passionate call to oneness.

The moral degeneracy that set in as the result of the Fall became so widespread that God decided to give the human race a chance to start all over again (Gen. 6:12). But even the purging by the Flood was unable to overcome the disruptions that had begun at the Fall. The old temptation that had been introduced in the garden for humans to defy God by deifying themselves found its way again into the hearts of the men of Babel. They decided to build a tower that would reach into the heavens and establish their own name as supreme (Gen. 11:4). But exactly the opposite happened. Instead of reaching up into heaven, they found themselves scattered all over the earth, and they discovered that when they spoke from one group to another, they could not understand each other's language (vv. 7–9). The destruction of the community of oneness was now complete. It had not, however, become final, for in the midst of this chaos God established a covenant, gave the Law, and sent prophets to announce and prepare the coming of redemption.

V. CURRENT VIEWS ON HUMAN BEINGS

We have discovered in this chapter that the biblical story of beginnings provides a gripping explanation of our human condition (Gen. 1–3). It tells us who we are as human beings, what the meaning of our lives is, why we suffer and die, and what the essence of sin is. It also tells us what God had intended life to be and describes his sorrow at the calamity that has befallen humans. The rest of the Bible is a long historical documentary on those themes.

Unfortunately, the first two chapters of Genesis are sometimes treated as if their main purpose is to provide a scientific explanation of the creation of the earth. It is possible to enter into endless arguments about the age of the earth, about whether the universe was created suddenly with a "big bang," or in geological ages, or a few thousand years ago. But the crucial issue in those chapters has to do with deeper matters, such as the definition of human nature. Is the origin of human life the result of random accidents in some haphazard evolutionary process, or is it the result of a purposeful divine initiative in creation? Much depends on the answer to this question.

If humans are random happenings, their lives and their personhood have no more significance than what they might or might not assign to themselves. Such definitions may vary from person to person, from country to country, from culture to culture, from time to time. Humans are then left at the mercy of whoever defines their worth, basing that worth on whatever criteria may seem convenient. From this humanistic perspective, there is no universally recognized standard to determine whether humans should have value or not, rights or not, granted by whom and on what basis, or whether those rights should be equal for all or discriminatory. There can be no appeal to any authority other than one's own or that of the leader(s) of the moment to determine the morality of law, social responsibility, civil rights, oppression, aggression, killing, euthanasia, war, abortion, suicide, capital punishment, genocide, torture, and holocausts. The denial of divine involvement in the emergence of human life results in its relativization and devaluation.

However, when God is recognized as the intentional designer of human life, such life acquires infinite worth and significance. Humans become accountable to a supreme authority other than their own for how they handle their lives, for what they accomplish with them, for how they steward them, and to what ends they use them. They also become responsible to love, protect, and enhance the lives of other human beings who matter to God as much as they do themselves. Without God, the cultivation of human solidarity and the establishment of responsible community are at best optional man-made ideals. With God at the center, they become compelling divine mandates to fulfill. The Scriptures clearly teach that God is the author of human life and that humans are accountable to him for their own lives and for the lives of others.

Discussions among Christians about the date of origin and the timing of creation are fairly recent. Historically, the dominant debate relative to the doctrine of "man" had to do with how badly human sin has affected the divine image. Some regard humans as having been so totally disabled by sin that we are incapable of doing any good without God undertaking it for us. Others agree that sin has badly impaired human capacity for good, yet believe that humans may do good, though it may require God's involvement on their behalf.

Although this discussion among theologians is still going on, it really began during the fifth century of our era, between two Christian leaders of great learning and high moral character. Pelagius was a monk from England who taught that human nature remained basically good after the Fall. He recognized that the individual will is now disposed to choose sin over righteousness, but he denied that this bent to sin was inherited from Adam. He taught that it resulted from the fact that humans are raised in a sinful environment and that they follow bad examples. Consequently, salvation comes to humans when they realize that it is in their best interest to accept the grace of God and to turn their lives over to him of their own free will.

If the Pelagian view of human nature may be described as "I'm OK, You're OK," the opposite definition may be called the "Wretched Worm" view. Its first propounder was Augustine, a bishop who lived at the same time as Pelagius. Born in North Africa, he had led a dissipated life during his youth until he experienced a dramatic conversion. He later became one of the greatest theologians of the church. According to Augustine, when Adam became a sinner, all of us were involved in his sin, since we were within him as his descendants. As a result, we are marked by sin even before our birth. We all bear the burden of "original sin," which is transmitted from parents to children through the sexual act—itself an expression of lust. Because of what was later termed "total depravity" of humans, no one has the will to seek God's grace. It is God who chooses those he will save and who causes them to accept his salvation. He is also the one who keeps them in his will so that they persevere in their salvation. In other words, humans are unable to do anything to be saved. It is all God's work.

The difference between those two positions is the "nature or nurture" polarity. *Augustinianism* teaches that human nature is evil, whereas *Pelagianism* teaches that the human environment is evil while human nature is basically good. Today, Christians fall in various camps in regard to this issue. Some, like the Roman Catholic Church, have combined the two traditions by keeping the doctrine of original sin but by maintaining that humans are born with the ability to choose the good. Some Protestants like those with a Lutheran or Calvinist heritage follow modified forms of Augustinian teaching, emphasizing human helplessness and divine initiative. Protestants in the Arminian, Wesleyan, and Anabaptist traditions insist on the necessity for the exercise of human responsibility in response to the grace of God. Such ongoing discussions are not purely academic. The issues involved and their outcome affect the definition of a number of other doctrines, not least of them the doctrine of salvation, the subject of the next chapter.

RESOURCES

For further study on the doctrine of human beings, see the following resources:

Alan F. Johnson and Robert E. Webber. *What Christians Believe: A Biblical and Historical Summary*. Grand Rapids: Zondervan, 1989, pp. 189–230.

James Fowler. *Stages of Faith: The Psychology of Human Development and the Quest for Meaning*. San Francisco: Harper, 1984.

Henri Nouwen. *Beyond the Mirror: Reflections on Death and Life*. New York: Crossroad, 1990.

The Doctrine of Salvation

Outline of Chapter Six

I. God Changes the Standing of Sinners
   1. The Saving Work of a Transcendent God
      a. Atonement
      b. Justification
   2. The Saving Work of a Dynamic God
      a. Ransom
      b. Salvation
   3. The Saving Work of a Good God
      a. Reconciliation
      b. Adoption

II. God Changes Sinners
   1. Calling
      a. Everybody matters to God
      b. Believers are predestined to salvation
      c. God chooses individuals for ministry
   2. Regeneration
      a. Phase one: conviction
      b. Phase two: conversion
   3. Sanctification
      a. Moralistic approaches
      b. Crisis-experience approaches
      c. Sanctification as a process
      d. The loss of salvation

III. Current Views on Redemption
   1. Liberation Theology
   2. Process Theology
   3. Universalism

CHAPTER SIX

The Doctrine of Salvation

Had God not been a holy, loving God, the disaster brought upon the world by the Fall would have spelled the end of the story of humankind. Having been held in contempt by his creatures, God had every right to abandon them to the destructive power of Satan. He could have turned his back on the human situation and let it rot into fine dust.

But God had created humans out of love and as the objects of his love. Like a parent who cannot disown a wayward child, he could not reject those who had rejected him. God therefore made a commitment to do his utmost to reclaim from humankind a people who would seek him and belong to him. This commitment was first hinted at in the promise of one who would crush the tempter's head (Gen. 3:15). It found full expression in a series of covenants that God made with humans to promise them the restoration of the community of oneness.

The first important covenant made by God was his promise to Abraham to make him the father of many nations. God told him that he would give birth to a people who would be used to bring his blessings among all the nations of the earth (Gen. 12:3). This promise was so important that God changed his name from Abram (meaning "exalted father" or "father of one family") to Abraham (meaning "father of a multitude of nations"; 17:1–7). Much later, reflecting on the church, the apostle Paul observed that the ultimate purpose of God's covenant with Abraham was to make him the father of all who believe, regardless of their racial background (Rom. 4:11–12, 16–18). In other words, God began the work of redemption with Abraham and brought it to fulfillment in the ministry of Jesus Christ.

In this chapter, we are concerned more with the outcome of the covenant than with the process that resulted in the ministry of redemption. The history of God's repeated attempts to form the racial descendants of Abraham into a community is told in the Old Testament. As instructive and interesting as the study of that failed

143

process may be, its outcome in Christ's redemptive ministry is of greater importance. Therefore, we will concentrate here on the doctrine of redemption, that is, on how God reclaims lost sinners so that they can become part of his new community. First, we will discover what God does for sinners as he changes their status in relation to himself; then we will study what God does to sinners as he changes them into saints.

I. GOD CHANGES THE STANDING OF SINNERS

After the Fall, humans found that they had cut themselves off from God and had become subject to death. In order to draw them back to himself, God laid down the basis for their acceptance in the redemptive ministry of Jesus Christ. While the great majority of those who were to benefit from the saving work of Christ were not yet alive, Christ obtained on their behalf all that was necessary to make them acceptable to God. In other words, long before we were born and before we could desire to be saved, Christ died for us, securing a *position* that we would later be able to claim for ourselves. For this reason, this aspect of the ministry of Christ is called *positional salvation*. Through Christ, we are given a new position, or a new standing, in relation to God.

1. The Saving Work of a Transcendent God

Human sin had violated the majesty and the sovereign rights of God. The principle of rightness or justice that God had established in the world when he gave Adam the warning about evil and death had been scorned. The sentence of death fell upon humans of their own choosing. Salvation meant that the sentence would be lifted. But for this to happen, another death had to take place, and the death of Christ met this need. Two kinds of images describe this aspect of redemption, one expressed in the language of the altar and the other in that of the court of law.

a. Atonement

The biblical words *expiation* and *propitiation* are also closely related to the concept of *atonement*. They all refer to the fact that, in the moral order, satisfaction has to be rendered for wrongdoing. In most ancient religions this satisfaction was offered by means of sacrifices. For Christians, the all-sufficient, once-for-all sacrifice was offered when Christ died on the cross for the sins of the world. The cross was like an altar on which Christ laid down his life in our stead (Rom. 3:25; Heb. 2:17; 1 John 2:2, 4:10; see also pages

71–72). Since he died as our substitute, we need not die for our sins; instead, we can claim eternal life through faith in him.

b. Justification

This word evokes the language of the court of law. To be *justified* in the biblical sense does not mean that one is suddenly made just or sinless. It means that since Christ has suffered the punishment for sin in our place, we can receive the verdict of "Not guilty" or "Sentence served," and thus be forgiven. According to this image, we are standing in the seat of the accused, sure to be sentenced, but the judge acquits us because Christ volunteered to be found guilty in our place (Rom. 3:23–26; 4:24–25; 5:1,9; 8:31–33; see also Col. 2:13–14).

2. The Saving Work of a Dynamic God

The God who gave of himself inexhaustibly in creation could not do less in redemption. The theme of God's activity in redemption is expressed in two images, one pertaining to the marketplace and the other to the battlefield.

a. Ransom

Christ's gift of his life as a *ransom* (Mark 10:45; 1 Tim. 2:6; 1 Pet. 1:18–19) suggests a transaction made in order to purchase freedom for slaves. Since this is a metaphor, we do not need to raise a question as to whom the price of the ransom was paid. The main idea is that of release obtained through the payment of a redemption price. We all, as it were, stood in chains at the auction block, sure to remain in the bondage of death, and suddenly Christ volunteered to pay the price of our freedom with his own life.

b. Salvation

With other biblical concepts like *deliverance* and *liberation*, the word *salvation* evokes the rescue of persons caught in a hopeless situation. The image suggests that we were all held prisoners by the evil one in the strongholds of death when Christ, through his own death, overcame the enemy, saved us from his power, and set us free (Mark 3:23–27; Col. 1:13, 15; 1 Thess. 1:10; Heb. 2:14–15). He still liberates from the power of sin and Satan those who appeal to him (John 8:32, 36; Rom. 6:17–18, 22; Gal. 5:1); he saves repentant sinners from this crooked generation, which is subject to the wrath of God (Acts 2:40; Rom. 5:9). Since God desires everyone to be saved and to come to the knowledge of the truth, Jesus Christ, the one mediator between God and humankind, came into the world to save us (1 Tim. 1:15; 2:4–5).

3. The Saving Work of a Good God

God proved his love for us in that Christ died for us when we were still sinners. It is conceivable that someone would accept death on behalf of a good person, but even this happens very rarely. The extraordinary thing about God's love is that Christ died for the ungodly (Rom. 5:6–8). God had every right to turn away from humans since they had treated him as the enemy. Instead, he extended himself to them in love, trying to bring about reconciliation so that he could reintegrate them as his adoptive family. This aspect of Christ's redemptive work is expressed in images that suggest the healing of social relations through *reconciliation* and the forming of family ties through *adoption*.

a. Reconciliation

At the Fall, humans slammed the door of rejection in God's face. Things have not changed since that time. Without cause, we treat the God who gave us life as if he were our enemy. Our disposition is to reject or ignore him, to exclude him from our decisions and concerns, and to give the advantage to the evil one who is bent on destroying us and our society. In the Old Testament, this readiness to turn away from God is compared to the unfaithfulness of a spouse who plays the harlot. In the New Testament, it becomes a hopeless condition of sinfulness that should cause God to give up on us (Rom. 1:24, 26, 28). But he doesn't! One of the most majestic sentences expressed in human language declares that "God was in Christ, reconciling the world to himself" (2 Cor. 5:19 KJV).

Normally, the offender is the one who is expected to make the first move in the process of reconciliation. But in this case, God comes to us in Jesus so that we can be reconciled to him in the death of his Son (Rom. 5:10). With God, it is the offended one who extends his hand of reconciliation to the offender. The image suggests that we betrayed and turned away from a dear and influential relative and, instead of our going back to him on our knees to beg for forgiveness, he is already at our door to offer his embrace of love (Rom. 5:10–11; 2 Cor. 5:18–21).

b. Adoption

God was not content to offer reconciliation. His love made him go the next step. God makes his children those whose sin had made strangers. He adopts them as sons and daughters so that they become a new family, God's household of faith (Eph. 2:19; Gal. 6:10).

Adoption was a legal act by which a person took a child born of someone else for the purpose of treating the child as one's own. The custom was not common among the Jews, though it was practiced widely in the Roman world. Through adoption, the newcomer became a member of the family and was entitled to all the rights and privileges of a natural-born child. The New Testament declares that God sent his Son so that we may receive adoption and enjoy all the privileges of natural children, even to the extent of sharing in his inheritance. God took pity on us and made us his children at the expense of his own Son (Rom. 8:14–17; Gal. 4:4–7).

In addition to the terms and images described above, the Bible offers others to convey the richness of the doctrine of salvation. But even in this brief survey we have already seen several important features of this doctrine. The first is that salvation is the result of God's initiative. Humans could not save themselves; it was God who accomplished the work of redemption. The choice before humans is to appropriate it or to reject it.

The second feature is that the person of Jesus is central to salvation. Each one of the various aspects of this doctrine as outlined above is focused on him as the true agent of redemption. Without him or outside of him, there can be no salvation (Acts 4:12).

Finally, our survey shows that the death of Christ on the cross is what makes salvation possible. In the great mystery of life and death, it was necessary for the death on the cross to occur in order to deliver humans from eternal death and to transfer them to the realm of eternal life. This implies that a substitution took place at the cross. When Christ died, he died in our place so that we could have access to all the blessings suggested by the images discussed above. Because of this substitution, God sees us as having a new standing in relation to himself.

But the blessing of redemption does not stop with us acquiring a new status. God also intervenes in the lives of believers to bring about changes within their beings that make them new creations (2 Cor. 5:17). It is this aspect of redemption that will be surveyed in the next section.

II. GOD CHANGES SINNERS

Like the governments of many other countries, every year the United States government allows a number of people from overseas to come and establish themselves on its shores. While the future immigrants are still in their own countries, preparations are made in the United States to receive them and to integrate them into American society. Visas are allocated to give them the status of residents in anticipation of their acquiring full citizenship. Up to this point, these future immigrants are not directly involved in the changes that will affect them; they are still in their own countries, leading their habitual lives. But in the United States, new identities are being prepared to be made available to them once they physically arrive on American soil.

As inadequate as it may be, this story illustrates what God has done to make a new standing available to sinners estranged from him. In Christ, he created all the right conditions for accepting us as his children. He prepared a new status, ready to be conferred upon us as soon as we accept his offer and "immigrate" into his kingdom. This aspect of redemption was surveyed in the previous section.

Returning to our immigrant analogy, it is obvious that making the status of resident available to people will be of no use unless they physically come to their new country. The government will not give them recognition unless they show up on its shores and become committed to and involved in becoming citizens. This will require them to go through certain standard procedures of naturalization. They will swear allegiance to their new country, and only then can they become legal residents and eventually citizens.

This stage of direct involvement that produces personal change is comparable to the phase of the redemption process that we will study in this section. As the title above indicates, God changes not only the standing of sinners but also the sinners themselves— meaning their actual beings, their inner selves, and all that gives them personhood as thinking and feeling individuals. From refugees emigrating out of the realm of sin, God makes citizens of the kingdom. This process of change will be summarized under the terms of *calling, regeneration,* and *sanctification.*

1. Calling

We often read in the Scriptures that believers are persons who have been called by God, according to his purpose, to belong to Christ and to become saints (for example, Rom. 1:6–7; 8:28; 1 Cor. 1:24; 1 Pet. 5:10). Frequently this idea of God's call is associated with that of his electing or choosing those who are to believe in him (1 Cor. 1:26–28). Amazingly—as if to emphasize this idea of selection—the concepts of calling and choosing are also linked to those of foreknowledge and predestination. Thus, those who are called according to God's purpose are also those whom he first foreknew and predestined (Rom. 8:28–30). Moreover, this selection does not happen on the spur of the moment; it reaches back before the time of creation. God chose the believers in Christ before the foundation of the world and destined them to be his children according to the purpose of his will (Eph. 1:4–5).

While there are differences between the ideas of *calling, choosing, election,* and *predestination,* the meaning of those terms overlaps sufficiently to indicate that there is in Scripture a massive amount of evidence to support the concept of predestination. At first sight, predestination seems to mean that, out of his sovereign will, God has preselected those individuals whom he will call to himself in salvation. This is precisely how this doctrine has been understood by some theologians—those who teach that God chose a limited number of individuals for salvation before the foundation of the world, that the benefits of Christ's redemptive work extend only to them, and that they cannot resist receiving the salvation for which they have been designated. Carried to its ultimate logic, this thinking results in the doctrine of double predestination, widely taught since it was popularized by John Calvin in the sixteenth century. According to it, God in his inscrutable wisdom has selected before all worlds some humans for salvation (election) while condemning others to eternal death (reprobation).

Obviously, such a doctrine does not square easily with our findings about the biblical teaching regarding the loving nature of God and Christ's saving work. Therefore, as we look again at the Bible's teaching on predestination, we make the following three observations.

a. Everybody matters to God

Because God is love, he created human life out of love. Love bears all things, endures all things, and never ends (1 Cor. 13:7). Therefore, as horrible as it was, the Fall could not make God stop loving the beings he had created in his image. "He yearns jealously for the spirit that he has made to dwell in us" (Jas. 4:5 NRSV). The one lost sheep is as important to him as the ninety-nine that are safe (Luke 15:3–7). In fact, that sheep is important enough for God to engage in a major search and rescue operation into which he throws everything he has, including his own Son.

Because of that same love, God wants every person to be saved and to come to the knowledge of the truth—not just a few, but everyone (1 Tim. 2:4). As a means of making the truth known, God has shown his eternal power and divine nature, invisible though they are, through the things he has made. Since humans did not know him as God, he also wrote his law on their hearts so that they might instinctively do what God's will requires. On the basis of this knowledge, their conflicting thoughts may accuse or excuse them on Judgment Day (Rom. 1:19–20; 2:14–16). Since those two forms of revelation, one in nature and the other in conscience, are universally available, every human is given a chance to know God's will and become aware of the need for salvation. Therefore, there can be no question of selectivity in God's intent to reach every human being.

The Scriptures also teach that, although humans are without excuse for not responding to these two forms of divine outreach, God went the extra mile. He sent the one mediator between himself and humankind, the one who gave himself as ransom for all (1 Tim. 2:5–6). The Father went all the way in his love for humans; he gave his Son. And the Son went all the way in his love for humans; he gave his life. Anticipating the kind of death he would experience as Savior, Jesus said, "And I, when I am lifted up from the earth, will draw all people to myself" (John 12:32 NRSV). He knew that his death held the potential to provide salvation for all people of all times—for two reasons. First, as already suggested, God does not want anyone to perish but he wants all to come to repentance (2 Pet. 3:9).

The second reason given is that Christ's death as the Son of God provides salvation to as many as receive him (see John 1:12). If we had been ransomed from sin with perishable things like silver and gold, there might have been a limit on how many the ransom price could cover. But since the ransom price was the precious blood of Christ, the Son of God, the number of those who can be saved by it is without limit. All of humanity on one side of the salvation scales could not outweigh the value of the life of the Son of God on the other side. By setting limits to the number of people who are to be saved by the sacrifice of Christ, we run the risk of reducing the value of his life. The Bible teaches that God so loved the world that he gave his Son so that whoever believes in him will be saved (John 3:16). Nowhere does the Bible teach that God has set a quota in order to limit access to salvation. To the contrary, the Bible teaches that admission to eternal life is available on the basis of open enrollment to all who believe because everybody matters to God (1 John 2:2).

b. Believers are predestined to salvation

Yet the question remains: If the "saved" refers to all those who respond freely to God's call, why are they named the *chosen* or the *elect*, as if God had selected them rather than they who had chosen God? For instance, what did Jesus mean when he flatly stated, "For many are called, but few are chosen" (Matt. 22:14, NRSV)?

This saying of Jesus provides an excellent opportunity to define the "chosen," since it concludes, summarizes, and explains a parable of Jesus on that very subject (Matt. 22:1–14). The parable is the story of a king who offered a wedding banquet, the kind that lasted several days. The invitation was either turned down (v. 5) or abused (vv. 11–13). As a result, the king's invitation was taken to the streets where all people, good or bad, were offered the chance to attend the banquet. Those who accepted the call of the king became his guests. They were the people whom Jesus named the "chosen," a select and privileged group of people who had made the right decision. They were "chosen" because they were a choice group of people who had freely responded to a choice opportunity. The king had not predetermined the decisions of those who turned down the invitation or of those who accepted it. Becoming part of the "chosen" had been their choice all along.

This principle is also well illustrated in the history of Israel as the "chosen people" of God. God had chosen them in Abraham "to be a people for his own possession, out of all the peoples that are on the face of the earth" (Deut. 14:2 RSV). This would seem to imply that every descendant of Abraham would automatically belong to the "chosen." However, as the following observations will show, this was far from being the case.

First, God did not guarantee the physical descendants of Abraham that everyone would be part of his chosen people just on the basis of their Hebrew birth. Belonging to the chosen people was dependent on a free decision on their part. Only if they obeyed God and kept his commandments would they become his possession (Ex. 19:5). To give them his blessing, God expected them to respond to him by loving him, walking in all his ways, and holding fast to him. But should they decide to disobey God and turn away from him, they would receive a curse instead of a blessing (Deut. 11:22, 26–28). Thus, participation in the blessings of the chosen was dependent on each descendant of Abraham making a decision to obey the Lord and choosing to have faith in him. Belonging to the chosen people was a matter of personal choice.

Second, according to God's original covenant with Abraham, the true descendants of Abraham were not limited to one nation. They were to be from a multitude of nations because Abraham would become the father of this multitude. As a result, God's covenant was established between God on one hand, and Abraham and his descendants from all the nations throughout their generations on the other. Likewise, and for the same reasons, his wife Sarah would be the mother of nations (Gen. 17:4–7, 16). Therefore, belonging to the chosen people was not a matter of physical birthright. Had this been the case, God would have limited the descendants of Abraham to just one nation. Instead, anyone, Jew or Gentile, who chooses to have faith like Abraham, becomes one of the true descendants of Abraham and a member of the chosen people. To be a child of Abraham and a part of the chosen people was not and is not a matter of racial descendance but the result of personal choice (Rom. 1:16–17; 4:16–25; 9:30–31; 10:12–13).

Finally, it must be sadly noted that God abides by the decisions of humans who exclude themselves from belonging to the chosen people, even when those decisions violate God's desire for all to be saved. In Christ's day, the believing minority from racial Israel had reduced itself to a small remnant of Jews who had chosen the kingdom of God (Luke 12:32). In the meantime, God had been extending his hands to a disobedient and contrary people—but in vain (Rom. 10:21). Consequently, according to Paul, though the number of children of Israel is as the sand of the sea, only a minority from among them will be saved. Why? Because the others do not have faith (9:27, 32). Yet the defection of the people who had been called to be chosen cannot thwart the purpose of God. God allows humans to have their own way, but his agenda will be accomplished regardless of their rejection (v. 28).

That which was true for so many Israelites was equally true for their enemy, the pharaoh of Egypt. Pharaoh hardened his heart against God seven times. Consequently and for good measure, God let Pharaoh have it his own way and hardened his heart three more times (vv. 17–18; compare Ex. 7–9). Yet, without knowing it, Pharaoh was actually helping God's work when he hardened his heart against him (Rom. 9:17). God does not force himself upon anyone. He is not a tyrant who imposes himself on humans against their own will. God respects the freedom of choice he has given us as his image-bearers.

What we have seen for the history of Israel applies also to the New Testament community of God's people. God had decreed *even before the creation of the world* that he would establish a chosen community of faith comprised of all nations. For example, when Christ receives the righteous into eternal life at the Last Judgment, he will tell them, "Come, O blessed of my Father, inherit the kingdom prepared for you from the foundation of the world" (Matt. 25:34 RSV). When the apostle Paul preached to the Gentiles in Antioch, "as many as were ordained to eternal life believed" (Acts 13:48 RSV). Paul describes believers as "those who are called according to God's purpose," and he adds that those whom God foreknew, he also predestined, called, justified, and

152

glorified (Rom. 8:28–30). He wrote to the Ephesian church that God chose believers before the foundation of the world and destined them to be his children according to the purpose of his will (Eph. 1:4–5). The Jewish minority is the remnant "chosen" by grace (Rom. 11:5). And the gopsel is a plan decreed by God before the ages (1 Cor. 2:7).

On the basis of such evidence, we must maintain that, although all humans matter to God, not all will be saved. God had decided even before the beginning of time that only people of faith would enter eternal life. In other words, he had ordained that believers should receive salvation.

Having said this, we must quickly add that Scripture *does not* teach that God has foreordained which individuals will become believers. All biblical statements about predestination, the ones listed above and several others, make reference to predestination as a *collective* reality. God has decided that there will be a community of faith, but he has not chosen the individuals who will be part of it. This choice is left to "whosoever will." God makes salvation available; it is up to individual people to accept it or to reject it.

The case of the chosen people of Israel discussed above can serve as a model for the method of admission into the ranks of the chosen. Being born a Jew did not give a Jew a ticket to salvation. To be a member of the "chosen people," a Jew had to profess faith. Otherwise he or she had no share in the promises of God. Likewise, God has appointed the existence of a new chosen people in Christ from before the foundation of the world. But he did not specifically appoint the persons who become part of this group, nor does he force or manipulate individuals to enter the body of the church. Like the king in Jesus' parable, God has prepared the banquet of salvation because he knows there will be takers. Then, he invites "whosoever will" to come off the streets to join the festivities as chosen ones.

Among all the references to predestination in the New Testament, there is one that might appear to support the view that God indiscriminately foreordains individuals because he loves some and hates others. In Romans, Paul quotes an Old Testament passage that states flatly, "Jacob I loved, but Esau I hated" (Rom. 9:13). However, in this segment of his letter to the Romans, Paul is explaining why the Jews failed to obtain salvation in Christ, except for a "believing remnant" minority, while the Gentiles have found access to it (vv. 27, 30). The reason he gives is that it was never enough to trace one's ancestry to Abraham to be included among the children of God (v. 8). Thus, of the two sons of Abraham only

Isaac was included in the promise, and of the two sons of Isaac only Jacob inherited it, so that God's purposes of election might continue through history (v. 11). To prove this point, Paul quotes the text from Malachi where *Jacob* stands for the people of Israel as God's people and *Esau* for the people of Edom who chose to be the enemy of Israel (Mal. 1:1–5). Again, a whole collectivity is designated as the object of divine election, not the selection of individuals within it.

The illustration of the immigrants cited at the beginning of this section may help convey this point. Periodically, the U.S. government opens its borders to immigrants from overseas. As a result, the immigration service knows that a whole group of people is, as it were, "predestined" to take residency in the United States. However, no U.S. official goes overseas to buttonhole aliens and to propose immigration to them, much less to force them to apply. At its embassies, the U.S. government receives applicants who come there on their own when they learn the good news of the availability of immigration, and upon meeting requirements they are admitted into their new country of adoption. Likewise, sinners who meet the requirements of repentance and faith, on learning the good news of salvation, are admitted into the body to form the new "chosen people . . . a people belonging to God" (1 Pet. 2:9 NIV).

c. God chooses individuals for ministry

God does not choose individuals for salvation, for he wants all to accept his invitation and be saved. But he does choose some individuals to perform specific tasks. Such individuals may or may not be saved. Even when they are not believers, they can be used to advance the purposes of God without being part of those purposes.

Before Jeremiah was born, he had been appointed to become a prophet to the nations (Jer. 1:5). He accepted the commission reluctantly (vv. 6–7) and, in a state of discouragement, he even wished he had been killed by human hands when he was still in his mother's womb—at the very moment God was appointing him to become a prophet (20:14–18). But the word of the Lord came to him repeatedly, and he faithfully accomplished his ministry as a prophet. Astoundingly, God also chose a pagan monarch, Cyrus of Persia, to perform a specific task on his behalf. God said he would use Cyrus as his shepherd to fulfill his purpose; he even called Cyrus his "messiah," the anointed one, whose right hand he was holding despite the fact that Cyrus did not know God (Isa. 44:28– 45:5).

Likewise, Jesus chose disciples like Peter, John, and James, who then devoted their lives to the work of the gospel (Mark 3:13–19). But he also chose Judas who, far from being "appointed to" salvation, was called a devil by Jesus (John 6:70–71). But all the disciples had ministries to accomplish, and they were chosen for that purpose.

The commissioning of the apostle Paul at the time of his call likewise illustrates this principle. The accounts of the conversion of Paul on the Damascus Road emphasize his appointment to ministry rather than his experience of redemption. The risen Christ who appeared to Paul told him to go into Damascus, where he would be shown what he was supposed to do (Acts 9:6). This task was described as Paul becoming a chosen instrument of the Lord to carry his name before the Gentiles and kings and the people of Israel (v. 15). Paul himself quotes the Lord as telling him at that very moment, "Rise and stand upon your feet; for I have appeared to you for this purpose, to appoint you to serve and bear witness . . ." (26:16 RSV). Like Jeremiah of old, Paul believed that God had set him apart for ministry when he was still in his mother's womb (Gal. 1:15). Accordingly, the gracious call of God and the revelation of his Son on the Damascus road were extended to him to appoint him for ministry. In Paul's own words, God revealed his Son to him "in order that I might preach him among the Gentiles" (v. 16 RSV). There is no text to the effect that Paul had been predestined to salvation—although he certainly became saved—but there are many statements revealing that he had been specifically chosen for ministry. However, as compelling as his call to ministry may have been, it was not binding. At the time of his commissioning, the risen Lord told him, "It hurts you to kick against the goads" (Acts 26:14). This saying, drawn from Greek folklore, evoked the efforts of an ox to resist the prod of the plowman. Paul could have rejected the call of Christ. He still had the freedom to do so, though it would have been a costly decision. Obviously, Paul bent his will to Christ's will, and he was used mightily to establish the gospel in the Gentile world.

The immigration analogy may help clarify this point one more time. When the U.S. government opens its doors to immigrants, aliens apply and, upon acceptance, they take residency and become citizens. Parallel to this program, another kind of immigration takes place. Both the U.S. government and the private sector often identify specific individuals in other countries who possess skills and expertise needed in the United States for specialized areas of research and production. This selective recruitment program is not conducted for the purpose of immigration (salvation) but for the sake of their usefulness to the receiving country (ministry). These individuals are approached and presented with an offer they usually cannot refuse. Then, the way is facilitated for them to enter the country and perform their tasks. Those individuals may or may not choose to become citizens and remain in the country. What is important is that they have been selectively recruited for a specific job and that they have complied with the call to serve.

Thus, we have been led to discover two kinds of predestination on the basis of scriptural data: one that is collective, where believers as a body are predestined to salvation, and the other individual, where specific persons are elected to accomplish specific tasks. It is important to keep these two forms of election separate so that they are not combined to make the Bible wrongly say that God predestines individuals to salvation and, consequently, dooms others to damnation. God is neither unfair nor unfeeling; he does not practice partiality. Every human being matters to him immensely, and he offers salvation to all without discrimination.

2. Regeneration

This long word means "re-birth." The Bible teaches that the men, women, and children who hear God's call and respond to it experience a divine visitation. God intervenes in their lives and works a miracle. He forgives their sins and wrongdoings and gives them a fresh start with their lives. In the Bible, this new beginning is called the "new birth." "If anyone is in Christ, there is a new creation: everything old has passed away; see, everything has become new!" (2 Cor. 5:17 NRSV).

Obviously, the new birth is a spiritual transaction between God and humans rather than a physical experience, though it has repercussions in the physical realm. But what is born of the flesh remains physical and what is born of the Spirit opens up to the realm of the spiritual (John 3:6). Those who receive Christ's calling and believe in him are born not of the flesh or from human desire, but of God (1:12–13). Their dormant spiritual natures become activated by God's power and, as a result, they receive a new nature that transforms them according to God's image (Col. 3:10; 2 Pet. 1:4). Or putting it differently, they receive the washing of regeneration and the renewal in the Holy Spirit (Tit. 3:5).

This renewal is so personality-shaking that it is likened to a resurrection from the dead. Since the Fall, the normal course of our earthly existence has been to live for some years and then die. No one can escape the power of death; it rules over all and is a disease that afflicts every person terminally. However, spiritual birth reverses the process. It is like passing from sure death into life and, at that, a supercharged kind of life that Jesus called "life to the full" or "life abundant" (John 10:10). By hearing Christ's word and believing in him, one receives eternal life and passes from death to life (5:24; Rom. 6:13). This new life in the spiritual dimension is so connected with God, the author of life and the enemy of death, that it makes physical death pale into relative insignificance. Actually, it turns physical death into the threshold of a swift passage into eternal life, God's kind of life.

Death was the result of the Fall. Redemption overcomes the Fall and its consequences. Those who believe in Christ, though they die, yet shall they live; and whoever believes in Christ and lives in him will never die (John 11:25–26). For Christians, in other words, death does not have the final word. It promotes them to glory. Although we are now like "dead men" through our sins and trespasses, God makes us alive in Christ by a resurrection not unlike his (Eph. 2:1–6). Anyone who has the Son has life, and anyone who does not have the Son does not have life (1 John 5:12). The exclamation of the father upon the return of the prodigal son provides a striking illustration of the new birth: "This son of mine was dead and is alive again" (Luke 15:24 NIV).

The mysterious transaction called the new birth is difficult to analyze, and even more so to describe. It is more easily experienced than explained. It involves very personal human needs and long-term divine activity in response to those specific needs. Since every individual is different from others and since God respects such differences, he deals with different people in different ways. Some people become believers through a long process of opening up to God and to his truth, while others experience a dramatic conversion that turns their lives around in an instant. Whatever the mode may be, the basic components of regeneration do not change. Scripture describes them as consisting of two phases: *conviction* and *conversion.*

a. Phase one: Conviction

This is a passive state of being that remains unproductive unless it is allowed to lead to the active phase of conversion. However, without conviction there can be no conversion. It is possible to distinguish two aspects of conviction, one negative and the other positive.

(1) **Negative conviction.** This is a state of feeling convicted of guilt, of inadequacy, and of need. One becomes aware that something is wrong and that nothing or no one may be able to help.

The conscience is stirred with a deep dissatisfaction about oneself and with life—the anxiety of missing out on what is important without even knowing what it might be, a consciousness of one's limitations and liabilities, a fear at the shallowness and the brevity of existence, a yearning for purity and simplicity, a sickness of the soul that seeks escape in drugs, alcohol, sexual adventures, work, toys, divorce, and the fast life. It is the condition of the son who, having decided to go for the "good life," left his father's home and, having done it all, found himself in a situation of "need" (Luke 15:14). He became aware that something was wrong with his life. This in itself was not a solution. Had he remained at this stage, he would have shriveled and died. This is why we call it "negative conviction." Unfortunately, many people find themselves in this condition and do not seek or cannot find a way out of it. They are afflicted with a malaise of the soul, a sickness unto death, but they do not go the next step. The Scriptures call this condition "worldly sorrow" that leads to death (2 Cor. 7:10).

(2) **Positive conviction.** The next step is to become convinced, however dimly, that there is hope, a source of mercy in this universe, that we are not abandoned, but that the One who has created the world has also provided a safe place within it. The Bible teaches that God seeks us even before we are aware of our own lostness (Luke 15:3–10). Conviction in this sense involves an openness to the idea of a secret divine love bent on meeting human need, a sensitivity to a patient presence that can be ignored and shut out but not dismissed, and a yearning for release, forgiveness, abandonment, and security. In the story of the prodigal son, conviction occurred when "he came to himself" and started thinking of the journey home (15:17). In our own life stories, the moment of conviction occurs when we despair enough of ourselves and begin hoping enough in God to ask as a desperate man once did: "What must I do to be saved?" (Acts 16:30).

b. Phase two: Conversion

Having come under conviction, the prodigal son became convinced that he should do something about his condition. "He got up and went to his father" (Luke 15:20). The decision to take action marks the passage to an active stage that seeks to resolve the tensions created by conviction. If conviction can be viewed as preparation, conversion is the result. It is an act of the will, as opposed to conviction's passive state. Conversion was the basic message preached by Jesus from the outset of his ministry: "Repent, and believe in the gospel" (Mark 1:15 RSV). Conversion, therefore, comprises two elements, one negative and the other positive: *repentance* and *faith*.

(1) **Negative conversion.** We describe repentance as the negative aspect of conversion because it implies a rejection of and a turning away from a whole condition of life. It is the prodigal son deciding to go back to the father and to cry out, "Father, I have sinned against heaven and against you" (Luke 15:18 NIV). Repentance is the heartfelt cry of King David, who lifted up this prayer toward God from his knees:

> Have mercy on me, O God,
>   according to your steadfast love;
> according to your abundant mercy
>   blot out my transgressions.
> Wash me thoroughly from my iniquity,
>   and cleanse me from my sin.
> For I know my transgressions,
>   and my sin is ever before me.
> Against you, you alone, have I sinned,
>   and done what is evil in your sight,
> so that you are justified in your sentence
>   and blameless when you pass judgment.
>
> (Ps. 51:1–4 NRSV)

Repentance is also evident in the man who went to the place of prayer but felt so unworthy that he stood apart, beating his own chest as a sign of remorse and daring not even to look up to heaven while he pleaded, "God, be merciful to me, a sinner!" (Luke 18:13 NRSV).

Obviously, there is more to repentance than a liturgical statement, a pat formula, or the emotion of a moment. It consists of two elements. The first element is a complete change of attitude toward ourselves that makes us willing to see ourselves as we really are in the sight of God. We must lay down pretense, self-deception, defensiveness, and pride; we must also be ruthlessly honest and admit to our sinful disposition, moral failure, and spiritual bankruptcy. The second element of repentance is asking God for forgiveness. The sin-sick soul turns to the God who has been ignored, dismissed, and disgraced by human arrogance. If sin is telling God to move over because we are taking over, repentance is falling on our knees so he can take over. "Godly sorrow brings repentance that leads to salvation and leaves no regret" (2 Cor. 7:10 NIV). This goes without saying: because sin and pride are ever-present realities, repentance needs to be a lifelong attitude in addition to an initial requirement for experiencing new birth.

(2) **Positive conversion.** Whereas repentance causes us to kneel

in brokenness, faith makes us rise in newness. In repentance, we ask for forgiveness; by faith, we receive it. Saving faith is acquiring the knowledge that God accepts our repentance when we tell him that we are sorry. It is the prodigal son getting up and actually going back to his father, knowing that he will be accepted (Luke 15:20).

The Bible teaches that "without faith it is impossible to please God, because anyone who comes to him must believe that he exists and that he rewards those who earnestly seek him" (Heb. 11:6 NIV). But the question arises as to how can we know this for sure? Does God really care? Can he wipe our slates clean? Can he make all things new and give a new beginning, a new birth? Will he forgive everything and keep on forgiving?

To such questions, God has provided one absolute, unshakable, indisputable proof of his unlimited saving love: the Cross. Pointing heavenward, the cross of Christ is the everlasting sign that God receives and forgives. Its outstretched arms embrace all who look to God for mercy. On the cross was offered "the atoning sacrifice for our sins, and not for ours only but also for the sins of the whole world" (1 John 2:2 NRSV). Its power to forgive is inexhaustible. "If we confess our sins, he who is faithful and just will forgive us our sins and cleanse us from all unrighteousness" (1:9). Therefore, in faith we accept the reality of God's offer and commit ourselves to a living God. By faith, we obtain peace with God and gain access to his forgiving grace—all this through Jesus Christ our Lord (Rom. 5:1–2). This is why, when the desperate man cried out, "What must I do to be saved?," the apostle answered him without a moment's hesitation, "Believe in the Lord Jesus, and you will be saved" (Acts 16:30–31 NIV). Saving faith is our acceptance of God's acceptance of us in Christ.

Repentance and faith produce together the conversion that makes regeneration possible. In our sinful state, we are disconnected from God; conversion reconnects us with God and takes us back to the garden of communion from which we had been expelled by sin. Like the father rushing to his repentant son to embrace him and to bring him home, conversion is God forgiving us, embracing us, and making us his children (Luke 15:20–24). It allows him to get a hold on us and to infuse us with new life. The new life that begins with the new birth is forever; it is life eternal.

3. Sanctification

In order to change sinners into saints and to bring them from death to life, God issues a call inviting them to receive the gospel.

He offers them rebirth and sets them on a new course. As important as these elements are, calling and regeneration mark only the first stages of an individual's redemption story. Following them is the process of change that Scripture describes as *sanctification*.

In biblical terms, to *sanctify* means to set apart for holiness, to purify, to make free from sin. As we have discovered previously, God is holy. Therefore, to be made holy is to be made in God's likeness, to be conformed to his nature, and to reflect his character. In other words, sanctification is nothing short of the restoration of God's image in human life, a return to the pristine purity that characterized humans before sin distorted that image at the Fall.

Since Christ is God made visible among humans, sanctification in its simplest definition is to become Christlike. Indeed, Scripture sets a goal for believers to grow in "the knowledge of the Son of God and become mature, attaining to the whole measure of the fullness of Christ" (Eph. 4:13 NIV); to strip off the old self and to get into a new self that is renewed in the image of the Creator (Eph. 4:24; Col. 3:10); to see the glory of the Lord and to be gradually transformed into the same image from one degree of glory to another by the working of the Holy Spirit (2 Cor. 3:18); to be imitators of God as his beloved children (Eph. 5:1); and, to put it in a nutshell, to walk as Jesus walked (1 John 2:6).

This goal of spiritual transformation applies equally to all believers without exception and without distinction. Scripture knows of no special kinds of spirituality for different groups of people. There is only one walk, one righteousness, one sanctification, and one model, Jesus Christ. Institutionalized misreading of isolated New Testament verses has caused some teachers to advocate one form of spirituality for men and a different one for women, under the guise of biblical manhood and womanhood. However, no such thing is taught in Scripture. The biblical sanctification ideal transcends the particularities of manhood and womanhood just as it does of Jew or Greek, slave or free (Gal. 3:28; Col. 3:11). As one author put it, spirituality does not come in "blue and pink"; for both man and woman it takes the color of the servant blood of Christ. It is the attainment of "the whole measure of the fullness of Christ" as "we all reach" for oneness in the faith (Eph. 4:13). Accordingly, the goal of ministry is to present "everyone perfect in Christ" (Col. 1:28) until "Christ is all, and is in all" (3:11 NIV). The attempt to draw a distinction between biblical manhood and biblical womanhood creates a false dichotomy, for both manhood and womanhood find their full expression in servanthood (Gal. 5:13) and in the cultivation of the fruit of the Spirit, which is exactly the same for both men and women (vv. 22–23). It is true that within the biblical definition of personhood exists a rich diversity of roles, functions, and ministries. But these are always predicated on spiritual gifts and competencies—never on gender, social status, or racial distinctions (1 Cor. 12:6–7, 11, except in the NIV which, singularly and unaccountably, inserts "men" in v. 6!). There is only one Christ and therefore one sanctification.

At first sight, this call to sanctification sounds like a totally unrealistic expectation. Who in the world can be holy but God alone? Is it fair of God to require of believers to be holy as he is when they live in sin-saturated environments and when they find within themselves that the disposition to sin battles vigorously against the desire for righteousness? When the saintly apostle Paul was struggling with the same questions, he asked in desperation, "Who will rescue me from this body of death?" Then suddenly, aware that God in Christ was the author of his sanctification, he answered his own question, "Thanks be to God—through Jesus Christ our Lord!" (Rom. 7:21–25 NIV).

Indeed, Scripture teaches that even before we achieve sanctification, God grants us the status or position of being sanctified as part of the salvation package. Thus, at the same time as Paul wrote that the Corinthian Christians were "called to be holy," he also said that they were already "sanctified in Christ Jesus" (1 Cor. 1:2), because he had become the righteousness, the sanctification, and the redemption of those who were in Christ Jesus (v. 30). Consequently, active sanctification means that we become what we already are before God.

Sanctification as described above looms as such a lofty task that it seems easier to define it than to do it. Who can claim to have become like Christ or to reflect God's image in its pre-fall purity? Because of his own cultivation of saintliness, the apostle Paul sometimes cited his conduct as a model to his converts (1 Cor. 4:16; 11:1; Phil. 3:17; 2 Thess. 3:7, 9). Yet even he admitted that he had not attained perfection but that he was straining forward and pressing on toward that goal (Phil. 3:12–14). Therefore, it is little wonder that much disagreement exists on how sanctification is to be achieved. Several approaches have been commonly advocated as means of obtaining or entering into sanctification.

a. Moralistic approaches

We call these methods to attain sanctification "moralistic" because they emphasize human effort in achieving it. They come in many forms, three of which will be briefly described.

Asceticism. This is the belief that one can reach a high moral and spiritual state of sanctification through the practice of rigorous discipline, self-mortification, and self-deprivation. Since the desires of the flesh are opposed to those of the Spirit (Gal. 5:16–17), it is assumed that the quality of one's spirituality can be enhanced by denying the body and ignoring its needs. This quest for spiritual perfection has caused Christians to withdraw from society, isolate themselves in caves and deserts, mutilate themselves by self-flagellation, and expose themselves to hunger and lack of shelter. Some even spent years on top of ancient pillars where they barely survived as they depended on the charity of passersby for subsistence.

While a life of rigor and deprivation may help in gaining control of one's physical appetites, it does not guarantee the transformation of the inner person. Some of those saints who make it a point to display how much they suffer for Christ are also the most difficult people to live with on a daily basis.

Legalism. According to this approach, Christian conduct consists in the observance of prescribed lists of "dos and don'ts." The Scriptures definitely contain some commandments that are binding for all Christians (for example, Matt. 5:44; 7:12; 19:18–19; 22:37–40). But outside of them, the New Testament offers only guidelines for each Christian to make his or her moral choices. Some such guidelines are the principle of expediency, according to which any action not beneficial or positive is not worth doing (1 Cor. 6:12a); the principle of protecting one's personal freedom, according to which potentially addictive behaviors are prohibited (v. 12b); and the principle of consideration for others, according to which any activities that may be offensive or detrimental to others are ruled out (10:23–24). Obviously, since what is or is not beneficial, addictive, or edifying varies from person to person, it would be impossible to establish a code of conduct that covers all situations for all Christians. Yet this is precisely what legalism tries to accomplish; it reduces Christian behavior to a predetermined set of regulations. Because legalism often elevates human rules to the status of divine law, because it emphasizes external behaviors at the expense of inner attitudes and motivations, and because it creates a false sanctification, the teachings of the New Testament severely forbid Christians from falling into its bondage (Matt. 23:23–28; Mark 7:1–23; Col. 2:20–23).

Self-improvement techniques. It is obvious that most of us do not live up to the level of our potential. This fact has been exploited by countless self-styled teachers who promise to train their followers in super-successful living through their programs of mental and spiritual exercises. Christianity is thus perverted into methods devised to secure health, wealth, beauty, and a flourishing sexual life. One can walk into any bookstore, religious or not, and find shelves of titles that promise such attainments in so many easy steps. These are great money-makers for their authors, but all too often, their approach promotes self-centered absorption with one's own success in life and falls short of producing the Christian virtues that reflect Christlikeness and the resulting acceptance of oneself.

Such moralistic approaches fail because of their overly optimistic expectations from human nature and the supposed ability of humans to improve character. They focus on external factors at the expense of the inner person, where attitudes and motivations take shape. They are bootstrap operations that reduce the pursuit of sanctification to a human-centered, narcissistic process that is bound to end in false security, frustration, or failure.

b. Crisis-experience approaches

If the moralistic methods for attaining sanctification overemphasize human involvement, other approaches exclude it almost completely by making God responsible for producing sanctification in the lives of believers. According to some teachings, perfect sanctification is produced automatically as the result of two separate divine visitations in the lives of believers. The first is conversion, when God grants salvation through Christ to repentant sinners. The second is an experience of grace, when the Holy Spirit accomplishes instant sanctification in their lives. This latter experience is said to follow conversion at varying intervals, depending on the individual. For some, it may happen shortly after their initial encounter with Christ; others must wait for years before they receive it.

Some maintain that this visitation occurs as a quiet, private infilling and renewal. For others, however, it is an ecstatic moment accompanied by visible and audible manifestations, such as "speaking in tongues." Such experiences are variously called "second conversion," "second grace," "second blessing," or the "baptism of the Holy Spirit." Their significance is usually the same. They allegedly produce complete spirituality through a direct intervention of the Holy Spirit, who enters believers in order to gain control of their lives. Paradoxically, this form of teaching that makes sanctification dependent on divine initiative is prevalent among groups and denominations that emphasize the freedom of choice of human beings.

c. Sanctification as a process

The New Testament teaching on the subject of sanctification suggests that there is no shortcut to attain it, but that it is a lifelong human endeavor. It also teaches that God is involved in the process. As sinners turn to God in saving faith, a two-way relationship is established between them and God. Believers "work out" their salvation while God is at work within them, enabling each one to will and to act for his good purpose (Phil. 2:12–13). Viewed from this perspective, the restoration of the integrity of God's image in human life is a task that requires the joint involvement of both God and believers. The need for a cooperative undertaking between divinity and humanity in effecting sanctification shows the severity of the damage that sin has inflicted upon human personality. It requires humans to assume their share of responsibility, and it requires God to undergird their goodwill with his power in order to counteract the effects of the Fall.

God's involvement in the task of rebuilding the human personality is indispensable. Jesus had anticipated it in his last prayer as he petitioned the Father on behalf of his followers, "Sanctify them in the truth; your word is truth" (John 17:17 NRSV). Accordingly, when the apostle Paul pronounced a benediction for his friends, he wrote, "May the God of peace himself sanctify you entirely; and may your spirit and soul and body be kept sound and blameless at the coming of our Lord Jesus Christ. The one who calls you is faithful, and he will do this" (1 Thess. 5:23–24 NRSV). Without God's participation there can be no sanctification.

Conversely, without human cooperation there can be no sanctification. When Jesus was teaching his disciples about loving others, even their enemies, he exhorted them to be perfect as the heavenly Father is perfect (Matt. 5:48). Believers must yield themselves "to righteousness for sanctification" (Rom. 6:19 RSV), because God wills their sanctification (1 Thess. 4:3). This means that they must maintain a daily openness to God's influence because he helps them make the right decisions. As the process of sanctification unfolds, there will be struggles. There may even be stumblings and setbacks. But, "if we confess our sins, he is faithful and just and will forgive us our sins and purify us from all unrighteousness" (1 John 1:9 NIV), so that "no one who is born of God will continue to sin, because God's seed remains in him; he cannot go on sinning, because he has been born of God" (3:9).

For this reason, no Christian travelling the road of salvation should be easily satisfied and stop advancing. The Scriptures exhort us to persist and to "purify ourselves from everything that contaminates body and spirit, perfecting holiness out of reverence for God" (2 Cor. 7:1 NIV). Such progress does not just happen randomly; it requires self-knowledge and the deliberate, purposeful, systematic cultivation of the basic Christian virtues. "For this very reason, make every effort to add to your faith goodness; and to goodness, knowledge; and to knowledge, self-control; and to self-control, perseverance; and to perseverance, godliness; and to godliness, brotherly kindness; and to brotherly kindness, love. For if you possess these qualities in increasing measure, they will keep you from being ineffective and unproductive in your knowledge of our Lord Jesus Christ" (2 Pet. 1:5–8 NIV). And lest such a program appear so demanding that we become tempted to give up on sanctification and think that it is an optional adornment of the Christian life, the Scriptures solemnly warn us to strive for sanctification because without it "no one will see the Lord" (Heb. 12:14).

On the basis of such biblical teaching, we can affirm that the process of sanctification begins with the new birth and goes on for a lifetime. It will eventually come to term but not before the end of time when, at his coming, the Lord Jesus will change our lowly bodies to become like his glorious body by the power that enables him to subject all things to himself (Phil. 3:20–21). In other words, the point of termination of the process of sanctification is the final resurrection when "we will be changed" (1 Cor. 15:52–53). "And just as we have borne the likeness of the earthly man, so shall we bear the image of the man from heaven" (v. 49). "We are God's children now; what we will be has not yet been revealed. What we do know is this: when he is revealed, we will be like him, for we will see him as he is. And all who have this hope in him purify themselves, just as he is pure" (1 John 3:2–3 NRSV). Our chief end as humans is to become again what God had intended us to be at creation, to help him restore in ourselves the purity of the image of God through sanctification. This glorifies God and enables us to enjoy him forever.

d. *The loss of salvation*

One more aspect of sanctification must be considered before we bring this discussion to a close. Obviously, the fact that the process of sanctification is partly dependent on human participation makes it vulnerable to human failure. God can be trusted to keep his end of the commitment, but humans are not as consistent as God is. They can fail, falter, fall, fold, or fizzle out. The question must be answered whether the process can be arrested, reversed, or worse, terminally reversed? In other words, can a Christian lose his or her salvation?

Among Christians there are two schools of thought on this subject. One teaches that backslidden Christians can lose their salvation. This belief is based on texts that teach the impossibility of restoring again to repentance those who "have fallen away" or "those who shrink back," because they "willfully persist in sin after having received the knowledge of the truth" (Heb. 6:6; 10:39, 26 NRSV). For them remains nothing but the fearful prospect of judgment, the "fury of fire that will consume" (10:27; cf. 6:8).

Other Christians look at the same texts and claim that a genuinely converted person cannot lose his or her salvation. They claim that the teaching in those passages does not refer to persons who have made the faith commitment of conversion but to individuals who have received the knowledge of the gospel without acting on it decisively (Heb. 6:4–8). Thus, it is impossible to restore to repentance those "who have once been enlightened," but who evidently did not fully receive the light and walk in it; who "have tasted the heavenly gift" of salvation, but did not make it their lasting menu; who "have shared in the Holy Spirit" without responding to him and receiving his fullness; who "have tasted the goodness of the word of God," but have only tasted it instead of obeying it.

These may be descriptions of people who have understood their need of salvation but who have refused to commit themselves to it. Instead, they have pulled consistently away from what they knew to be right and have rendered, on their own account, the death of Christ useless. They have been under the conviction of the gospel repeatedly but have resisted it for so long that they have passed the point of no return in their unbelief (6:7–8). They have developed "an evil, unbelieving heart that turns away from the living God" instead of surrendering to him (3:12). They have terminally rejected the Holy Spirit's work within them and committed the unpardonable sin against the Holy Spirit in that they have hardened their hearts to the point where they cannot even bring themselves to repent again (Matt. 12:31–32; Heb. 6:4). They profane the Holy Spirit by rejecting the grace he was bringing to them (Heb. 10:26–31). Such persons become "hardened by the deceitfulness of sin" (3:13); the message of salvation they heard did not benefit them because they did not respond in faith like those who believed (4:2).

Such texts do not seem to describe the garden variety of backsliding Christians who commit sin or fall away out of weakness but who remain recuperable to repentance and, like straying sheep, can be brought back to the fold (Jas. 5:19–20). Rather, they may describe people who, having understood their need for salvation, began the process of conviction and repentance but stopped short of crossing the line of faith, repeatedly refusing to do so. The Scriptures teach that such people may become so hardened by resisting the Holy Spirit that they cannot surrender to God but deliberately place themselves in a position of mortal defiance and enmity against God (1 John 5:16–17). By willfully and consistently rejecting the work of the Holy Spirit within them, they join the ranks of the opposition and they become so hardened to the Spirit's influence that they become unreachable. They thus commit the unpardonable sin (Matt. 12:30–32).

Perhaps, therefore, the best resolution of differences between the views of those who claim that it is possible to fall out of grace and lose one's salvation, and those who believe that salvation is eternally secure ("once saved, always saved"), is to make a distinction between two categories of persons. The first comprises Christians who have committed themselves genuinely and irreversibly to the gospel in a faith relationship that binds them to God and God to them through a covenant that neither wants to be broken. Despite their faltering ways, those Christians will persevere because their yearning is genuine and because God will not abandon them. They enjoy the double protection of being held securely in the hand of Christ from which no power in heaven or earth can snatch them away, and of being covered at the same time by the mighty hand of the Father who is greater than all and from whom no one can snatch them away (John 10:27–29). Consequently, there is no power present or past, physical or spiritual, that can "separate us from the love of God in Christ Jesus our Lord" (Rom. 8:38–39 NRSV). God always remains faithful to his commitment because he cannot deny his own nature (2 Tim. 2:13). Of course, believers retain the freedom to return to a state of lostness. But they will never want to do so if their faith is authentic. Because God deals with humans according to his grace rather than according to what they deserve, their salvation is dependent on God's faithfulness to them much more than on their faithfulness to him. God's love for his children is unconditional. He forces no one to become saved or to remain saved. However, he can be trusted to keep his side of the covenant with Christians who abide by their own commitment to him. And God's commitment to the salvation of his creatures surpasses by far their ability to remain faithful to him.

However, there is also another category that consists of tentative, would-be Christians who remain forever at the stage of inconstant seekers. They are the rocky ground on which the seed of the gospel fell without being able to take hold (Matt. 13:5–6). They are the son who consented to go and work in his father's vineyard but who never went; there was no genuine commitment on his part (21:30). Of such people it was said, "They went out from us, but they did not belong to us; for if they belonged to us, they would have remained with us. But by going out they made it plain that none of them belongs to us" (1 John 2:19 NRSV). Their rejection of Christ is tantamount to his recrucifixion on their own account (Heb. 6:6). By turning away from the faith, those who quit show that their heart was not in it unreservedly or that their Christian experience remained incomplete.

In view of this sobering truth, the Scriptures forbid speculating about who will be saved and who will not (Rom. 10:6–10). These are matters that pertain exclusively to the sovereignty of Christ, since he is the one who does the saving work. Rather than making judgments about others, God calls us to look at ourselves to make sure that our own commitment is genuine. Salvation is ours only if the confession of our mouth is a genuine expression of the belief in our heart. God is the one who in Jesus Christ "will judge the secret thoughts of all" (2:16 NRSV).

III. CURRENT VIEWS ON REDEMPTION

The doctrine of redemption is at the heart of the Christian faith. In a significant way, it marks the difference between Christianity and other world religions. How to appease divinity in order to make oneself acceptable and to gain the favor of the gods or of the spirits is the concern that dictates the cultic and sacrificial practices of many religions of the world. Christianity turns those expectations around by showing the extent to which God is willing to sacrifice himself to reclaim humankind and to offer salvation as a free gift of his grace to fallen creatures. It is the religion of divine love. However, the manner in which this love is manifested is described differently by some Christians. Besides the view of redemption presented in this chapter, three others should be mentioned.

1. Liberation Theology

This is a broad designation that covers the teachings of many people of Christian persuasion, especially in Third World countries. While some of them hold to the validity of justification as the means of individual salvation, they generally believe that Christ's redemptive work was intended to change the sinful structures of society in order to liberate disadvantaged people from economic, social, and political oppression. Some liberationists teach that the purpose of the death of Christ was to affirm God's victory over the forces of evil at work in history; others believe that its intention was to launch and energize a movement of human revolt against injustice by showing that even Christ fell victim to it and, in so doing, registered God's disapproval of it; still others believe that the death of Christ set an example for us to follow as we endeavor to live and die for those who suffer under the heel of oppression. While such programs of social redemption represent worthy goals, their chances for success remain improbable without the recognition of the human need for individual regeneration.

2. Process Theology

According to this view, the relationship between God and the world is essential to the being of God. Although God is greater than his creation, creation is part of his being. As a result, he is dependent on the world to maintain his own existence and to rise up toward perfection. All of reality, including the being of God, is involved in a dynamic process of transformation that makes it move ever closer to ultimate salvation for all parties. According to such views, the redemptive ministry of Christ played an important role in that he added impetus to the process of change and provided a new dynamic to the world's response to divine love.

Undoubtedly, the ministry of Christ has had a beneficial impact on human history. However, it is the created world that is in a state of transition and in need of redemption, not its Creator. God is the provider of redemption, not its beneficiary.

3. Universalism

This is the belief that all humans will finally be saved regardless of whether they sought righteousness or rejected it. Against such a belief, the Bible teaches that Christ is the only source of salvation and that those who have rejected him in this life have excluded themselves from that salvation (John 14:6; Acts 4:12). This raises the issue of seekers after God who are deprived of the knowledge of the gospel but who attempt to worship him with the means available to them within their own cultures. The Scriptures teach that such people may be guided in the ways of God by their own conscience and that God will judge them on the basis of the secrets of their hearts (Rom. 2:14–16; 1 Cor. 4:5). Many Bible teachers believe that God can extend to them the benefits of the redemptive ministry of Christ whom they are seeking without having access to his gospel. Should this be true, the quest of such people for the

170

knowledge of the gospel and the need to convince the indifferent and convert the wicked make the necessity of obeying Christ's command to preach the gospel throughout the world even more pressing and more binding upon the church.

RESOURCES

For further study on the doctrine of salvation, see the following resources:

Alan F. Johnson and Robert E. Webber. *What Christians Believe: A Biblical and Historical Summary*. Grand Rapids: Zondervan, 1989, pp. 231–321.

William W. Klein. *The New Chosen People: A Corporate View of Election*. Grand Rapids: Zondervan, 1990. (This book offers an excellent treatment of the doctrine of predestination.)

Terry Muck. *Those Other Religions in Your Neighborhood*. Grand Rapids: Zondervan, 1992.

Robert Shank. *Elect in the Son*. Minneapolis: Bethany, 1989.

Robert Shank. *Life in the Son*. Minneapolis: Bethany, 1989.

DISCUSSION QUESTIONS

1. Does justification mean becoming righteous?
2. Did God predestine the unsaved to go to hell?
3. Is there any connection between sanctification and the image of God?
4. Can Christians who lose their salvation regain it?
5. Can seekers after God who do not have access to the Gospel be saved?

CHAPTER SEVEN

The Doctrine of the Church

Outline of Chapter Seven

I. The Making of the Church
   1. The Primacy of the Church
   2. The Centrality of the Church
      a. The church in the old covenant
      b. The church in Christ's ministry
      c. The church in the new covenant
   3. The Finality of the Church

II. The Ministries of the Church
   1. Oneness in Community
      a. A shared faith
      b. A shared purpose
      c. A shared lifestyle
      d. A shared authority
   2. Oneness in Worship
      a. Definition of worship
      b. Hindrances to worship
      c. Creative worship: Baptism and communion
   3. Oneness in Outreach
      a. The ministry of conversion
      b. The ministry of compassion
      c. The ministry of confrontation

III. Current Views on the Church
   1. The Syncretistic Church
   2. The Antithetical Church
   3. The Transformational Church

The Doctrine of the Church

The following text is excerpted, with slight alterations, from an article describing the early experiences of one person with the church (quoted with permission from the *Willow Creek Magazine*, September/October, 1990). We cite it here because it expresses the joys and frustrations of many churchgoers and because it raises basic issues regarding the nature and the task of the church.

My first awareness of the significance of the church came when my father, on the eve of moving away, said his good-byes to the church in which he had been active for many years. Speaking under great emotion, his last words to that tiny congregation were, "Love the church; take good care of her. She is the bride of Christ." Rarely had I seen my father weep. At the time, I was puzzled by the depth of his sentiments. How could the church inspire any tears but tears of boredom?

During the years of my youth, my participation in church had been casual and sporadic. As a child, I attended Sunday School in a small neighborhood church close to my parents' home in the heart of the city. Later, I drifted away from it and occasionally attended my parents' church that was even smaller. Church held no interest for me. Because those churches viewed themselves as culturally segregated, beleaguered minorities trying to survive on the fringes of a hostile secular environment, they had little impact on my life.

At the age of 20, during a vacation in the mountains, I became a committed Christian through a private conversion experience. Having become a believer apart from the church, I felt little need to become involved in the church. Participation in church life seemed to be an optional decision, somewhat desirable but not indispensable or mandated by Scripture.

After a few years, a change of vocation and location caused me to become deeply involved in a young and dynamic church. It was during this time that I discovered the biblical doctrine of the church. Far from being a motley gathering of wimpy people, I discovered the church to be the new community that God was preparing on earth for an eternal destiny in heaven. The Bible

175

pointed to the centrality and the ultimacy of the church in God's eternal purposes. The church is the reason for history. The church is at the very center of everything that God is doing from the creation-beginning through redemption in Christ and on to the final consummation. And when the end comes and time is no more, all that will be left of this universe will be the church united with her Redeemer in an eternal embrace of love.

Once I had acquired this perspective on the primacy of the church, the implications became clear for the conduct of our lives as Christians, for the use of our gifts and resources, for evangelism and outreach, and for the building up and energizing of the local church as the body of Christ. The church was to be the warm, open, pulsating, dynamic, loving, attractive new community of God's people that would penetrate culture and claim it for Christ.

However, after five exciting years of involvement with this church, my family and I moved again to a new locality. This became a painful period of our lives in regard to church affiliation. After the exuberance of our involvement with our former church and with new-found convictions about the pre-eminence of the church in God's purposes, identifying a suitable church home in the suburb where we now lived became an exasperating frustration.

Attending church on Sundays became a torment from which I would return home livid with anger. It seemed that almost everything that took place in most churches was devised to kill the spirit of believers and to deaden vital Christians. As for unbelievers, it seemed that every aspect of church life had been calculated so that, if perchance an outsider had wandered in, he or she would be discouraged from ever setting foot in the place again. It was as if the ideals that were assiduously pursued were tedium, inertia, mediocrity, rigidity, and close-mindedness—and all in the name of Christ who had actually established the church in the world to turn it upside down!

It occurred to me that the church had unthinkingly become captive to irrelevant traditions and to worldly values that stifled the energies, the gifts and the dreams generated by the Spirit. Where the gospel teaches that everyone matters to God and that Christ died for all, many churches claim that Christ died only for them and the rest of the world be damned. Where the gospel proclaims God's forgiveness and acceptance, many preach condemnation and rejection. Where the gospel brings a message of hope, they preach a message of doom. Where the gospel grants freedom in Christ, they impose man-made rules and regulations. Where the gospel requires every believer to do ministry, they watch their minister do everything. Where the gospel is a force, they make it a farce.

I longed for a church that was modeled after God's vision.

It is the purpose of this chapter to define God's vision for the church. To proceed biblically, we will first survey the development of the idea of the church throughout biblical history. Then we will define the tasks assigned in Scripture to the church. These two aspects of the doctrine of the church will be discussed as the making of the church and the ministries of the church.

I. THE MAKING OF THE CHURCH

The *church* is the community made up of those who believe in God as revealed in the Scripures and who unite for worship and service to him. Our discussion of the doctrines of God and of redemption has shown that God willed such a community to exist from before the foundation of the world. When God established Adam and Eve in a community of oneness, he demonstrated how important community was in his eternal purposes. Of all his creation, the making of community had primacy. The Bible goes on to show the centrality of the church in God's plan of redemption. Indeed, the focus of both the old and the new covenant is the making of the new community. Lastly, the Bible also shows the finality of the church. When history comes to an end and the worlds disappear, the church alone will remain in eternity. These three phases of the making of the church will be surveyed in that order: the primacy, the centrality, and the finality of the church in God's designs.

1. The Primacy of the Church

This means that from the very beginning, the church was at the forefront of God's designs. When God created infinite space and scattered galaxies across it, when he put in place sun, moon, and earth, when he caused plants to grow and animals to populate the earth, he finally created beings in his own image. Because God is a plurality of persons (Father, Son, Holy Spirit), he cast his image into a plurality of human persons by creating them male and female. And because God is one, he created these two beings into a community of oneness: they shall "become one flesh" (Gen. 2:24). This was the pure essence of the church, untouched by the Fall and free from the stain of sin. As long as Adam and Eve remained within the will of God, they formed the community of oneness as God had originally intended it to be. It was God's primary project, his cherished accomplishment, and the pinnacle of all his created works.

The creation of human beings was an act of divine love. In making them in his image, God tenderly entrusted a most precious aspect of himself to their care. Even more so, the creation of the "one flesh" relationship was supremely an act of love, as if God were outdoing himself in expressing his love to humans. Because it was "not good" for humans to be alone, God provided them with their most valuable possession, the community of oneness.

In the church, this divine gift of love is multiplied many times over. In the Garden of Eden, the community of oneness consisted of two humans united in the "one flesh" relationship. In the church, that community of oneness is extended and multiplied into the "one body" relationship of multitudes from every nation, from all tribes and peoples and tongues. It becomes God's gift of companionship on the grand scale of the church because it is still not good for anyone to be alone. In other words, the oneness in the garden was a microcosmic anticipation or a scaled-down preview of the oneness that the church was intended to bring about. The church has the same kind of primacy within the unfolding of world history as the primacy God gave humans at the beginning of all things.

2. The Centrality of the Church

Not only was the church at the forefront of God's concerns from the beginning of time, but it also remains at the center of what God has been doing throughout history. In this sense, we can speak of the centrality of the church in all things. In order to trace this theme in Scripture, we will consider the making of the church through the old covenant, in the teaching of Jesus, and in the new covenant.

a. The church in the old covenant

If the church is to be defined as the community of those who believe in the God of the Scriptures and who unite to worship and serve him, then obviously such people were around long before Christ came into this world. The Bible describes how God's revelation had been entrusted to Abraham and to his descendants as a people of faith. Abraham believed in God, and God treated him as special because of his faith in him (Gen. 15:6; Rom. 4:9).

The Bible goes on to teach that the focus of their faith was the coming of Christ and the making of the new community. The object of Abraham's faith deserves special attention. When God first spoke to Abraham, he gave him the promise of a personal blessing saying, "I will bless you" (Gen. 12:2). But God's blessing on one man out of the whole world's population would have held no significance for history if this personal blessing had been an end in itself. It would have disappeared with Abraham when he died.

Precisely for this reason, God also gave Abraham the promise of a national blessing, saying, "I will make you into a great nation" (v. 2). The personal blessing to Abraham would be extended to his descendants.

But even this broader blessing was limited. It concerned only a tiny nation out of a whole world that was so loved by God that he was ready to give his Son for its salvation. This is why God expanded the personal and the national blessings promised to Abraham into a universal blessing: "and all peoples on earth will be blessed through you" (v. 3). In making this promise of salvation for the Gentile world, God was actually preaching the gospel to Abraham. This truth may sound like a wild idea, but that is precisely what the Bible teaches: "The Scripture foresaw that God would justify the Gentiles by faith, and announced the gospel in advance to Abraham" (Gal. 3:8 NIV). The passage goes on to say that the promises given by God to Abraham and his offspring were not meant for many people, but for just one person, namely Christ (v. 16). In other words, God intended the blessings and promises he gave to Abraham to benefit the ministry of Christ and to be passed on through Christ to a church community drawn from all believing people on earth.

Jesus confirmed the same teaching when he asserted that Abraham's vision had anticipated his ministry with such intensity that Abraham saw it from afar and rejoiced in it (John 8:56). The apostle Paul agreed with this Gentile understanding of the promises made by God to the ancestors of the Jewish nation beginning with Abraham. He declared that Christ became a servant to the Jews in order "to confirm the promises made to the patriarchs so that the Gentiles may glorify God for his mercy" (Rom. 15:8–9). The promises made to Abraham and his descendants were intended to be fulfilled in the ministry of Christ, so as to bless believers from all nations gathered in the church community.

The purpose of the covenant given by God to Abraham received an even sharper definition when God came to him and changed his name to "Father of many nations," because his descendants would be many nations (Gen. 17:1–8; see p. 143). The New Testament clearly recognizes that Abraham's real descendants are identified not on the basis of race but of grace—a people from among both Jews and Gentiles who have faith just as Abraham had faith. "Those who believe are the descendants of Abraham" (Gal. 3:7, NRSV) because "those who believe are blessed with Abraham who believed" (v. 9), "in order that in Christ Jesus the blessing of Abraham might come to the Gentiles" (v. 14). Consequently, there is no longer Jew or Gentile, but "if you belong to Christ, then you are Abraham's offspring, heirs according to the promise" (v. 29). Indeed, Abraham "is the father of us all, as it is written: 'I have made you a father of many nations'" (Rom. 4:16–17; see also 2:28–29; 3:29–30; 4:11–12).

Thus the theme of the centrality of the church in God's purposes provides the key for the understanding of the relationship between old and new covenants. The fulfillment in the church of God's promise to Abraham was the perspective of every New Testament author who dealt with the issue of the role of the old covenant in light of the new. After having drawn a breathtaking list of the great figures of the Old Testament, the author of the letter to the Hebrews summarized the whole issue from a new covenant perspective in these words, "These were all commended for their faith, yet none of them received what had been promised. God had planned something better for us so that only together with us would they be made perfect" (Heb. 11:39–40 NIV). Likewise, the apostle Peter, reflecting on the prophetic ministry of the old covenant, concluded that the object of the ministry of the old covenant prophets was not to benefit their own times or their own people, but that it concerned the church in the new covenant:

> Concerning this salvation, the prophets, who spoke of the grace that was to come to you, searched intently and with the greatest care, trying to find out the time and circumstances to which the Spirit of Christ in them was pointing when he predicted the sufferings of Christ and the glories that would follow. It was revealed to them that they were not serving themselves but you, when they spoke of the things that have now been told you by those who have preached the gospel to you by the Holy Spirit sent from heaven (1 Pet. 1:10–12 NIV).

According to Peter's insight here, the Spirit of Christ was working within the old covenant prophets, enabling them to perform their ministry on behalf of the church. Likewise, in Acts, Peter declared that all the prophets of the old covenant had foretold the days of the church (Acts 3:24). In another bold word-picture, the apostle Paul traced the ministry of Christ as far back as the time of the Exodus when the people experienced collectively the sacraments of the church. They received a baptism that prefigured Christian baptism and were provided by Christ with spiritual bread and spiritual drink that prefigured the Lord's Supper (1 Cor. 10:1–5).

This development of the church may be illustrated with the sign ◀. The point on the left represents Abraham, then his descendants through faith, and at its widest point, the extension of the promise to believers from all nations through the ministry of Christ. From Abraham to the end, God gathers a believing people. The making of the church remains consistently central to God's purposes at work in history.

b. The church in Christ's ministry

The whole ministry of Jesus was devoted to the preparation and the launching of the new community. He came and preached peace to the Gentiles who were far away from God, and he preached peace to the Jews who were near, in order to unite them in the oneness of faith and to establish the church community on the foundation of the apostles and prophets (Eph. 2:17–22).

Jesus purposely chose twelve disciples from among the people of Israel to show the continuity between the community of faith of the old covenant and the church community of the new covenant. The twelve and the many other followers who surrounded him, including the female disciples and the seventy, were to become the core of the new community (Luke 8:1–3; 10:1–24; Acts 1:23–25). In keeping with God's promise to Abraham that he would have descendants among all the nations, Jesus ordered his followers to go and to make disciples among all the nations and to be his witnesses to the end of the earth, knowing that this endeavor would extend until the end of the age (Matt. 28:16–20; Acts 1:8). The scope of Jesus' vision for the church was universal, spanning the full extent of history. Beyond history, Jesus anticipated the resurrection of believers to life eternal (John 5:24–29) and the gathering of the church in eternal glory (Matt. 24:31; John 14:3). Jesus' coming into this world and his death and resurrection were designed to establish the church (John 12:32).

Jesus dedicated his three years of earthly ministry to teach his followers how to relate to God, to the world, and to each other (see, for example, his Sermon on the Mount, Matt. 5–7). He also taught them how to dissociate themselves from the corrupt religion of the Pharisees (the "Law" or "the tradition of the elders," Matt. 23) and of the Sadducees (the temple system, John 2). Most importantly, he taught them how the new community would embody the kingdom of God (see his parables of the kingdom, Matt. 13). Finally, Jesus gave his life and rose again to make it possible for ordinary women and men to be transformed into kingdom-builders as members of the new community. The nature and the effects of this transformation were made explicit in the story of the commissioning of the apostle Peter (Matt. 16:13–18) and in Lord's last prayer for his disciples (John 17); we will survey these passages briefly.

(1) **Building the church (Matt. 16:13–19).** About midway

181

through his ministry, Jesus took the disciples for a time of retreat, away from the crowds, to a resort area up the foothills of Mount Hermon. While there, he questioned them to test their understanding of his real identity. It was Simon Peter who affirmed, "You are the Christ, the Son of the living God." In this answer, Peter showed that he had identified Jesus in terms of both his mission and his nature. Christ was the long-awaited *Messiah* (a Hebrew word) or *Christ* (a Greek word), that is, God's anointed one, the fulfiller of God's purposes. He was also the Son of God, because he was uniquely related to God as Son to Father and because he was God in the flesh. Peter was the first human to pierce the mystery of Jesus' supernatural identity and mission.

By far the most startling part of this episode was Jesus' response to Peter. Because Peter had recognized Jesus' true identity and mission, Jesus gave him a new identity and a new mission, both designated in a new name: Simon son of Jonah was made Peter, which means "rock" (v. 18, see NIV note); on this rock Christ would build his church.

The identification of the "rock" on which Christ would build the church is hotly debated. Historically, it was held that Peter was the rock. However, this belief was challenged by the Protestant Reformation. Since then, some hold that the rock is Christ himself, and others that a faith like Peter's is the foundation for the church. Fortunately, Peter provided his own commentary on the imagery of rocks, foundations, and the church as a building. In his first epistle, he stated emphatically that Christ was the cornerstone of the church. But he also expanded the imagery to apply to each believer as he or she becomes basic building material used for the making of the church community. Believers are like living stones joined together to form God's spiritual house, the church (1 Pet. 2:4–8). In other words, Peter received Christ's designation of him as "rock," but he also understood it to apply to all believers, not just to himself.

Because of Peter's new-found faith, Jesus conferred upon him the quality of "rock" that would be instrumental for the building of his church. From Peter's own later admission, he was only one of a series. He was the model and the symbol of multitudes of others who would join him in the same faith to form the living organism that is the church (see also Eph. 2:19–22). The following equation may help clarify the point:

Simon son of Jonah + Christ's revelation = Peter the rock

The name Jonah is translated in the English language as John. Therefore, Simon son of Jonah means Simon, the son of John.

Today, we would call him Simon Johnson. Without the knowledge of who Christ is, Simon Johnson is just that, an ordinary person with no claim to fame, a man on the street, Mr. Anonymous. But suddenly, the divine revelation of Christ pulls Simon Johnson out of meaningless insignificance. Christ makes of him a hero, the very material out of which he builds the church. To simplify our equation:

$$\text{Johnson} + \text{Christ} = \text{rock}$$

And to do justice to Peter's own understanding of the interrelationship between all believers, Christ, and the church, we may again summarize it in this fashion:

$$\text{Anyone} + \text{Christ} = \text{living stone}$$

$$\text{All of us} + \text{Christ} = \text{living stones} = \text{the church}$$

Not only was Peter transformed into construction matériel to build the church but he also received a new mission. Christ gave him the keys of the kingdom of heaven so that whatever he would bind on earth would be bound in heaven, and whatever he would loose on earth would be loosed in heaven. Jesus conferred an authority on Peter that would cause his decisions to have eternal consequences. This authority has been interpreted in various ways. One view is that Jesus gave Peter primacy over other Christian leaders so that he had a Christ-derived authority over them. Then the inference is drawn that the successors of Peter were to inherit the same authority as representatives of Christ upon the earth. However, a closer reading of the text in Matthew 16:13–19 shows that it makes no such claims for a privileged position of Peter in relation to the other disciples, nor is there any reference to delegated powers or to the transmission of authority through succession.

Another approach to the meaning of the keys is that Peter was the apostle who played a crucial role in the launching of the church, since he was the first to verify the resurrection of Jesus (1 Cor. 15:5) and to preach the gospel to the Jews (Acts 2:14–36) and to the Gentiles (10:34–43). However, the best interpretation of the power of the keys must be derived from Peter's own treatment of the rock/stone imagery. According to the text, the authority given to Peter to bind and to loose accompanies the quality of him becoming "rock" (Matt. 16:18–19). Since, as noted above, Peter extended that quality to all believers (1 Pet. 2:4–8), it follows that the binding and loosing authority is a shared responsibility that pertains to the church as a whole. Indeed, Jesus repeated the mandate to bind and to loose with reference to the disciplinary and prayer functions of the church (Matt. 18:15–20), conferring that authority on the whole community: "I tell you the truth, whatever you [plural] bind on earth will be bound in heaven, and whatever you [plural] loose on earth will be loosed in heaven" (v. 18 NIV). This corporate exercise of authority expressed itself especially in the ministry of the forgiveness of sins through the Spirit-energized preaching of the gospel so that, in Christ's words, "If you [plural] forgive the sins of any, they are forgiven them; if you [plural] retain the sins of any, they are retained" (John 20:23, RSV).

Too often, such discussions as those just mentioned have overshadowed the main thrust of Jesus' affirmation that on the confessing Peter, "I will build my church." Jesus uses "I" and "my." The church belongs to him and he is its builder. All he needs is willing human lives to become living stones by receiving the revelation of his significance. Then Christ takes charge and builds a beautiful and powerful community. However, when humans think it is their church and build it according to their own wisdom and traditions, the church becomes a pathetic parody of what it was intended to be, and the gates of hell prevail easily against it. But Christ must be in charge; the church belongs truly to him and not to the clergy. He is the church's builder and establishes the centrality of the church in God's purposes. Under his leadership, the church becomes an irresistible community that moves on to crush the gates of hell.

(2) The community of oneness (John 17:21–26). As darkness fell over Jerusalem, Jesus whispered, "The hour has come" (John 17:1). In a few moments, he would leave the security of the Upper Room where he had gathered with his disciples for a last meal together and would lead them outside the city walls through the eastern gate. They would wind their way down to the Kidron valley, cross it, and climb the lower slope of the Mount of Olives to a garden. There his ordeal would begin.

For a while yet they were together. The disciples all sensed imminent disaster. Jesus had spoken at length to them, but words would not suffice now. So in the silence of the night, Jesus prayed. He looked up to heaven and poured out his soul. As the disciples listened in awe and fear, Jesus communed with the Father. He told how much his ministry had meant to him and how much it had accomplished in heaven and on earth, and he offered to God his hopes and desires for the future of his work in this world.

Suddenly, the disciples heard Jesus pray for them. He was thanking the Father for their having become his disciples, and he prayed for their protection from the evil one and from the world. But strangely, Jesus was not petitioning God for their safety

184

through the coming upheaval, nor even for their protection from persecution and death. At this crucial moment on the eve of his own death, when their world would collapse and their dreams shatter, Jesus was asking God to protect the disciples "so that they may be one" (John 17:11).

To say the least, this was a strange prayer request at such a critical time. More reasonably, Jesus could have prayed for the disciples' survival, for their future success, and for the effectiveness of their service to the kingdom. The very last thought of a person usually expresses the passion of his or her life. A loving wife on her deathbed will think of her husband, the workaholic of his accounts, the addict of one last shot, the miser of his gold, and the wounded soldier dying on a distant battlefield of home. For Jesus, the central passion of his life was the new community. He had come into the world to reconcile humans with God. He had taught reconciliation and lived it, and now he was dying for it. Understandably, therefore, during his last moments of quietness with his followers, he prayed for the community of reconciliation. He knew there could be no such community unless it had oneness; thus, he prayed for their oneness.

He did not just pray. He implored the Father insistently to protect the oneness of his followers for the sake of the oneness he himself enjoyed with the Father. The oneness of the community was as central to Jesus' concerns as his own relationship with the Father (John 17:11). And because Jesus knew that the church had an eternal destiny, he anticipated that it would expand beyond the disciples who surrounded him. He visualized his people dispersed to the ends of the earth and down the ages of time, and he prayed for us as well (v. 20).

Not surprisingly, his prayer for us was the same as his plea for the oneness of his first followers (v. 21). Jesus saw each one of us as part of a pilgrim family that would travel the length of history to its end. On their journey, this people would model God's intentions of oneness to a fragmented, community-starved world. In Jesus' vision, the proof of the gospel's truth in an unbelieving world would be the demonstration of genuine oneness in the community life of his followers. Such oneness would actually be fleshed out in the church community because Christ had given it as much of himself as the Father had given of himself to the Son (v. 22). And the essential quality of the gift transmitted by the Son from the Father to the community was his love (v. 23). The reality of this love within the community would prove to the world the real nature of Christ's mission—because love was the divine reality that existed before the foundation of the world and was the cause of its existence (vv. 23–24). This was the same love that caused the Father to send his Son into the world in order to form the new community, a love that now binds together that community in oneness (vv. 25–26).

Three years before this time, Jesus had begun his ministry among the disciples by teaching them how to pray (Matt. 6:9–13). They had, of course, already known how to pray. The Jewish religion demanded that prayer be one of the compulsory requirements of their lives. Prayers were offered several times a day in the temple and in synagogues. There were also prescribed family prayers and individual prayers for morning, noon, and night. But Jesus had taught the disciples to pray all over again, emphasizing a community aspect to prayer. He taught them to say, *"Our* Father," *"give us,"* *"our* daily bread," "forgive *us,"* and "deliver *us."* He had trained them to think of themselves as community—not as isolated individuals trying to relate to a private God. However, during his last moments with his disciples, Jesus was entrusting them in prayer to the loving Father, and central to that last prayer was his plea for the protection of the oneness of his church.

c. The church in the new covenant

For a definition of what that oneness means, we must go to those passages in the New Testament epistles that develop the theme. They present so many references to the oneness of the church community that it would be impossible to survey all of them within the scope of this chapter. However, two aspects of oneness stand out in the texts we will examine.

The first is a correlation between the "one flesh" relationship of man and woman in creation, when God declared "the two shall become one flesh" (Gen. 2:24), and the "one body" relationship that merges individual believers into community (Rom. 12:5). The concept of the community of oneness carries from the couple to the church—though, of course, the oneness of the church obviously involves more people (Eph. 5:31–32). The difference between both kinds of oneness is more quantitative than qualitative. Both find their origin and their definition in God's nature. Satan's designs at the Fall resulted in separation and stratification, but oneness is God's gift to the couple in creation and to the church in redemption. It reflects the fact that, within the Trinity, the Creator is himself three in one.

The second main idea that emerges from a thematic study of oneness is that oneness is impossible unless the constituent parts of the body are different from each other. Sameness results in uniformity, but this is not oneness. The world hates and rejects diversity. It strives for everyone to be conformed to this world. It responds to racial, ethnic, social, and sexual differences with segregations, polarizations, and stratifications. However, God loves the diversity he has built into his creation. There is diversity within the very being of God in that the Father, Son, and Spirit are different from one another, but there is also oneness since God is one being. Similarly, God celebrates the diversity that exists among humans as the expression of his own creative versatility, and he uses those differences as tools in the making of oneness. The pieces of a jigsaw puzzle are different from each other, but assembled together they form one picture. The man and woman at creation were different from each other, but together they formed one flesh. The members of a church are different from each other, but together they form one body. Diversity provides the building blocks that form oneness.

(1) **Oneness at the center (Gal. 3:26–29).** When the leaders of the Jews were plotting the death of Jesus, one of them rationalized his forthcoming murder as a national security measure. Without knowing it, he was predicting that Jesus was going to die "to gather into one the dispersed children of God" (John 11:52 NRSV). God's agelong purpose for the human race to produce community finally began to happen in Christ. God's promise that he would bless all the nations through Abraham's descendants and gather for himself a people of faith to be his community was now being fulfilled in the church. Without hesitation, Paul could declare to Gentile believers, "If you belong to Christ, then you are Abraham's offspring, heirs according to the promise" (Gal. 3:29 NRSV). In Christ, God was accomplishing his promise of creating a new chosen people.

The old chosen people had been drawn mainly from the Jewish race. When the members of the new chosen people looked around at each other in church, they were struck at the diversity among them. There was Greek and Jew, circumcised and uncircumcised, barbarian, Scythian, slave, and free (Col. 3:11). Each of those categories came with a history of ethnic and religious exclusiveness that made it impossible, under normal circumstances, for them to be found together under the same roof. For instance, it was unthinkable that a Gentile slave female could have any rapport with a Jewish free male. Strongly delineated racial, class, and sex segregations would guarantee that such a woman and such a man would live worlds apart with no opportunity for their lives to touch. But as believers, the Gentile slave woman and the Jewish free man had become one in Christ. Not only could they get to know each other but they also worshiped the same Lord together.

Best of all, they had now become servants to each other on the same basis of equality because the segregations of their past lives had become irrelevant in the new community. Paul triumphantly made this declaration when he announced that the promise to Abraham had now been fulfilled in the church: "There is no longer Jew or Greek, there is no longer slave or free, there is no longer male or female; for all of you are one in Christ Jesus" (Gal. 3:28 NRSV).

Accordingly, oneness was at the center of the new community as its centripedal force. All the old distinctions had become secondary issues, mere accidents of birth or fortune. Race, skin color, gender, and wealth had formerly provided the criteria to pigeonhole people on the social ladder. Now, however, oneness in Christ had become the basis for accepting each other as equals. For example, outside the church the Jew viewed himself as being above the Gentile. But in the new community Jews were not above Gentiles because they were all one, and because Jewishness and Gentileness were not a factor in the life of oneness. Similarly, outside the church, the free person viewed himself above the slave. But in the new community free persons were not above slaves because they were all one, and because being free or slave was not a factor in the life of oneness. Outside the church, the male viewed himself as being above the female. But in the new community men were not above women because they were all one, and because manhood and womanhood were not a factor in the life of oneness. As Paul declared, "We, who are many, are one body" (1 Cor. 10:17 NIV).

As we shall see below, the only differences among Christians that are relevant to the functioning and structure of the church are those that pertain to ministry, differences based on individual gifting. The Holy Spirit distributes the spiritual gifts not on the basis of the old racial, class, and sex discriminations, but as he wills (1 Cor. 12:11).

This teaching on transformed relations and structures within the new community is often threatening to those who wish to maintain old community patterns in the new community. For this reason, they have claimed that the content of Paul's statement in Galatians 3:28 refers not to the life of the church but applies only to new believers at their point of entrance into the community through justification by faith and baptism. This interpretation should be examined with its implications.

According to this approach, Paul would be saying, "When you become a believer, there is neither Jew nor Greek; but after you enter into the life of the church, there is a distinction made between Jew and Greek. When you become a believer, there is neither slave nor free, but after you enter into the life of the church, there is a distinction made between slave and free. When you become a believer, there is neither male nor female; but after you enter into the life of the church, there is a distinction made between male and female. In other words, when you become believers you are all one in Christ Jesus. But after you enter into the life of the church, you are no longer one in Christ." The inconsistency of such a position is obvious. It results in the denial of the oneness of the church.

To get around this pitfall, other defenders of the male/female hierarchy offer a slightly different interpretation of Galatians 3:28. According to them, this pasasge would be teaching that men and women are equal in status and worth but not equal in functions and roles. It is claimed that there can be spiritual equality between men and women in worth without equality in function. On such premises the biblical texts would be stating: "Whether you are Jew or Gentile, slave or free, you are equal in worth and, therefore, you are equally worthy to function as one body. However, if you are a woman, you have equal worth, but not equal enough for you to participate equally in the functional oneness of the church." The scriptural text does not seem to make such discriminatory exceptions.

According to the New Testament, the spiritual oneness of the church necessarily results in functional oneness, since a foremost sign of the oneness of the church is the inclusive availability of spiritual gifts distributed on the basis of divine grace—never in consideration of race, social status, or gender. "We who are many form one body, and each member belongs to all the others. We have different gifts, according to the grace given us" (Rom. 12:5–6; in the next part of v. 6, the NIV unjustifiably inserts "man"). The oneness of the church as described in the New Testament confers on its members spiritual worth that transcends considerations of race, social status, and gender (Gal. 3:28; Col. 3:11-15). That very same oneness is what requires the functional participation of all its members in the church's ministry, on the basis of their gifting and never in consideration of race, social status, or gender (1 Cor. 12:4–26; Eph. 4:4–7). The biblical equation of worth and oneness and the analogous equation of function and oneness render worth and function inseparable. Oneness requires the free and total functional participation of each member by reason of the supreme worth of each person for God and for the community.

Scripture teaches that oneness is more central to a Christian's identity as a member of the body of Christ than his or her racial, class, or sexual identity. And when the center collapses, the church becomes something other than what the divine Founder intended it to be. The oneness of the community is central to the definition of the church.

(2) **Oneness through diversity (1 Cor. 12:12–26).** In 1 Corinthians, the church is compared to a body with its many parts. Surprisingly, the metaphor is not, as elsewhere, that of Christ as head and the body as the church. The head is included, but only as one of the parts of the body, equal to them with its own responsibility to be a servant (v. 21). As his body, the church does not function through just one of its members, such as a pontiff or a head bishop, neither is it ruled by a few people such as the clergy. "For the body does not consist of one member but of many" (v. 14 RSV). All the members together make up the body, the church (v. 12). To function properly, it needs the active participation of all its members. Should the foot or hand go dead, the body becomes disabled. This is why the Holy Spirit utilizes for the common good the gifts with which he has endowed all individual believers (vv. 7, 11).

Just as the life of the human body is dependent on the functioning of all its parts, so the life of the church is dependent on the utilization of each person's gift. The use of only a few parts of the human body cannot make it function properly. Neither can the church function when only some of the people's gifts are utilized. If the people in the congregation should say, "Because I am not a clergyman, I cannot serve the church," where would the church be? Or if a pastor should say, "Because you are not an ordained minister, we have no need of you," what would happen to the body?

In the light of this passage, it is wrong to designate some people in the church as ministers and to leave the ministry functions of the church solely to them. Each member of the church is a minister, and the church makes it possible for each member to contribute his or her spiritual gift to the ministry of the church. The variety of gifts distributed by the Holy Spirit is to be valued and exploited for ministry without comparison or competition (1 Cor. 12:14–20). Each member with his or her gift is needed by the others (v. 21). The very gifts that we consider less glamorous and less valuable from our human perspective, God treats with greater honor than the visible, up-front gifts, so that there may be equality among the members (vv. 22–24). The purpose for this divine adjustment is that the members of the church may treat each other with equal consideration without elevating some, such as the clergy or men, above the others (v. 25). The church is one group of people and not two, with one at a higher level and the root below them—for example, the clergy above and the congregation below, or men above and women below them. The test of such balanced, nondiscriminatory treatment of people within the church is whether there exists "equal concern for each other" (v. 25). A church passes this test if all parts are equally affected when something good or bad happens to a member, regardless of rank, position, influence, or function within the body (v. 26).

Because Christ is at the center of every believer's life, all believers are inevitably joined to the same center. Just as the human body unites all its parts into one living organism, so Christ brings believers into the oneness of the church. The church is the *body of Christ* in the world. Without it, Christ's presence in the world would not be felt. As individual members of the body of Christ, believers are the key players in the unfolding of the most important of all the stories that compete for headlines on the front page of history.

3. The Finality of the Church

If the church is the most important thing that God is doing in history, it is also because God has assigned for it an eternal destiny. Jesus made it clear to his followers that though they would experience hardships in this life, they would receive eternal life in the age to come (Mark 10:30). He depicted the end of history as the separation of the righteous for their entrance into eternal life (Matt. 25:46). And referring to his followers he declared, "I give them eternal life, and they shall never perish" (John 10:28 NIV). Commitment to Christ has a significance that outlasts a Christian's earthly experience. According to the apostle Paul, the eternal purpose of God is for the church to become the supreme expression of his wisdom for the whole universe to behold for ever and ever (Eph. 3:10–11, 21). And according to the apostle John, the world will pass away; only those who do the will of God will remain for eternity (1 John 2:17). To put it simply, only the church will survive the present order and remain for God's eternal kingdom; only the church is forever.

As amazing as it may seem, the Scripture teaches that this was precisely how Abraham understood the promise made to him by God (Heb. 11:8–10). When God told Abraham to leave his home and to go to the land that was promised to him as an inheritance, he travelled to it but he never claimed the land as his own. He lived in Canaan like an alien, refusing to stake out any part of it. His descendants Isaac and Jacob, also beneficiaries of the same promise, followed the same strange behavior.

191

Fortunately, Hebrews provides the explanation for their reluctance to claim the land. Through the eyes of faith, Abraham and his descendants saw that the land was only the image of an infinitely greater reality that was to be theirs. They considered themselves as aliens and strangers while walking on the land. They were looking for their real country, a much better country than Canaan because it is a heavenly home (Heb. 11:13–16).

Within this symbolism of a better, heavenly country, the spotlight is on the city of God; Abraham looked forward to the city whose builder is God (Heb. 11:10). In return, God complied with his desire and prepared a city for them (v. 16). But neither Abraham nor his descendants entered that promised city. They all saw it from afar through the eyes of faith and died without receiving the promise, because God had planned that we, of this present church age, should also be included in the fulfillment of the promise (vv. 39–40). God had put on hold the cosmic unveiling of the mysterious heavenly city until the coming of Christ and the birth of the church.

But what is the city? Fortunately, we do not have to guess because the author of Hebrews provides us with a dazzling description of it. He writes to Christians about entering the spiritual Jerusalem, not the earthly city of Jerusalem in Palestine which, at the time of writing, was either destroyed or close to being razed by the Romans.

> You have come to Mount Zion, to the heavenly Jerusalem, the city of the living God. You have come to thousands upon thousands of angels in joyful assembly, to the church of the firstborn, whose names are written in heaven. You have come to God, the judge of all men, to the spirits of righteous men made perfect, to Jesus the mediator of a new covenant, and to the sprinkled blood. . . . (Heb. 12:22–24 NIV)

Through the imagery of a holy city in heaven, he describes God in his glory and Jesus, the author of the new covenant, surrounded with innumerable worshiping angels and with the community of those made righteous by the sprinkled blood. Should we wonder what this blood is, the author later explains that Jesus suffered outside the city walls of earthly Jerusalem in order to create a holy people through his blood (13:12). Consequently, on this earth, we as believers have no lasting city. But we are looking for the spiritual, heavenly city that is to come (v. 13).

In other words, the heavenly city that Abraham saw at a great distance and that Christians are now waiting for is the spiritual Jerusalem in heaven, the church ushered from earth into eternity, the community of faith from Abraham to the last believers on earth, all gathered with their God forever. Even at their best, the land of Canaan and the old earthly Jerusalem were only pale and passing tokens of the glorious church community gathered to her Savior for all eternity.

Abraham's vision of the land of Canaan as a predictive image of the church is perfectly consistent with God's original promise of the land to Abraham (Gen. 17:4–8). The main point of the everlasting covenant given by God to Abraham (meaning "father of many") was that it applied to him and his descendants forever (v. 7). In the same covenant, the descendants of Abraham were defined, not as a single nation, but as "many nations." God told him, "Your name will be Abraham, for I have made you a father of many nations. I will make you very fruitful; I will make nations of you" (vv. 5–6 NIV). When God added, "The whole land of Canaan, where you are now an alien, I will give as an everlasting possession to you and your descendants after you" (v. 8), he was actually promising the land not just to one nation but to Abraham's descendants "from many nations." For this reason, the author of Hebrews viewed the land where Abraham wandered about as representing the church, the real descendants of Abraham from "many nations." Obviously, neither God nor the church has an everlasting interest in a piece of real estate that will pass with the rest of the world. But the church reality represented by the land and by the city in it will last forever.

Further explanations of the church as a heavenly city can be found in the last chapters of Revelation, where the city as community becomes the symbol for the church in eternity.

> Then I saw a new heaven and a new earth, for the first heaven and the first earth had passed away, and there was no longer any sea. I saw the Holy City, the new Jerusalem, coming down out of heaven from God, prepared as a bride beautifully dressed for her husband. And I heard a loud voice from the throne saying, "Now the dwelling of God is with men, and he will live with them. They will be his people, and God himself will be with them and be their God. He will wipe every tear from their eyes. There will be no more death or mourning or crying or pain, for the old order of things has passed away." (Rev. 21:1–4 NIV)

In this passage, the apostle John anticipates the day when our universe will disappear and be replaced by a new reality. At the very center of this new order appears the new Jerusalem coming out of heaven from the hands of God. She is his special creation, the eternal centerpiece of all his works, the new dwelling of God with his people, prepared as a bride for her husband. Under the imagery of a city-community made by God, John sees all believers from old and new covenant, the church in its completeness, gathered in its finality for eternity (21:9–14; see pages 268–69). This great multitude cries with one voice, "Let us rejoice and be glad and give him glory! For the wedding of the Lamb has come, and his bride has made herself ready" (19:7 NIV).

The finality of the church in God's purposes shows that the church is not just the most important thing that God is doing in history. The church is the *only* thing that God is doing in this world that will last through time and eternity, because it is the only earthly reality that will survive time and last throughout eternity.

II. THE MINISTRIES OF THE CHURCH

Although God has entrusted the church with many responsibilities to fulfill on this earth, we must remember that above all else, the church exists for God's sake. God made the church primarily because he loves it. It is his special creation within all of creation. God's love for the church is reason enough for it to be. A good man takes a bride because he loves her and wants to serve her and enhance her life. Whatever she may do in service to him is the result of their union rather than the purpose for it. In a similar manner, Christ loved the church as his bride and gave himself up for her to make her beautiful and exalted (Eph. 5:25–27). In return for Christ's servant love, the church submits herself to him in all things as his servant (v. 24). In this section, we will survey some aspects of the servant *ministry* of the church as it unites believers in community, in worship, and in outreach.

1. Oneness in Community

In the previous section we explored the church as God's community of oneness. He delights in oneness among humans and desires to be part of it. When two or three are gathered in Christ's name, he promises to be present in the midst of them (Matt. 18:20). He lives among them by his Spirit (Eph. 2:22). However, such oneness does not just happen. It is generated and nurtured by the sharing of authentic faith, with the pursuit of clearly defined objectives, by conformity to patterns of behavior consistent with the teaching of Scripture, and by methods of communal organization that encourage participation. Each of these will now be considered in sequence.

a. A shared faith

The apostle Paul testifies that the church has "one faith" (Eph. 4:5) and is "built on the foundation of the apostles and prophets" (2:20). It is important to define what this foundation consists of. The Christian faith is founded on Scripture. But the Bible is a huge book, and people often understand its contents differently. What some stress as the foremost parts of the Bible other Christians ignore completely, and some draw ideas from Bible texts that others interpret in an opposite manner. Therefore every church needs to formulate clearly its understanding of the Christian faith in a document commonly called a "creed," a "statement of faith," or a "confession of faith."

Obviously, such a document cannot be exhaustive. It cannot be made to say all that could be said. It should normally cover the main areas of the Christian faith, such as those suggested by the outline of this book: Revelation, God, Christ, the Holy Spirit, human beings, redemption, the church, and the endtimes. But in doing so, two dangers must be avoided. One is to draw a statement so vague that it requires virtually no faith commitment to subscribe to it. Some groups adopt such broad formulations that Christians, Moslems, and Hindus can all endorse them. In this case the church risks losing its Christian distinctiveness.

The opposite pitfall is to draw a statement of faith so detailed on minor points of doctrine that it becomes divisive. In this case, a church tends to become cultic and separatist. The long history of church tradition supplies us with a number of great faith documents, such as the Apostles' Creed (so called!), the Nicene and Chalcedonian Creeds, and certain denominational confessions, that can serve as models for the formulation of balanced statements that emphasize the essential tenets of the faith with integrity and fairness. Such a statement can provide guidance for the preaching and teaching ministries of the local church. At the same time, it provides a common basis for the commitment of new believers to church membership.

b. A shared purpose

A clear statement of faith also enables a congregation to draw from it a definition of its mission. A church that does not know precisely what it is supposed to accomplish will either do nothing or will spread itself too thin by trying to do everything. Each congregation needs to draw a clear and concise strategy statement for what it believes God calls it to accomplish within the particular location where it is planted. Since needs and opportunities vary from place to place, the approaches must be defined accordingly.

Obviously, such a statement of purpose should include the elements of communal life, shared worship, and corporate outreach as vital areas of a church's life. But such goals will not likely be attained if it does not adopt specific methods for attaining them. Therefore, the statement of purpose should also suggest carefully designed strategies to work out those objectives. A church takes too great a risk in leaving the fulfillment of its mission to the happenstance of improvisation. The challenges facing churches in modern society require them to follow carefully considered plans so that they can focus their efforts on what needs to be accomplished without being distracted by the many worthy causes that clamor for their involvement when those are not central to their purpose. As Jesus commissioned the disciples for a short-term outreach effort, he told them to be as wise as serpents within their generation (Matt. 10:16). The command still applies today. Such strategizing does not preclude reliance on the Holy Spirit; rather, wise planning enhances and multiplies the effectiveness of the Spirit.

c. A shared lifestyle

One of the most consistent themes of Scripture is that in order to be authentic, faith in God is to be lived out in this world. Faith has implications for how we think, talk, act, and relate to others. Without faith, the values that determine behavior are borrowed from a world ignorant of divine guidance. With the commitment of faith comes commitment to a new life informed by God's word. The Bible rejects some behaviors as being incompatible with God's will, and it requires in their place other forms of conduct derived from God's will. In the chapter on salvation, this change from one lifestyle to another was defined as the result of the restoration of God's image in human life through the process of sanctification (see pages 165–66).

In order to provide clear guidance in those areas to its people, it is appropriate for a church to draw up a statement of responsibilities outlining its expectations for its members as well as the means of enforcement. The absence of such a statement sends the message that anything goes. When this happens, the line between the church and society becomes blurred, and the church fails to impact society because it is not modeling a Christian lifestyle. On the other hand, a statement of conduct may be so restrictive that it appears cultic and controlling. Some churches seem to be so intent on protecting their members from worldly influences that, through detailed sets of rules and regulations, they segregate them from society so much that they have no channels left for ministry to the world.

For this reason, it is advisable for churches to refrain from placing legalistic prohibitions and expectations on their members that go beyond the clear teaching of Scripture. For instance, the Scriptures clearly forbid drunkenness but permit the drinking of wine for a variety of reasons (John 2:1–11; Eph. 5:18; 1 Tim. 5:23). Churches that require total abstinence as a condition for membership should realize that Jesus himself would be rejected as a member, since he once changed 120 gallons of water into wine for people who had already drunk enough to be unable to discern its high quality. In view of the enormous social problems caused by alcoholic addiction in contemporary society, churches may legitimately advise abstinence rather than require it as if it were a biblical command. More important, however, is that churches exercise strict discipline in areas clearly defined by Scripture. Note that the same biblical text that prohibits drunkenness also requires the excommunication of people who love money (the "greedy") and who badmouth other people (the "revilers"; see 1 Cor. 5:11–13).

This raises the issue of church discipline. Having a statement of conduct is useless if it cannot be enforced. The New Testament places on the congregation the responsibility to watch over its members both to correct offending members and to protect the body in case of misbehavior. It ordains a graded approach of confrontation so that opportunity for repentance is offered at every stage of the process (Matt. 18:15–18). Should the process lead to excommunication, its purpose is not the permanent exclusion of the offenders, but their eventual restoration to the body (2 Thess. 3:14–15). Thus, through this watchcare Christians can maintain good conduct in the world so that unbelievers may see how honorably they live and may themselves be brought to God (1 Pet. 2:10).

d. A shared authority

As just noted, concern for the purity of the church and for the welfare of its members requires the exercise of oversight. Some may stray away from the faith or err in their behavior and, as a result, may need to be rebuked or even disciplined. A progressive and dynamic church ministry requires decisions to be made in regard to policies, personnel, and planning. So the question arises as to who should exercise leadership in those areas. Historically, churches have come up with three basic forms of governance.

One model places the authority for the conduct of the affairs of the church community in one person who decides from the top down what is good for the group. In this case, the leader stands at the uppermost point of a pyramid of authority and sees to it that his or her decisions are carried out at every level of execution down the chain of command. This form of administration is comparable to the hierarchic organization of the military or of management in traditionally structured corporations.

The model at the opposite end of the spectrum puts the responsibility for making decisions in the hands of the congregation as a whole. In this case, the "leaders" of the group are appointed by it and have only an advisory function. They bring the business of the church to the community, and the group as a whole makes the decisions that affect its life and ministry.

A third model looks like a compromise between the two described above. It might be pictured as a sawed-off pyramid. The congregation appoints a group of representative leaders who act on its behalf while remaining accountable to it. The leadership is represented by the top of the truncated pyramid. It forms a part of the congregation it serves, and the plurality of leadership provides checks and balances that the one-man leadership model does not have. This group of leaders—who may be called elders, deacons, the session, or the vestry, depending on the church's denomination—has the authority to manage the affairs of the church. But because they are elected to their position of responsibility by the people of the church, they remain answerable to the community for the administration of its affairs.

The diversity of views on this subject may cause us to wonder what exactly is the teaching of the New Testament on church governance. In order to find out, we must first consider the teaching of Jesus on this subject. He anticipated the establishment of the community of faith and gave instructions for its functioning.

Jesus absolutely forbade one individual to hold authority over others in Christian communities. The disciples were upset at the fact that he was not structuring their own group with one of them in charge and the others under him. That was the only model of group organization they knew. So, behind his back, they apparently decided to elect their own leader as the one "greatest" among them (Mark 9:33–35). Upon learning this, Jesus rebuked them and told them that anyone who wants to be the top man in a Christian community should instead make himself servant to all. A servant does not exercise authority over others but places himself or herself under the authority of the group.

This one strong lesson should have been enough to put the

point across to the disciples. But they were so used to the principle of people being under the authority of strong individual leaders that they could not grasp the radical nature of Jesus' teaching. Thus, two of them approached Jesus privately and asked him to make them number one and number two in his community (Mark 10:35–45). They had completely missed the point. Again, Jesus explained to the two disciples that in order to become leaders according to his definition of leadership, they had to share in his own ministry of self-sacrifice, humiliation, and suffering instead of seeking positions of authority.

On hearing this, the other ten disciples became angry at James and John for their attempt to supplant them. Once more, Jesus gathered the disciples and gave them a strong teaching on how to structure Christian communities. He gave them the illustration of the imperial political system under which they were all living. They were ruled by one person (the Roman emperor), who exercised authority all the way down the pyramid of society. Jesus had no objection to that form of government for non-Christian communities. He said it was acceptable for the world to structure its communities in this manner but not for Christians. The only person who rules Christian communities is the Lord himself (Matt. 23:8–11). Under him, we are all equals.

Jesus emphatically rejected the top-down authority model by declaring, "It shall not be so among you" (Mark 10:43 RSV). He also added that the very people who desire to run the show should instead become servants and slaves to the community. Single leaders tell other people what to do; servants and slaves ask others what they can do for them. The servant attitude is the antidote Jesus prescribed for the poison of single-person leadership structures. And to emphasize this point, Jesus cited as his reason the precedent he had himself set by giving up his position of supreme authority to become a servant among humans (Mark 10:45). With this teaching, Jesus grasped in his mighty hands the worldly concept of community as a pyramid of power and turned it upside down on its head. For true oneness to happen in Christian communities, those who aspire to lead from the top must instead serve at the bottom. Thus the strength of the strong can balance and support the efforts of the weak.

Jesus knew that without supervision and therefore without the exercise of authority the work of the church cannot go on. Decisions must be made and responsibilities must be carried out. The call to servanthood does not absolve the church from the responsibility of making decisions and seeing to it that they are put into effect. However, in Christian communities the slogan "Somebody's got to be in charge," does not apply because the whole body is mobilized by the Spirit to be in charge. Out in the world, one person may make the decisions for the whole group. But in the church, it is the group that decides for itself. In Christian communities, authority is not vested in one dominant individual but in the body as a whole or in a representative plurality of leaders.

Jesus illustrated this principle with one of the most critical decisions a group may be called to make: that of ruling on who may or may not be part of the community (Matt. 18:15–20). In the community of oneness, such matters ultimately come to the body, not just to one individual (v. 17). And the decisions made by the group are binding because they have an eternal relevance (v. 18) since Christ is present in the group, providing guidance to it (v. 20). When Jesus placed the base of authority in the congregation rather than in one person, he was not being anti-authority. In fact, he was giving greater strength to the authority principle since decisions are more binding when they are made by many people than when they issue from a single individual. Jesus denied any one person the right to control the community, for that power belongs to him alone and he shares it only with the body of which he is the only Lord.

As a result of this teaching by the Lord, there is no church mentioned or described in the New Testament that was governed by a single leader, and there is no discussion of a practice called *ordination* whereby selected persons are designated as "ministers" or "priests"—except for the formal recognition of spiritual gifts among believers (1 Tim. 4:14; 5:22; 2 Tim. 1:6). The New Testament recognizes all believers as "ministers" and "priests" (Rom. 12:6–8; 1 Cor. 12:4–7; 1 Pet. 2:5, 9; Rev. 1:6). Because these churches were at different stages of development, because they had attained different levels of maturity, because they were located in different social environments, and because they all had different corporate personalities, their particular methods of self-governance were not the same. But in every case, leadership was a shared responsibility.

When the apostle Paul dealt with the congregations of Corinth, Galatia, and Colosse, he did not appeal to a leader or even to a group of leaders to resolve their problems. He set his case before the whole church and asked for congregational resolutions. Some churches had designated groups of representative members, called *elders* (or *bishops*) and *deacons,* to provide leadership to the congregation on its own behalf. This was true for the church in Ephesus (1 Tim. 3) and in Philippi (Phil. 1:1). But even in these cases, a careful study of the required qualifications for such leaders and of the very scant information provided in Scripture about their job descriptions indicates that the mode of their administration was designed after the pattern of the sawed-off pyramid. Moreover, the New Testament shows that this pattern of church governance is best illustrated by turning the shortened pyramid upside-down on its small base, with the leaders caring for the people from the bottom as their servants, not lording it over them but being examples to the flock and empowering them for ministry (1 Pet. 5:2–3).

In the church, as in most human organizations, there is a need for strong leaders who are farsighted, proactive, and intentional in promoting the purposes of the group. But their leadership gifts should never be misused as a pretext for the exercise of personal dominance (1 Pet. 5:3). The scriptural mandate for leaders is to use their gifts to enable, empower, and facilitate the development of leadership skills among other members of the group, within each one's area of competence. Moreover, the Scripture requires that individual leadership be exercised within the context of a leadership team (plurality of elders) so that decisions will be made consensually on the basis of broad participation. The members of a church's leadership team (whether called elders, deacons, session, or vestry) are the real *pastors* of the church. Together they are accountable to keep watch over the souls of their charges (Heb. 13:17 NRSV). In this perspective, the appointive pastor or "senior" pastor should act as one of the regular members of the leadership team and, preferably, not as its chairperson. Christ alone is the Chief Shepherd of the church (1 Pet. 5:4).

In our day, much emphasis is given to church structure, with a tendency to make it rigidly uniform for different churches on the basis of the one pattern derived from 1 Timothy 3. However, we must remember that this pattern reflected the governance model of only one church in New Testament times and that other churches had other forms of governance. Accordingly, each church should decide under the Spirit's guidance what form of governance will work best for it, rather than model itself after some other church. In fact, the changing needs of any church in process of development may call for the consideration of different forms of governance at each significant stage of its growth. Both the availability of leadership and the size and maturity of the congregation will affect the choice of structure. Contemporary churches must be as adaptable and as flexible in this regard as New Testament churches were under the guidance of the Spirit during the first century. We must realize that institutionalized misreadings of

Scripture that define Christian community as hierarchy instead of oneness eventually result in the disablement of community.

One of the obvious advantages of churches with consensual and adaptable forms of governance is the openness they offer for the use of the spiritual gifts invested by God in each member of the congregation. Within rigid structures, the leaders at the top monopolize access to ministry. But where the Spirit of the Lord is allowed to be active, there we find freedom and opportunity (2 Cor. 3:17). Each individual may become involved in service on the basis of his or her spiritual gift(s), knowing that every gift is important for the work of the kingdom. Some gifts we regard as being authority-intensive, such as that of apostles (church-planting pioneers), prophets (preachers), evangelists, pastors, and teachers. Scripture describes those very gifts as service ministries provided by God to facilitate the work of the congregation and to enable it to carry on the ministry of the church (Eph. 4:11–12). The congregation does not exist to enable the clergy to do ministry. The New Testament teaches precisely the opposite; the clergy exist in order to enable the congregation to do ministry (v. 12). According to the inverted-truncated pyramid model, they are at the base of the structure empowering the congregation above it to do the church's work of ministry by facilitating the use of all the spiritual gifts made available by God to the congregation. The authority of ministry belongs to all of God's people, not to a spiritual elite above them.

2. Oneness in Worship

The first priority for a community of Christians is to enter into communion with God. The oneness in community surveyed in the previous section finds its strength and meaning in the fact that believers can share a corporate relationship with God in corporate worship. It is like a group of musical instrumentalists. Each of them has his or her own integrity as a musician. Each one can make beautiful solo music in the privacy of one's own place. But their most complete and powerful performance occurs when they come together and combine their talents in orchestral music. As they play together, they enhance each other's contribution and reach heights of musical achievement that could not be attained individually. Similarly, corporate worship expresses the essence of what the church is, a community of believers in communion with God.

a. Definition of worship

Worship is more easily done than defined. Attempts at defining it often end up with the listing of its components—like praying, praising, singing, listening, giving, receiving, and edifying. But the more basic question is: What is the reason for doing those things? What do they accomplish? Is worship limited to the formal occasions set apart to do it? What does the Scripture mean when it tells us to do all, whether we eat or drink or whatever we do, to the glory of God (1 Cor. 10:31)?

It is obvious that worship takes this world into account since it happens here. But it also reaches beyond this world to divine transcendence. It recognizes the relevance of the triune God as Creator, Redeemer, and Sustainer to the totality of life, past, present, and future. Through faith, worship perceives God at the center. Therefore, we might suggest that worship is the acknowledgement and the celebration of the centrality of God in all of life. Of course, we live in a fallen world, every parcel of which has been vandalized by Satan. But beyond, above, and within the fallenness, signs of God's goodness still shine through the pollution of sin. Christians rejoice at the signs of the presence of God and make it the focus of their devotion when they worship. They pool together the richness of their individual perceptions of God into one experience of exaltation, and they tell God in as many ways as possible that they love him above all else.

When addressed, God does not remain silent. He eagerly enters into the proposed dialogue. In many ways, but essentially through his word, the Lord tells his people that they are at the center of his purposes for time and eternity. Therefore, worship is also the celebration of the centrality of the church within the purposes of God. When we worship, God tells us that he loves us above all else.

At the same time, we acknowledge the importance of other believers in our own lives. We recognize that people matter to God supremely. Since they matter to God, they also matter to us. Therefore, worship is also our sharing with God in his celebration of the community of oneness.

This definition of worship as the recognition of God's centrality to our lives and of our centrality in God's purposes implies that worship is an integral element in the everyday life of every Christian. Whether we eat or drink, or whatever we do, we can indeed do it in an attitude of worship by recognizing God at the center. But designated times of worship, both private and public, afford opportunities for unhindered, focused, and planned experiences of reverence and enjoyment: reverence, because we are relating to transcendent God; enjoyment, because worship pleases God and is good for us. This means that our experiences of worship should be well prepared and creatively crafted, drawing on the multiple talents and gifts available within the community of believers. All gifts of the mind and the imagination are needed to render worship to God since he has created both. Inasmuch as the arts express meaning, display beauty, embody feeling, and facilitate perception, they are relevant to worship. Sloppy, boring, predictable, and tradition-bound forms of worship are an insult to God. If God deserves our best, he especially deserves it when we approach him in worship. Creative worship is the grateful acknowledgment of the Creator and of the gifts of creativity that he has bestowed on his creatures through the use of these very gifts.

In addition to being pleasant to God, worship is good for us. God seeks to fulfill us, to renew us, to teach us, and to help us grow. All the means and the gifts present in the community ought to be made available for worship. This may require a broad sharing among qualified people of the responsibilities of teaching and preaching, praying and singing, and whatever else is integrated in the church's worship experiences. In churches where those gifts abound, programming the ministries of worship on the basis of specialized teams offers the best chance for providing freshness and diversity and for striving for excellence in worship.

b. Hindrances to worship

Many churches have needlessly impaired the quality of their worship potential because they have uncritically accepted unscriptural restrictions about participation in worship. Some believe that the only persons authorized to lead in worship are ordained ministers. One of the dangers of this concept is that worship can become a one-person show performed before an audience of spectators instead of a community experience involving broad participation on the basis of spiritual giftings. Another drawback is its suggestion that the church is a "split-level" arrangement composed of two classes of people: the clergy above and the congregation below, a distinction that sabotages the oneness of the church as community.

The nature of women's participation in worship is also a matter of debate among some churchgoers. On one side, many Christians believe that the Bible forbids women to lead in public worship. They interpret the words of Paul in 1 Corinthians 14:33–35 and 1 Timothy 2:11–15 as applying universally to all women, in all churches and in all ages. They believe that God has ordained a hierarchy of authority between men and women. Inasmuch as leading in worship and teaching represent the assumption of spiritual authority, such activities are considered off-limits to women.

Other Christians claim that in New Testament churches, women had access to the highest levels of ministry, including that of prophecy (Acts 2:17–18; 21:9), a gift that was equivalent to preaching as defined in 1 Corinthians 14:3. They believe that since the ministry of prophecy was the second highest divine appointment in the church, just below the apostles and just above the teaching function (12:28), women could lead in worship and prophesy on the same basis as men, provided they had the spiritual gift for doing so (11:4–5; 12:7; 14:31).

According to this view, the only condition for participation was that such gifted people be properly trained (2 Tim. 2:2 NRSV) and that they first receive instruction quietly prior to becoming teachers (1 Tim. 2:11). Owing to the lack of adequate training, some Ephesian women were apparently straying after Satan (5:15) and leading others into error (v. 13). According to Paul, they acted like Eve, who took it upon herself to dialogue with Satan about matters that lay outside of her competence, since they had been explained to Adam prior to her existence and she had obtained them only secondhand (2:13–14). Accordingly, Paul's prohibition for women to teach (v. 12) would have applied specifically to the untrained women in Ephesus, and universally to any untrained or incompetent would-be teacher (see also James 3:1).

Other restrictions that must be mentioned are those of location and numbers. Jesus dealt with both of those matters when he declared that wherever two or three believers gather in his name, he is present with them (Matt. 18:20). The "wherever" points to Christ's universal availability to worshipers. He does not confine his presence to cathedrals or to churches at eleven o'clock on Sunday mornings. He is willing to meet with the faithful in consecrated buildings as well as in any other place where they can assemble—in an upper room, by the seashore, while breaking bread at the table, and even on the Emmaus road. Churches are not "houses of worship" but convenient gathering places for worshiping people. The homes of those people are the real houses of worship.

The regular gathering of the whole congregation for the purpose of worship is essential to the life of a church. But it is equally important for the members of a congregation to have the freedom and the opportunity to get together in smaller groups for the purpose of worship, mutual support, discipling, Bible study, prayer, and service to the body as specialized ministry teams. The intimacy of small groups is conducive to the sharing of personal concerns, mutual watchcare, and accountability. It lends itself better than large gatherings to the dynamics of community life. The congregations mentioned in the New Testament gathered in places large enough to accommodate them as a group, such as in the temple area at Jerusalem and the hall of Tyrannus in Ephesus (Acts 2:46; 19:9). But they also met as smaller groups in homes so that the ministry of the church was decentralized and disseminated wherever its people lived (Acts 2:46b; Rom. 16:5; 1 Cor. 16:19). This made it possible for each home to function all week long as a micro-church. Such flexibility in worship structures facilitates broad participation in the life and ministry of the church by its constituency.

The New Testament doctrine of the priesthood of all believers finds its most vivid and visible application in the congregation's participation in the worship ministry of the community. Together, believers form a spiritual house, a living temple within which they act as one holy priesthood. Like the priests of the old covenant in the temple, they offer sacrifices that are acceptable to God. But unlike the specialized old covenant priesthood, the new covenant priesthood involves all believers in ministry to God. They all offer spiritual sacrifices—not according to the law of Moses but through Jesus Christ (Rom. 12:1; 1 Pet. 2:5, 9).

The sacrifices offered in the church by believer-priests come as two forms of worship: first, the sacrifice of praise that is offered up to God as the tribute of lips that acknowledges and celebrates his centrality in life (Heb. 13:15). But Scripture also describes worship as something that goes beyond making sounds with our mouths; it is defined as relating with other people in a godly manner, by acting kindly toward them and sharing resources with any in need (v. 16). Such attitudes and deeds are also expressions of worship and bring joy to God.

c. Creative worship: Baptism and communion

Worship defined as the recognition and the celebration of God's centrality for us and of our centrality for God makes it obvious that all of life is relevant to worship. Therefore, there is little in the realms of communications and creativity that cannot be used in worship. Jesus recognized this fact, and he exploited all the resources of creativity to enhance the effectiveness of his ministry as an offering of his own life to the Father. His speech was rich in imagery, drawn from the world of nature and relationships. He used a variety of readily available means, such as little children, sheep, and a mustard seed, as object lessons to dramatize teachings about our relationship with God.

But nothing better demonstrates Jesus' ability to put creativity at the service of worship than his institution of the *sacraments*. When Jesus gave baptism and communion as observances to be practiced throughout the ages, he committed his followers to worship at the most significant points of their Christian experience with the benefit of his masterful use of creativity. Water, bread, and wine were ordinary elements of everyday life. Yet Jesus used them as powerful symbols of truths that reach deeply into the heart of spirituality.

Some church traditions regard the very substance of the elements of the sacraments (water, bread, and wine) as having a saving power of their own (a *sacramentalist* view of the sacraments). Our understanding of the biblical teaching about the sacraments is that the elements used in the sacraments are tangible signs that point to, illustrate, and confirm spiritual truths that pertain to our salvation (a *sacramentarian* view). The water, bread, and wine are not endowed with a supernatural power to forgive sins and to save. Rather, they represent and celebrate the forgiveness and salvation already acquired through Christ's ministry on earth. As such, the sacraments may also be called the *ordinances*, because they were ordained by Christ. He explicitly commanded his followers to practice baptism and communion. They are "sacred" only inasmuch as they convey sacred truth. Some churches add foot-washing as a regular practice, and others add the rites of confirmation, penance, ordination, marriage, and extreme unction to the sacraments of baptism and communion.

(1) **Baptism.** By being baptized we tell our stories as individual believers. Jesus commanded his disciples to go throughout the world and to make more disciples. As a sign of their commitment, the new disciples were to be baptized in the name of Father, Son, and Holy Spirit (Matt. 28:19). The obvious symbolism conveyed by the ceremony of baptism is that of cleansing. Water is used everywhere as the basic purifying agent. Therefore, someone who receives baptism acts out a statement about having received spiritual cleansing through forgiveness and renewal. Peter told his hearers to be baptized for the forgiveness of their sins, which they had obtained by repenting of them (Acts 2:38). He also wrote that it was not the physical action of washing the body that saves, but rather the spiritual reality portrayed by that baptismal washing, a purged selfhood relating to God in a new way (1 Pet. 3:21). The symbolic washing of our bodies with the water of baptism is the

visible sign that our hearts have also been sprinkled clean from an evil conscience (Heb. 10:22).

Since the forgiveness portrayed by baptism was obtained for us by the death and resurrection of Christ, baptism is also a sign of our identification with Christ in his death and resurrection. When he was still walking on this earth, Jesus described his forthcoming death as a baptism (see pages 65–66). By this he meant that his own baptism by the prophet John at the beginning of his ministry had signified his identification with our human condition, an identification that became total at the time of his death. In response, our baptism as new believers expresses our acceptance of the forgiving power of the death of Christ and our own identification with the death that he suffered for us. In baptism we state that we have died to ourselves as we have been spiritually buried in death with Christ. And as he rose from the dead, we also rise with him to walk in newness of life (Rom. 6:1–10). Thus defined, baptism is the ceremony that tells our spiritual story to the church community as we become part of it. It announces that we now belong to Christ and walk with him the road of life.

This raises questions as to who should be baptized, how, and by whom. Practically all biblical Christians agree that everyone who becomes a committed follower of Christ should receive baptism as a sign of that commitment. In addition, some Christians believe that the children of believers should also be baptized since they are considered to be part of the family of faith. They believe that the baptism of infants born to Christian parents places a claim upon them that will come true when the infants grow up as believers. However, those who advocate "believers' baptism" cite numerous instances that form a consistent pattern in the New Testament of people who were baptized only after professing personal faith. They also make the point that there is no mention in the New Testament of babies qualifying for baptism. Instead, they prefer to "dedicate" their children to God and to wait for baptism until they come of age and make their own commitment to Christ.

As to the mode of baptism, some people think that a few drops of water suffice (baptism by "sprinkling"), while others believe that it is necessary to dip the whole person in a body of water (baptism by "immersion"). In truth, it is neither the water nor the act of baptism that saves. We are saved through faith by divine grace, and baptism is an image representing that reality. Therefore, as long as the symbolism of purification is made clear, the amount of water used for baptism does not matter. A little water can suggest cleansing and renewal as well as a whole lake. The amounts of water, bread, and wine used to perform the ordinances are never a matter of concern in the New Testament. The focus of the sacraments is always on the great spiritual truths that these elements are intended to proclaim.

Such a perspective on the meaning of the sacraments has implications for the people authorized to administer them. According to the New Testament, the focus of the sacraments is Christ and the spiritual truths they represent; it is never the people dispensing them. Therefore, any member of the community who is in good standing and who has facility to lead in worship should be qualified to minister in this manner. Since the sacraments involve no magic, they do not require individuals endowed with special powers to administer them. The sacraments are intended to be community events. As such, their purpose is to enrich the lives of each of the participants and of the community as a whole. Therefore, the people best qualified to serve the sacraments are those who represent the community authentically and have its respect. And those people are not necessarily men who have placed themselves over and above the community by virtue of rank or position.

(2) Communion. If baptism tells the story of believers as individuals, communion tells their collective story as community. In Jesus' day, the most important religious festival of the year was the Passover. This observance reminded the people of their deliverance from the bondage in Egypt when God first made them a nation. The main event of the seven-day festival was the sharing of the Passover meal; it required the sacrifice of a lamb, whose blood symbolized the salvation of the Israelites from sure death (Ex. 12:1–14).

The last time Jesus gathered with his disciples prior to his crucifixion was in connection with the Passover meal. Later that same evening he was arrested and put on trial by the leaders of the people. The next day he was falsely accused of being a criminal, convicted, and sentenced to death on a cross. During the Passover meal Jesus chose to establish the Christian meal that celebrates the new deliverance from sin and death. It was his way of showing that something greater and more universally significant than the Exodus from Egypt was now happening through his own death. The Passover lamb that had given salvation to Israel from Egypt was only a pale foreshadowing of the real Lamb of God, whose blood could save the whole world from sin (John 1:29). Of him, Christians would later say, "Christ, our Passover lamb, has been sacrificed" (1 Cor. 5:7 NIV).

The meal given to the church by Jesus goes by several names. It is called communion or holy communion (1 Cor. 10:16), the Lord's

Supper (11:20), the Lord's table (10:21), the Eucharist (from giving "thanks," 10:16, 11:24; see also Matt. 26:27), and the breaking of bread (Acts 2:42; 20:7). This diversity of designations gives an idea of the richness of meanings conveyed by the symbolism of communion. Each component of communion has its significance: the gathering, the sharing, the bread and the wine, the explanations as "This is my body . . . my blood," the invitations to "take and eat . . . drink," and the mention of the new covenant, of the resurrection, and of the kingdom of God. The accounts of Jesus' institution of communion reveal additional meanings (most notably Matt. 26:26–29 and 1 Cor. 11:23–32). But the most penetrating commentary on communion was given by Christ himself in his famous "Bread of Life" speech (John 6:35–65). Here Jesus spoke to his followers about eating his flesh and drinking his blood. The narrative reports that some were offended at the cannibalistic notions suggested by a literal interpretation of Jesus' words (vv. 60–61).

Jesus intended his teaching to correct such misconceptions. He provided a framework for the proper understanding of the offering of his body and blood as food and drink. He said, "The Spirit gives life; the flesh counts for nothing. The words I have spoken to you are spirit and they are life" (v. 63 NIV). Here Jesus made it clear that his teaching about eating his body and drinking his blood was to be understood in spiritual rather than physical terms. Eating and drinking do not save, but entering into a spiritual relationship with God by trusting in the merits of the broken body and the shed blood of Jesus Christ does save an individual. The bread and wine are outward signs of our inner ownership of the eternal benefits gained for us by the death of Jesus. Faith in Jesus whose body was broken and whose blood was shed is the only source of our salvation. Eating and drinking of the communion bread and wine without discerning the body and without having faith in the Christ they represent does nothing for our salvation. In fact, the mere physical act of partaking of communion without faith in Christ is an invitation to judgment and disaster (1 Cor. 11:29–32).

Therefore, taking communion does not save. It is Christ who saves those who believe in him and in his death on the cross on their behalf. If we do not satisfy our hunger for what Christ has to offer by appropriating it in our innermost being, we have no life in ourselves (John 6:53). We could take communion every day of the week and still be bound for hell. On the other hand, one could believe and never have communion, and still be saved. However, whenever saving faith has force and reality, it seeks to be professed through the imagery of the sacrament. This is why Christians love to have communion, for it provides them with Christ-ordained opportunities to celebrate their salvation. Each time they gather for communion, Christians proclaim that Christ is as indispensable to their spiritual survival as food and drink are to their physical survival, and they rejoice because Christ and his salvation are as easily accessible to them as bread and wine are available at a rich man's table.

The sacrament of the Lord's Supper as described in the pages of Scripture is a marvel of creativity. It is like an acted-out drama in three acts—the past, the present, and the future—with Christ at the center of each. The stage is the whole sweep of the new covenant, the new arrangement between God and humans that began with the ministry of Jesus and that will end with his Second Coming. As he offered the bread and the wine, he told the disciples, "Do this in remembrance of me" (1 Cor. 11:24–25). In communion, the spotlight is not on the bread and wine but on the Savior whom they represent.

In the first act of the drama, we remember him in conjunction with the *past*. We remember that our spiritual story began with Jesus and with his cross. As we survey the wondrous cross on which the Prince of Glory died, we realize that on it, his body was broken and his blood was shed—and that this happened for the forgiveness of our sins (Matt. 26:28). We thus proclaim his death as often as we eat the bread and drink the cup (1 Cor. 11:26).

In the second act, we remember him in conjunction with the *present*. He is the one who keeps us alive. As he gave the bread, he said, "This is my body, which is for you" (1 Cor. 11:24). As a loving parent prepares a meal that will give life and strength to the children, so Christ offers his life and strength to his followers in every new generation. Communion symbolizes our continued communion with the Savior: "Those who eat my flesh and drink my blood abide in me, and I in them" (John 6:56 NRSV). Communion gives proof that he is with us, even within us.

In the third act, we acknowledge him in conjunction with the *future*. We remember where he is taking us. Communion points to the time yet to come when our communion with him will be whole, perfect, and unhindered, when the promise of his return that we proclaim every time we eat the bread and drink the cup will be fulfilled (1 Cor. 11:26), when he will raise on the last day those who have eternal life because they have received it from his body and blood (John 6:54), and when the church finally gathered unto the Savior will drink with him the new wine of the Father's kingdom (Matt. 26:29).

Because of the richness and the variety of symbolisms conveyed by the Lord's Supper, participation in communion inevitably becomes a subjective experience. Closeness with Christ is sought out of a multitude of needs. Each person comes to the Lord's table at a different stage of his or her spiritual pilgrimage and from different circumstances—carrying one's own burden, facing one's own temptations, fears, and joys, and understanding the very meanings of the sacrament in different ways. There are enough spiritual resources available in the sacrament to minister to each believer according to his or her need. As a result, it might appear that this sacrament isolates each participant in his or her private encounter with God and that communion therefore conflicts with community.

The answer of Scripture to this suggestion is a unanimous and emphatic NO! As meaningful as participation in the Lord's Supper may be for each individual, the sacrament symbolizes enough vitally important truths held in common by all Christians to make it also, and primarily, an experience of corporate worship. Before being anything else, the Lord's Supper is an assembly of believers in communion with their Lord and with each other. As Jesus gave the sacrament to the disciples, he emphasized that they were sharing in it as a community. He did not simply pass out the cup to them, but he also commanded *all* of them to drink of it (Matt. 26:27). More graphically, Luke's account reports that Jesus instructed the disciples to divide the contents of the cup among themselves (Luke 22:17). In obedience to his command, "they all drank from it" (Mark 14:23 NIV). For this reason, the apostle could declare, "We who are many are one body, for we all partake of the one bread" (1 Cor. 10:17 NRSV).

Communion both demonstrates the oneness of the community and reinforces it. Communion is not merely Christians, with heads bowed, receiving the bread and the cup. It is Christians with heads bowed together, receiving the *same* bread and the *same* cup, and remembering and communing with their one Savior. As such, communion is an earthly anticipation of the eternal union of the church with her Savior, an event that is, not surprisingly, described as the marriage supper of the bride with the Lamb (Rev. 19:8–9).

3. Oneness in Outreach

The church exists for its own sake as the eternal community. Only the church is destined to survive when everything else ceases to exist. But while on this earth, the church has been entrusted with a mission, one that was important enough for Jesus to commit to his followers on the very day of his resurrection. That evening, he suddenly appeared among the assembled disciples, greeted them, showed them his torn hands, and uncovered the spear wound on his chest. Then, pointing again to the wounds that had obtained their redemption, he told them, "As the Father has sent me, even so I send you" (John 20:21 RSV). Before leaving this earth, he was entrusting to his followers the task of extending his redemptive ministry to the world. They were to continue his servant work, empowered by the Holy Spirit (v. 22). He who had come into the world not to be served but rather to serve was sending his disciples to deliver his ministry of redemption to a needy world.

This mandate to minister to the world as Christ's representatives is consistent with the mission that God had entrusted to believers in the old covenant. He had called them to be "a light for the Gentiles, to open eyes that are blind, to free captives from prison and to release from the dungeon those who sit in darkness" (Isa. 42:6–7 NIV). More pointedly, God had designated ancient Israel as his "servant," describing their mission on his behalf with these words, "I will also make you a light for the Gentiles, that you may bring my salvation to the ends of the earth" (49:6). By New Testament times, this mission had ended in failure. Under the leadership of the Sadducees, the temple had become a corrupt racist business enterprise (Mark 11:17), and the law had been turned by the Pharisees into a hypocritical legalism that damned their Gentile converts rather than saved them (Matt. 23:15). Jesus rebuked them all for promoting their own agendas rather than doing God's will.

Aware of such dangers for the future of the church, Jesus carefully defined the mission of his disciples. He summarized his mandate for his followers by charging them to go out into the world and to make more disciples—believers who would obey all that Jesus had commanded (Matt. 28:18–20). The New Testament's description of this formidable task can be discussed as the outward thrust of the church in three main dimensions: the ministries of *conversion*, *compassion*, and *confrontation*.

a. The ministry of conversion

Because conversion is a personal transaction between God and individual seekers, the church is neither the author of conversions nor their distributor. However, it has been ordered by Christ to be vitally involved both in facilitating conversions and in turning converts into disciples. This is the task of evangelism.

(1) The mandate. The last orders of Jesus to his disciples were to be his witnesses "to the ends of the earth" and to "go and make disciples of all nations" (Acts 1:8 and Matt. 28:19). The scope of this mandate indicates that Jesus intended this order to apply not just to the original disciples but also to all Christians throughout the ages. Jesus knew that it was a practical impossibility for the Eleven to reach "all nations" and to take the message "to the ends of the earth" during their lifetime. There were too few of them and the territory to cover was immense. All that the first disciples could do was to begin to carry out the assignment. It would take the concerted and consistent efforts of generation upon generation of disciples to bring the commission to completion. Through the disciples, Jesus entrusted the task of evangelizing the world to all Christians, in all ages, to the end of time. Therefore, every local community of believers is under divine obligation to bear witness to Christ and to "make disciples of all nations," beginning with people in their own neighborhoods.

This mandate to evangelize is not optional, a kind of volunteer proposal that churches may or may not adopt. It is a binding command of Christ that reflects his deepest passion to reclaim the world for which he died. Nevertheless, one comes upon church after church that has become ingrown and isolated, settling for barely subsisting instead of reaching out effectively into the world and making disciples. Being found in flagrant disobedience to Christ's order, they then satisfy their conscience by paying someone to do evangelism on their behalf in "revivals," "special meetings," "evangelistic crusades," or missionary work in far away lands.

Such efforts are no substitute for consistent and effective involvement of each church community in the task of evangelism. Any church that is not actively involved in bearing productive witness among unbelievers and in discipling converts into community life stands in violation of Christ's commission and denies itself the fullness of his blessing.

(2) **The means.** If this last sentence sounds like a judgment instead of a challenge, it is because many Christians feel uneasy about witnessing and evangelizing. They assume that doing evangelism is the task of gifted people, such as professional evangelists and pastors. But the New Testament teaches differently. Christ's mandate to tell the good news about Jesus engages the personal responsibility of every member of each local church (see Acts 8:4).

This is not, of course, to deny that some may have a special *gift* for evangelism (see Eph. 4:11), which probably describes both pioneer church planting by missionaries in places devoid of a Christian witness and a specialized ministry of soul-winning within existing churches. Only one person is called an "evangelist" in the New Testament (Acts 21:8), and his work is described as that of a pioneer ministry, planting a church where there was none (8:5). Today, we would call such a person a "missionary." When Paul exhorted young Timothy to "do the work of an evangelist," he apparently was challenging him to engage in pioneer work just as Paul had done himself at Antioch, Iconium, and Lystra (2 Tim. 4:5; 3:11; see Acts 3:14; 14:1,6).

If the fulfillment of the church's mandate for local evangelism is not the exclusive responsibility of designated individuals such as pastors and evangelists, who then should carry it out? The New Testament is absolutely clear on this subject: Every member of every church community is personally responsible for doing evangelism (Matt. 5:16; Phil. 2:14–16; 1 Thess. 5:5; 1 Pet. 2:12). This places the burden of evangelistic outreach not on professional clergy but on the woman and the man in the pew. These God-designated evangelists are not the few individuals who stand behind a pulpit; they are the people who make up the congregation.

(3) **The method.** This assignment of the evangelistic task to every believer may seem unrealistic and intimidating, for most Christians have neither the skills nor the disposition to act as evangelists. How could God require them to do a ministry for which they feel neither called nor gifted? In answer, it is important to note that most Christians refuse to view themselves as evangelists because they cannot identify with the only model of evangelism they know, that of a sermon followed by an altar-call. For them, to do evangelism is to engage in a forceful speech that presses non-Christians to make a dramatic "decision for Christ." They wrongly think that personal evangelism is doing on a small scale what TV or crusade evangelists do in front of large crowds. And since they cannot mimic the evangelists, even on a person-to-person basis, they leave it to clergy or itinerant evangelists to do their thing.

Christ's promise to make of his followers "fishers of men" applies to all Christians (Matt. 4:19), though not all Christians understand this kind of fishing. Some confuse fishing with hunting. They go after the fish with a Bible-shotgun loaded full of verses and blast the fish into shreds. Others think they are fishing when they retreat to the safety of their churches and applaud powerful gospel sermons preached at irreligious people who are not there. This attitude is like laying bait inside a boat and singing hymns while waiting for fish to jump in and go for the bait. Jesus commanded, "Go and make disciples"; he did not say, "Wait for sinners to come to you and beg you to make them disciples."

215

Fishing is an endeavor that requires common sense, knowledge of the fish and of their environment, and appropriate equipment. In other words, church-based evangelism needs to be carefully strategized and designed to reach a target audience. Because of all the variables present in church communities and their prospects, no single strategy will be uniformly applicable to all churches. Each church must develop its own evangelistic strategy in consideration of its collective personality, its gifts, and the demographics of the locality where it is planted. However, some general principles may be derived from the teaching of Scriptures.

- The best qualified people to do evangelism are lay Christians going about the business of their daily lives. With relatives, friends, and acquaintances at work, in school, and in neighborhoods, they are constantly in contact with people who need the gospel and who are otherwise unreachable. The teachings of Jesus and his own example require every Christian to get close to such people and to be available as a resource person. This does not necessitate special evangelistic skills. Every Christian should be willing and able to befriend a non-Christian and to be available to serve and counsel in case of need or crisis. Once trust has been gained, it is then appropriate to share how important God and church are in one's own life.
- The church should provide appropriate settings where Christians can bring their seeker friends to familiarize them with the gospel and with the Christian community without the fear of embarrassing or overwhelming them. For this interaction to happen, it is necessary to separate worship from evangelism. The two do not mix, since they address different publics with entirely different needs. Worship is for believers only; it is mostly irrelevant, and often incomprehensible or even offensive, to non-Christians; their presence may even be a hindrance to a worshiping congregation. Therefore, churches should schedule carefully prepared seeker-sensitive opportunities where the gospel and its relevance can be presented at an introductory level, in a nonthreatening manner, and in idioms familiar to secular people. Church members are more likely to invite their non-Christian friends to such gatherings and thereby to mentor their approach to Christ.
- Once the conversion of seekers is secured, they should be taught and discipled, incorporated into the life of the church through involvement in small groups and ministry teams, guided into discovering and using their spiritual gifts, encour-

216

aged to become participating and contributing members of the community, and motivated to make friends with unbelievers so as to become themselves "fishers of men."

Thus the ministry of conversion becomes a natural expression of the life of the whole community all year long, rather than the privilege of designated individuals casting their own nets on "special" occasions. Nothing is more detrimental to church-based lay evangelism than the word "special"—as in "special evangelistic services" or "special speaker."

b. The ministry of compassion

At no time does the church resemble more the Savior than when it emulates him in self-giving servanthood in response to situations of human need. During his ministry, Jesus viewed himself as fulfilling a servant role among God's needy creatures, and he commissioned the disciples to do likewise. He was overwhelmed with compassion whenever he came across the sick and the blind (Matt. 4:24; 20:34), the oppressed and the helpless (9:36), the hungry and the bereaved (15:32; Luke 7:13). He entered into their pain and, as a result, he was moved to action, dispensing relief, comfort, and healing. He lived for others.

Some came to Jesus seeking eternal life for themselves. He told them that to obtain eternal life they should love God and love others as themselves (Luke 10:25–28). And just in case they did not know what loving others meant, he made the point crystal clear with the story of the good Samaritan. The Samaritan was "moved to compassion" by the distress of a total stranger. He gave of himself and of his possessions to the stranger without thought of self, rescuing him from sure death. Jesus' terse command to his listeners was: "Go and do likewise" (vv. 29–37).

More specifically, Jesus taught what it meant to "do likewise." If his followers wanted to be blessed and inherit eternal life, they were to feed the hungry, give drink to the thirsty, shelter the homeless, clothe the naked, take care of the sick, and visit those in prison. And should they refuse to meet the needs of people less fortunate than themselves, they would become accursed and go into eternal punishment. According to Jesus, to meet human need is to recognize the hidden bond that connects the suffering of the needy with the suffering of the One who died to meet that need. Therefore, to serve the least of those who suffer is to serve Christ himself (Matt. 25:31–46).

Thus, through direct commands and personal demonstrations, Jesus charged the church to extend itself in compassion to situations of need both within its own fellowship and in the outside world. All the evidence indicates that the church of the early days was obedient to Christ's command. As previously noted (pages 102–4), after the coming of the Holy Spirit the Jerusalem church spontaneously instituted a welfare system to help the indigent among them (Acts 2:45). As a result, there was not a needy person among them. Those who had more than they required turned their unused assets over to the community. To make it clear that this outreach in compassion was the expression of the community of oneness rather than exceptional acts of individual charity, they brought their contributions to the leaders of the group, who then distributed the funds to the needy on behalf of the whole church (4:34–35).

This concern for the needy was not confined to local congregations. When Gentile churches in distant lands heard that the Christians in Jerusalem had fallen upon hard times because of an economic downturn, they banded together and sent relief to Jerusalem through the apostle Paul (2 Cor. 8–9). It was intolerable for those with wealth beyond their own needs to keep it for themselves when others did not have enough to meet their basic needs. Their commitment to Christ compelled them to follow his example (8:9) and to obey his command (9:13). The oneness of the people of Christ was expressed in concrete ways across national boundaries, despite ethnic or economic differences.

Today, many Christians and many churches regard this stewardship of sharing as a good-will option rather than as an obligation dictated by the gospel itself. Two main factors promote this heresy. The first is the easy acceptance of a view of personal property that is derived from the individualistic and materialistic values that prevail in the pagan world. The world teaches that what you own belongs to you and what you do with it is your own business. Against this, the Scripture teaches that everything you own belongs to God and that you are accountable to him for how you use it. According to Scripture, the welfare of the group takes precedence over the individual interests of private persons (1 Cor. 6:7; 10:24,33; 13:5; Gal. 5:13–14; Phil. 2:3–4; 1 Tim. 6:18–19).

The second hindrance to the proper stewardship of money among Christians derives from misleading teachings about the tithe. From many pulpits, the giving of one tenth of one's income is presented as the Christian standard of stewardship. This teaching is wrong. The giving of the tithe was a requirement in the old covenant, one that the New Testament never confirms as the standard of giving valid for Christians. In fact, it teaches something entirely different: The measure for giving is based on the principle of the total disposition for God's work of who we are and of all that we own (Matt. 19:16–30; Mark 12:41–44; Luke 12:33–34; Acts 5:32–37; Rom. 12:1; 1 Tim. 6:17–19).

This means that the goal for poor Christians is to become solvent and then to set the tithe as a minimum level of giving to attain. For affluent Christians, the rule of total disposition requires that we keep enough to provide for ourselves and our families so that we do not become a burden for anyone, and that we then make available the remainder of our income to God's work. Accordingly, if we need only the tenth of our income to guarantee self-sufficiency, the remaining ninety percent belongs to God; or if we need only half of our income for ourselves, the other half should be an offering to God's work and to the poor. Such a high concept of Christian stewardship leaves the Old Testament tithe far behind as an extinct stage of minimal divine expectations. It allows Christians to give "according to their means" (2 Cor. 8:3 RSV) rather than according to a uniformly restrictive percentage. Only thus may the resources needed for the church to accomplish its mission of compassion in a God-honoring manner be released within the Christian community.

In actual practice, the Scripture teaches that our financial stewardship should be allocated according to four areas of responsibility. The first duty of each Christian is to earn enough through his or her work so as to be self-sufficient and avoid being a burden on anyone else (1 Thess. 4:11–12; 2 Thess. 3:12). In other words, the priority of a Christian is to establish an economic base strong enough to be in a position to help others instead of draining public or private welfare resources (Acts 20:33–35; 2 Thess. 3:7–10). At the same time, while the New Testament is favorable to believers achieving financial independence, it contains strong warnings against the ever-present danger of becoming greedy (1 Cor. 5:11–13; 6:9–10) and of seeking to acquire greater wealth than needed (Matt. 6:19–24; 1 Tim. 6:6–10). A profit-driven and prosperity-obsessed society claims that there is great contentment in gain. But the Scripture reverses this pagan value and teaches that there is great gain in contentment (Phil. 4:11–12; 1 Tim. 6:6). For this reason, the Scripture enjoins already wealthy Christians to use their wealth in a manner that will not cause it to be a hindrance to their entering eternal life (1 Tim. 6:17–19).

The second line of responsibility is to provide for one's dependents. Both Jesus and Paul were merciless in denouncing the hypocrisy of religious people who put on a good show of piety to the extent of giving to God's work but who did not take care of their needy relatives (Matt. 15:3–9; 1 Tim. 5:8).

Third, Christians must use their resources to extend themselves "to those who belong to the family of believers," though they are to make such contributions to the church's work only as they "have opportunity" (Gal. 6:10). To strive to tithe out of a budget that is riddled with debts and that does not suffice for the needs of one's family is dishonoring to God and harmful to his work. The first order of business for people with financial troubles is to get their budgeting practices straightened out with the help of qualified Christian counselors. Once they achieve solvency and are able to take care of their families, they may then contribute responsibly to the work of the larger family of faith (1 Tim. 3:4–5, 12).

Finally, Scripture teaches that we are to "do good to all people" (Gal. 6:10). More than any other private or public organization, the church should be attentive to the plight of the hungry, the homeless, the oppressed, and the despairing. Apart from simple obedience to Christ's commands, the church bears its most credible witness to the love of God, to the servant nature of Jesus Christ, and to the authenticity of the work of the Holy Spirit when it reaches out to help the helpless. This principle is deeply imbedded in the very being of God. When we were yet helpless, Christ came to our rescue, thus demonstrating the love of God (Rom. 5:6–8). One deed of mercy done in the name of Christ speaks more forcefully of his love than a dozen evangelistic sermons preached from a pulpit.

c. The ministry of confrontation

The word of God calls individuals to repentance. But God also has something to say about how institutions and political systems run their affairs. Collective sins committed by organized groups of people are as much an affront to God as sins committed by individuals. They both require repentance and redress since they both fall under the judgment of God.

Scripture calls Christians to confront both personal and corporate sin with the message of God's displeasure at evil. This ministry of confrontation directed at institutional sin is called the "prophetic" ministry of the church. Such a ministry requires Christians to look with objectivity and discernment at their political and religious institutions and at the social structures of which they are a part. It also requires boldness and courage to speak critically on behalf of God in order to denounce injustice and oppression when their practice is easily accepted by society at large. The overwhelming message of the old covenant prophets was that to remain silent or passive in the presence of injustice or oppression is to enter into complicity with evil and to incur God's judgment with those who perpetrate it. Because the ministry of prophecy is so demanding, it is easily ignored and replaced by cheap substitutes. Some evangelical teachers reduce prophecy to futuristic fantasies predicting schedules for the "Rapture" rather than coming to grips with the present realities of history and speaking God's judgment on them. Others define prophecy as privileged individuals receiving a spontaneous fax of divine "revelations" from heaven which may or may not have biblical validity, but which allows them to avoid becoming involved in the hard work required by prophecy in confronting corporate sin.

Such a ministry of confrontation characterized the prophets in both Old and New Testaments. Amos was a quiet Judean shepherd who minded his own business in the southern kingdom town of Tekoa. God called him to leave his own nation and to confront the evil ways of the northern kingdom of Israel. At the peak of its prosperity, Israel's social and moral life had so degenerated that God warned it of judgment. Amos violently rebuked the Israelite religious and political leaders for their unjust and oppressive practices. He stood as a witness to the radical truths that God wanted righteousness in public life, that he expected people to deal justly with each other, and that worship was a mockery unless it was accompanied with ethical living. He called the entire nation to repentance in order to save it from impending doom. But his prophetic confrontation probably cost him his life, and the nation that rejected his message was eventually destroyed.

A few years later, the farmer Hosea was called to denounce the repeated infidelities of Israel as this nation continued to forsake the ways of God and to adopt the idolatrous practices of surrounding pagan peoples. A lonely figure, Hosea suffered intensely in fulfilling his ministry of confrontation to a society plagued with crime and corruption.

Isaiah was born of noble blood in the royal family of Judah. But instead of pandering to the people in power and seeking their favor, he stood in defiance of the rulers of his own nation and reproved them on God's behalf for their crimes of oppression and for their promotion of national wickedness. Tradition reports that the evil king Manasseh silenced Isaiah's protest by having him tied between two pieces of lumber and sawn in two.

About a century later, Jeremiah appeared and denounced the sins of both the common people and their leaders—promiscuous sexual indulgence, corruption in the government, robbery, and oppression of the poor. Jeremiah's reward was to be cast in a cistern where he sank into the mire.

In New Testament times, the prophet John the Baptist cried out to the multitudes, announcing impending judgment for their sins. As they sought repentance, he demanded that they demonstrate their sincerity by sharing their goods with the poor, practicing equality of treatment before the law, and abstaining from extortion, falsehood, and greed (Luke 3:10–14). When King Herod brazenly scorned the laws of God by taking his brother's wife, John thundered God's disapproval. As a result of his protest, he was beheaded in the king's dungeon.

From the outset of his ministry, Jesus was recognized as the prophet from Nazareth. His radical message struck at the core of the wickedness in personal life and in the power structures of society. He denounced political and religious leaders for their deceit and their selfish abuse of public institutions. He took his protest to the very center of their stronghold, the Jerusalem temple. Singlehandedly staging demonstrations in the temple on two occasions, Jesus struck at the seat of the Jewish leaders' power. As he proclaimed the love of God to the meek and the humble, he also announced divine wrath upon arrogant oppressors. In response, the defenders of the status quo plotted for his death and had him crucified.

The Lord entrusted the apostle Paul to preach the message of the gospel to the Gentiles. Under the impact of his ministry, a chain of Christian communities was established, each of which became a pulsating, radiating center of a revolutionary spiritual life that challenged by word and deed the pagan pretensions of their culture. Paul claimed that Christians had divine power to demolish pagan strongholds, to destroy arguments and every obstacle to the knowledge of God thrown up by human pride, and to take every thought captive to obey Christ (2 Cor. 10:4–5). Eventually, the Roman sword brought Paul's life to an end, but it never conquered the power of the gospel. The gospel of Jesus Christ has marched on through the ages, winning men and women to the kingdom, transforming narrow-minded bigots into world citizens, hidebound chauvinists into apostles of compassion, and hate-filled zealots into prophets of righteousness. Through them, the church has often acted as the conscience of the world.

Today more than ever, God has something vital to say about the way communities and institutions conduct their affairs. Our secularized society desperately needs such guidance, and Christians are in a unique position to communicate God's message to the world. But in order to exercise credibly their prophetic ministry, Christians must meet certain conditions.

First, Scripture makes it clear that God expects believers to model his ethical imperatives both in their individual and corporate lives. Christians must put their own churches in order before they may address prophetically the evils of their generation. They must exhort each other to exercise watchcare and self-discipline in order to remain uncompromised by the evils of secular society. Whenever Christians conform to worldly ways and uncritically accept pagan values by becoming as materialistic, competitive, self-promoting, possessive, prejudiced, racist, and sexist as their non-Christian neighbors, they forfeit the right to speak prophetically to their generation and sabotage the church's witness to Christ. The very lifestyle of Christians and of their communities should constitute a protest against the misdirected values and practices of a godless world-system.

Second, in order to face the moral issues that torment a derelict society bereft of God's standards, Christians should be able to articulate clearly the biblical principles relevant to those issues. A shallow devotional approach to Scripture, coupled with the memorization of a few favorite verses, proves woefully inadequate to address problems such as moral decay, political corruption, inequities in human and civil rights, iniquitous use of resources and of wealth distribution, pornography, war, crime, violence, abortion, divorce, and a dozen global scourges that clamor for solutions derived from spiritual truths.

Even a superficial glance at the writings of the Old Testament prophets reveals that they were people who had done their homework; they had pondered deeply the crises of their times and the implications of God's will upon them. Too often, the modern church has retreated into obscurantist, anticultural positions by decrying from a safe distance those areas of public sin that it should confront but feels too threatened to address. A prophetic church, guided by the Spirit, should be able to articulate clear alternatives to the evils of the day and to present countercultural solutions drawn from God's Word instead of withdrawing into sterile, anticultural negativisms.

Finally, in order to protect its freedom to speak critically against societal evil, the church must guard itself from forming alliances with political bodies. Because confronting society prophetically looms as such a formidable task, the church has often been tempted to take sides with political leaders and parties that seemed to support its agenda. However, the same biblically based rule that calls for the separation of church and state applies to the church and partisan politics. The bride of Christ should never be mismated with unbelievers. It can be demonstrated historically that whenever the church has tried to use political power to its advantage, the opposite has happened; the political process has used the church, controlled it, and stripped it of its distinctive witness.

Rather than becoming enmeshed in partisan causes as a body, the church must educate its members to assume their own responsibilities as citizens and to influence the political process on the basis of their conscience and biblically informed convictions. In so doing, the church protects the legitimate diversity of opinion that may exist within its constituency; it also protects its own freedom to apply God's wisdom to matters clearly addressed in his word.

III. CURRENT VIEWS ON THE CHURCH

From the Vatican to storefront mom and pop meeting halls, there are multitudes of churches or church groups that claim to embody the expression of the true church, each with a different definition of what the true church is. To summarize such definitions in this space would be an impossible task. However, we may characterize churches on how they conceive their roles as God's people in relation to the society of which they are a part. Three broad categories may be defined from this vantage point.

1. The Syncretistic Church

According to this view, the church is only one of the agencies used by God to fulfill his redemptive purposes in history. Secular organizations, political movements, and non-Christian religions may do as much. In this light, the mission of the church is to make itself available to society as Christ made himself available to the world; it is the extension of Christ to the world. The church should view itself as servant to society and join the forces aimed at liberating the oppressed and the poor. From this perspective, the church is neither the place of salvation nor the upholder of the truth. It makes its symbols and its metaphors available to the world to be used creatively in meeting the challenges of the moment. In order to accomplish its mission, it has to be also of the world. This definition of the church blurs the lines of distinction between church and secular society and loses track of its purpose—hence, the term "syncretistic," which suggests the merging of disparate beliefs and the abdication of distinctiveness. For this reason, this theologically liberal church is sometimes called the "secular church."

2. The Antithetical Church

According to this view, the church is not only apart from society but also stands against it or in opposition to it. The world is the place of lostness, and the church is the place of salvation. In actual practice, this view of the church is expressed in either of two attitudes toward society, both of them falling generally within the camp of "fundamentalism." The "separatist" church flees the sinful world and protects itself from a culture it considers degenerate by segregating itself within the closed fellowship of the saved. The "triumphalist" church is also against a culture that it regards as corrupt, but a culture that it also considers to be redeemable. Instead of abandoning the world to its doom, this church views itself as the agent for its reconstruction according to the laws of the old covenant. Whenever possible, the triumphalist church attempts to gain control of the vital nerve centers of pagan society in order to bring it in subjection to God's agenda. Through such reconstruction, it seeks to establish the kingdom of God on earth and to recover the medieval ideal of political systems dominated by an imperial church. But through the centuries, many Christians have painfully discovered that attempts to use the methods of Caesar to glorify God only end up serving Caesar.

3. The Transformational Church

According to this view, the church bears witness before the world to God's desire to have its fragmented communities become the eternal community within which peace, justice, equality, and oneness prevail. To this effect, the church reaches out into the world and proclaims the good news of redemption through which sinners become new creatures in Christ. Thus transformed individuals become integrated into the new community, which is the embodiment on earth of the kingdom of God. Because transformational churches rely on the gospel (or *evangel*) as the dynamic for change, they are often called "evangelical churches." By way of persuasion rather than coercion, these churches seek to model before society and establish within it the reality and the values of the new community that was decreed into existence by God before the foundation of the world and which alone will survive the end of all things

RESOURCES

For further study on the doctrine of the church, see the following resources:

Gilbert Bilezikian. *Beyond Sex Roles: What the Bible Says About a Woman's Place in Church and Family*. Grand Rapids: Baker, 1985; especially pp. 104–18.

Gilbert Bilezikian, *Community 101: Reclaiming the Local Church as Community of Oneness*. Grand Rapids: Zondervan, 1997.

Greg Ogden. *The New Reformation*. Grand Rapids: Zondervan, 1990. (This book should be required reading for each pastor and church member.)

The Doctrine of the End Times

Outline of Chapter Eight

I. The Parousia as an "Imminent" Event
   1. Sign One: The Fall of Jerusalem
   2. Sign Two: The Gentile Mission
   3. Sign Three: The Distress and the Tribulation
      a. The tribulation
      b. The antichrist
   4. Parousia Behavior

II. The Parousia as an Absolute Event
   1. The Teaching of Jesus
      a. Matthew 13:24–30, 36–43, 47–50
      b. Matthew 24:29–31, 37–42
   2. The Teaching of Paul
      a. 1 Corinthians 15:23–26, 51–57
      b. 1 Thessalonians 4:14–5:4
   3. The Teaching of Peter—2 Peter 3:1–15
   4. The Teaching of John—The Book of Revelation

III. The Parousia as a Universal Event
   1. The Universal Renewal
      a. The resurrection
      b. The reunion
   2. The Universal Removal
      a. The resolution of the presence of evil
      b. The retribution by judgment

IV. Current Views on the End Times
   1. Anti-eschatological Attitudes
   2. Indifferent Attitudes
   3. Obsessive Attitudes

The Doctrine of the End Times

No Christian belief has created more controversy among well-meaning students of the Bible as the doctrine of the second coming of Jesus Christ. Practically every generation of Christians has had its contingent of Bible interpreters who have read the crises of their day into various Bible verses to predict imminent doom. History has proven each one of them wrong. Yet, the deception continues. The business of seeking the signs of the End has become a multi-million dollar enterprise supported by TV shows, radio programs, innumerable books and pamphlets, specialized magazines, study Bible notes, and a legion of "prophecy" speakers, all competing to titillate the public with the most sensational and the most exotic predictions of the End. They make their million, then wait for the next international crisis or the next war in the Middle East to revise their charts, face-lift their books, readjust their timetables, and fleece the gullible public out of another million.

Partly in reaction to such excesses, many Christians refuse to commit themselves to a specific line of belief on the doctrine of the end times and prefer to keep an open mind on the subject. They may believe that some catastrophic global events will usher the end of history, but they nurture a cautious skepticism toward a systematic approach to the study of this topic in Scripture. Yet they yearn to know what the Bible teaches on this subject.

Much of the confusion that prevails on the subject of the end times derives from the lack of a coherent method for interpreting the biblical data. The Bible is a large book; its very size makes it susceptible to misuse. Isolated verses can be taken out of context and coupled together with others to fabricate theories never taught in Scripture. The approach taken in this chapter, however, follows the three principles of Bible interpretion explored in the first chapter (pages 15–20): first, a thematic book-by-book approach to the Bible rather than cross-referencing isolated verses; second, the recognition of the finality and fullness of the revelation of Christ as found in the New Testament; and third, the exercise of extreme caution with hapaxic passages that are unclear or whose meaning is generally contested among biblical scholars.

For convenience's sake, the term *eschatology* will be used to refer to matters that pertain to the end times. This term comes from the Greek word *eschatos*, meaning "furthest" or "last"; it therefore refers to the doctrine or the teaching about the last things. The other word we shall use in this chapter is *Parousia*, taken from a Greek word meaning "presence" or "arrival." In the New Testament, it is often used to refer to the second coming of Christ (Matt. 24:3, 27, 37; 1 Cor. 15:23; 1 Thess. 2:19; 3:13; Jas. 5:7–8; 2 Pet. 3:4, 12; 1 John 2:28). These two words are part of the English language and are found in most dictionaries. Their use will facilitate our progress through this chapter.

The Bible presents Jesus Christ as the one who executes the counsels of the Trinity in regard to this world. As the eternal Word, he is the source of all created things, including life and light (John 1:3–5). In other words, Christ was vitally associated with the purposes for which the world came into existence at the very beginning.

When God's purposes were thwarted by the intrusion of evil, it was again Christ who intervened to reclaim the world and to form the future community. He came forth preaching, "The time is fulfilled, and the kingdom of God has come near" (Mark 1:15 NRSV). His first coming signaled the beginning of the end; it ushered in the last phase of history, what the New Testament calls the "last days" (Acts 2:16–17; Heb. 1:2; 1 Pet. 1:5, 20). As Redeemer, Christ was vitally involved in the events at the center of history.

The same Christ will intervene again to implement God's triumphant resolution of history at the end of time. He will destroy the invading satanic powers that captured the divinely titled domains of creation and submit them again to God's sovereign rule (1 Cor. 15:24). But he will also draw unto himself all the purged realms of creation and establish them in community for eternity according to God's original plan for the fullness of time (Eph. 1:9–10).

In summary, in Christ all things were made, in him all things were reclaimed, and in him all things will be fulfilled. He is the Alpha and the Omega, the beginning and the end (Rev. 21:6; 22:13). History finds its meaning in him alone. Since he will bring history to its final consummation, the doctrine of the end times necessarily revolves around his second coming. In other words, the Parousia is central to Christian eschatology. All other features of the end times are incidental to the Parousia, and the Parousia alone is the focus and the object of the Christian hope (Tit. 2:13).

In view of these considerations, it is appropriate to study biblical eschatology from the perspective of the second coming of Christ as its central event, rather than making events incidental to it the mainstay of the doctrine. Or to put it differently, the doctrine of the Parousia should be the starting point and it should remain the organizing center of Christian eschatology. This observation generates two consequences for the study of this topic.

First, the study of the Parousia will necessarily begin with an examination of the books and texts within the Bible that deal directly with this event. Since these are found mostly in the New Testament, the main focus of our study for this chapter will be the New Testament. From the vantage point of the Parousia, it will then be possible to work our way to other eschatological issues and to the biblical texts that pertain to them.

Second, since the Parousia is described in the New Testament as an event, it is appropriate to raise the basic questions that pertain to an event, such as "when, how, and where?" These three questions and the corresponding biblical answers will provide the outline for the structure of this chapter. "When?" has to do with the timing of the Parousia; the answer from Scripture is, "The Parousia is an *imminent* event." "How?" has to do with the manner of the Parousia; the answer from Scripture is, "The Parousia is an *absolute* event." "Where?" has to do with the place of the Parousia; the answer from Scripture is, "The Parousia is a *universal* event."

I. THE PAROUSIA AS AN "IMMINENT" EVENT

Practically every church creed or statement of faith that mentions the Second Coming confesses that no one knows for certain the time of the Parousia, but acknowledges that it will surely happen. It could happen at the present moment or in a million years, but its eventual occurrence is certain. From a human perspective, the time of the event is unknown, but the fact is unquestionably confirmed in Scripture.

Generally, this is the meaning that the word "imminent" is intended to convey when it is used in relation to the Parousia. Strictly speaking, however, the word "imminent" means something else. According to the dictionary an event is imminent when it is just about to happen. For instance, should someone pull the pin off a hand grenade and let go of it, the explosion of the grenade would be imminent, in the sense that it would happen almost immediately. But should the pin have corroded and seem weak enough to let go on its own, we could not say that the explosion is imminent. All we could say is that it is "possibly imminent," with the exact time being unpredictable.

Likewise for our own individual demise, we all know that death is inevitable. Any of us could die at any moment. But people in reasonably good health do not say that their death is "imminent." This can be said only of people whose vital signs are down and who are visibly on their way out of this life. Thus, to speak accurately, the word "imminent" must be qualified when it is applied to the Second Coming. That is why we have placed it in quotation marks in the title above. We are using the term as a concession to tradition and as an attempt to communicate the concept in familiar terms. But we qualify its meaning here to convey the idea of the *possible* imminence of the Parousia, an event that will happen for sure but at a time that cannot be accurately anticipated by humans. Indeed, the occurrence of the Parousia could be imminent, but it could also be a long time in the making.

Any discussion of the time frame for the Parousia must be grounded in Scripture. Fortunately, the New Testament yields abundant data in this area. The New Testament gives ample evidence that the early Christians believed in the possible imminence of the Parousia and that they lived in a mode of active expectancy for the Lord's return, yet without attempting to seek signs or to set dates. A sampling of Scriptures that reflect this theme of the possible imminence of the Parousia at the time of their writing follows.

- **Acts.** The coming of the Holy Spirit at Pentecost inaugurated the period of the "last days" (2:16–17). Early Christians believed that the church age was the last phase of history, and that the time period that began with Pentecost (vv. 17–18) would end with the coming of the Day of the Lord (vv. 19–20).
- **Romans.** Because the Day is at hand and salvation has drawn near, Christians, including those in Rome, should be alert and lead lives of holiness befitting their vivid expectancy of the return of the Lord (13:11–12).
- **1 Corinthians.** The Corinthian Christians were waiting for the Parousia to happen, possibly within their lifetime (1:7–8; see also 10:11).
- **Philippians.** The real homeland of a Christian is the kingdom of God. The Philippian believers were actively waiting for

232

the Savior to come from heaven and to change their bodies to become like his resurrection body (3:20–21; see also 4:5).

- **1 Thessalonians.** Some Thessalonian Christians had died, but those to whom Paul was writing might still be alive at the coming of the Lord. Paul wrote that all living Christians at the time of Christ's return would be gathered with the resurrected dead to be with the Lord for eternity. Paul and the Thessalonians believed that the Parousia could happen during their lifetime (4:15–17; see also 1:9–10).

- **2 Timothy.** In the last days, there will come times of stress when people will be exceptionally godless. Timothy was told to avoid these people because they were already present. He was already living in the time of stress characteristic of the last days (3:1–5).

- **Titus.** Paul told Titus, who shepherded the Christians in Crete, that they should lead holy lives because they were actively waiting for the Parousia. Those early Christians were rightfully waiting for Christ to return, possibly within their lifetime (2:11–13).

- **Hebrews.** The first coming of God's Son signaled the beginning of the "last days"; this is now the last phase of history, which will end when the Son becomes "heir of all things." The Hebrew Christians knew that they were living in the terminal phase of history (1:1–2; see also 9:26–28; 10:25).

- **James.** The Christians to whom James was writing were suffering under oppression. He advised them to bear their suffering with patience in the light of the Parousia and the great judgment, which was ready to take place at any time (5:7–9).

- **1 Peter.** Peter wrote that everything was ready for the judgment of the living and of the dead to take place, possibly within the lifetime of his original hearers (4:5; see also 1:5, 13; 4:7, 17; 2 Pet. 3:12–17).

- **1 John.** When John wrote, he solemnly acknowledged that this was the "last hour." All the conditions for the occurrence of the Parousia were fulfilled. It could have happened at any time then or since (2:18).

- **Revelation.** The book of Revelation dealt with matters that would happen soon, because the time was near (1:1, 3) and because Christ himself had promised that he was coming soon (3:11; 22:6–7, 12, 20).

This massive evidence marshaled from the inspired documents of the church in apostolic times indicates two facts. First, the early

Christians (as most Christians since those days) lived in a mode of active expectancy of Christ's return within their own lifetime instead of relegating its occurrence to a distant future. Second and more surprisingly, New Testament believers waited not for signs but for Jesus himself. In all the texts surveyed above, not one indicates that they were waiting for preconditions, for intermediate events, or for preliminary signs to take place before the Parousia. Their hope was directly focused on the sovereign appearing of Christ because they believed it was the next great event to occur in God's timetable for the end of all things.

That expectation of the imminent return of Jesus stands in tension with the teachings of Jesus given toward the end of his earthly ministry. He gathered his disciples and taught them extensively on matters relative to the end times. This is recorded in the "Olivet Discourse,"called that because Jesus gave it while he sat on the western slope of the Mount of Olives, facing the city of Jerusalem (Matt. 23:37–25:46; Mark 13; Luke 21:5–36).

In this teaching, Jesus clearly and unmistakably indicated several signs that were to occur before the Parousia could take place. Yet within one or two generations after having received Christ's teaching, his followers were not watching and waiting for signs of Christ's second coming, but they were watching and waiting for the Second Coming itself. This apparent contradiction might suggest that either Jesus was mistaken in setting conditions for the Parousia or that the Holy Spirit deceived the early church by revealing that not signs but the Parousia was the next thing to happen.

As will be shown below, however, neither Jesus nor the Holy Spirit was mistaken. It is true that Jesus set signs that were to be accomplished before the Second Coming, but the New Testament clearly shows that each one of those signs was accomplished during the lifetime of the first generation of his followers, so that the early Christians could rightfully wait for the Parousia instead of the signs. In other words, the signs and the conditions set by Jesus were all taken care of before the death of his original disciples. Therefore, they could legitimately watch and wait for the Parousia instead of watching and waiting for signs. In so doing, they set the model for our own attitude toward the Parousia.

Jesus outlined three basic signs that were to take place as preconditions for his Parousia (Matt. 24:1–28): the fall of Jerusalem (vv. 1–2, 15–21), the preaching of the gospel to all nations (v. 14), and the time of distress and tribulation (vv. 3–13, 22–28).

As we trace the church's understanding of these three signs through the New Testament letters, note that Jesus was addressing this teaching to the disciples in person, that he was speaking to them face to face, and that he was referring to them directly and to their own involvement in the events he was predicting. He spoke to them in the second personal pronoun "you" (vv. 4–5, 6, 9, 15, 20, 23, 25–26, 33, 42, 44) and told them that the signs that would precede the Parousia were relevant to them personally within their own life span. Although Jesus' teaching in the Olivet Discourse is relevant to all Christians in all ages, when Jesus spoke it he was addressing his first followers, and the content of this teaching was applicable first to them and to their own times.

1. Sign One: The Fall of Jerusalem

Jesus uttered a lament over Jerusalem, calling it the killer city that kept rejecting God's offer of salvation (Matt. 23:37–39). As a result, Jerusalem was bringing on itself a judgment that would leave it troubled and desolate (v. 38). The Parousia would ultimately compel it to acknowledge the Lord (v. 39). But then, the whole universe will do as much (24:30; see also Phil. 2:10–11; Rev. 1:7).

At that point, Jesus' strong reproof of the Jewish religious establishment should have caused the disciples to speak guardedly about the temple. Instead, they came to Jesus and pointed to its architectural beauty (see Mark 13:1). Jesus' response was terse, almost exasperated; in sharp tones, he predicted the total destruction of the place (Matt. 24:1–2, 15–21).

Such a catastrophic event seemed so improbable to the disciples that they linked it in their minds with Jesus' second coming at the end of time. They could not conceive of the end of Jerusalem apart from the end of the world (v. 3). So Jesus proceeded to teach them that the fall of Jerusalem was not the end of the world but only one of the developments that would take place before the end of the world. In fact, Jesus told the disciples that the destruction of Jerusalem would happen during their lifetime and that they would see it with their own eyes (v. 15). Because the Christian church would begin in Jerusalem, Jesus expected that the fall of the city would deeply affect the lives of his followers residing there (vv. 15–21). Thus, he gave them specific instructions for their escape (v. 20).

Jesus represented the disaster to befall Jerusalem as "great tribulation," unprecedented and unrepeatable in its severity (v. 21). Therefore, he was naturally concerned that the Jerusalem Christians be forewarned and protected. He interpreted the ancient prophecy of Daniel in relation to the fall of the temple (v. 15). The Gospel of Luke reports the same teaching of Jesus in even more vivid details, providing the additional prediction that Jerusalem (meaning the temple area) will remain under Gentile rule until the End (Luke 21:20–24).

The disaster predicted by Jesus struck some thirty-five years later. Under the pretense of putting down a Jewish civil war, Roman legions swept down the country, quickly laid siege around Jerusalem, finally entered it in A.D. 70, utterly decimated its population, and razed its buildings, including the temple. Having been forewarned by Jesus' predictions, the Jerusalem Christians fled the city in time to escape destruction. Gentile dominion over the temple began in A.D. 70 and has lasted to this day as the temple area remains under Moslem jurisdiction.

The Olivet Discourse contains a curious parenthetical editorial comment, a "Please, pay attention" note, that was designed to challenge the original readers' comprehension (Matt. 24:15; Mark 13:14). Whereas in the context Jesus was speaking to the disciples in the direct "you" address form, the parenthetical interjection ("let the reader understand") is in the third person. This footnote-like comment inserted by the Gospel writers seems to have been intended to call the attention of their first readers to the fact that the event predicted by Jesus was about to happen or was actually happening at the time of writing.

As history unfolded toward the tragic downfall of Jerusalem in A.D. 70, the followers of Jesus were able to verify the accuracy of Jesus' prediction. In the upheavals of the day, they discerned the passing of a covenant become obsolete (Heb. 8:13). They realized that the temple had been only a foreshadowing of the good things to come (10:1) and that in the new covenant, the real temple was no longer a building but the community of believers among whom God lived (1 Cor. 3:16–17; 2 Cor. 6:16; Eph. 2:20–22; 1 Pet. 2:5). They were told that when the End finally brings about the consummation of the union between Christ and his church, there will be no need for a temple because God will become their eternal dwelling place (Rev. 21:22).

Jesus had predicted that the temple would be destroyed before his Second Coming. The disciples who anticipated this tragic event and who saw it happening had every right to believe and to proclaim that, at least on this score, the Parousia could happen at any time. This element of fulfillment provides an explanation for the early church's vivid expectancy of the Parousia within their generation.

2. Sign Two: The Gentile Mission

The second condition given by Jesus for the End to occur could not have been stated more clearly: the preaching of the gospel to the nations as the sole reason for the continuation of history. God desires all people to be saved and to come to a knowledge of the truth (1 Tim. 2:4). He does not wish that any should perish but that all should reach repentance (2 Pet. 3:9). Therefore, "this gospel of the kingdom" must be preached universally before the End can come (Matt. 24:14). This gospel was defined early in Matthew as Christ's own message of repentance for kingdom readiness (4:17). It alone could guarantee salvation (24:13), and it is intended to make disciples of all the nations (28:18–20).

This precondition of worldwide evangelism is most baffling, however, for it seems to rob the Christian hope of its "any moment" expectancy for the Parousia. Moreover, it makes the timing of the end dependent upon the diligence of the church in preaching the gospel to the nations and upon the receptivity of the nations to the gospel. In other words, this condition appears to rob God of his sovereign right to determine the timing for the end of history and to give control over it to humans. Thus, the question must be raised as to why the early church lived with the vivid expectancy of the End to occur within their lifetime when they knew that this condition was far from being completed.

Fortunately, the letters of the New Testament provide the answer to this dilemma. Paul makes several statements indicating that the early church considered this condition to have been sufficiently fulfilled to justify the imminent expectancy of the Parousia. A thematic listing of a few such references follows.

- **Romans.** Paul describes himself as the divinely anointed apostle to the Gentiles entrusted with the mandate to propagate faith in Christ "among all the Gentiles" (1:5 NRSV). He believed the scope of his mission to be universal and thanked God that the faith held by the Christians in Rome was "proclaimed throughout the world" (1:8 NRSV; see also 16:25–26).
- **1 Thessalonians.** After receiving the gospel, the church at Thessalonica had spread the "word of the Lord" in the surrounding provinces of Macedonia and Achaia. In addition, the Thessalonians' faith in God had become known "in every place" (1:8 NRSV), to the extent that Paul did not have to say anything about it.
- **Colossians.** The Colossians' faith in Jesus Christ was based on the gospel that they had received (1:6, NRSV), the same gospel

that was "bearing fruit and growing in the whole world." At the latest, Paul wrote this epistle during his first Roman imprisonment (A.D. 61–63). At that time, the gospel had hardly gone beyond Rome to the west and Syria to the east. Yet Paul claimed that it was expanding in the whole world. A few verses later, he stated that the gospel "had been proclaimed to every creature under heaven" (v. 23, NRSV).

Paul did not write these sentences flippantly. The tone of the Colossians 1:23 passage is solemn and its content profound. It deals with the central doctrines of the Christian faith: reconciliation, redemption, sanctification, and the universality of the gospel's proclamation. Yet it is clear that Paul's claim that the gospel had been preached to every creature under heaven was not intended to be interpreted literally. The key for properly interpreting this verse is to place it in the context of the theme of the completion of the Gentile mission as traced above. Whether Paul meant that the gospel could be considered to have been universally preached through ethnic representation, or through geographic distribution, or through cultural penetration, or in any other manner that escapes us today, he emphasized that the early Christians viewed the Gentile mission as a success. This did not deter Paul and his missionary companions from pressing on relentlessly to take the gospel into new frontiers (see Rom. 15:23–24, 28). But based on their own assessment of the state of the Gentile mission as reflected in Paul's letters, we must conclude that the early Christians considered Jesus' precondition of the Gentile mission sufficiently fulfilled to justify their belief in the possible occurrence of the Parousia within their lifetime.

3. Sign Three: The Distress and the Tribulation

The third sign that Jesus gave his disciples regarding events occurring between his first and second coming was an acceleration in the process of deterioration within history (Matt. 24:6–8) and severe opposition directed against his followers (vv. 4–5, 9–13, 22–28). Jesus compared this increased distress to the birth pangs that precede the birth of a child (vv. 6–8). The Parousia would be the final outcome of this time of crisis. As Jesus taught the twelve disciples about this worldwide turbulence, he was speaking to them directly, telling them that they would *personally* suffer the crises of the tribulation (vv. 9, 20–21), but that they should not be alarmed at the first signs of trouble and conclude that the End would happen imminently (v. 6). The "you" form of address indicates that Jesus' teaching had the same relevance for the early disciples as it would have for future generations of Christians. To relegate this time of world distress to a period yet to come is not justified by the teaching of Jesus.

At least two explanations may account for Jesus' anticipation of political, economic, and natural upheavals during the church age. One is that the church age represents a period of transition between the time when the kingdom of God has been manifested in the person of Christ at his first coming and the time when it will be fully realized at the Parousia. The satanic powers know that though the battle rages on, they have already been defeated at the cross (Col. 2:15) and their doom is sure (1 Cor. 15:24–25). In the meantime, they lash out and thrash around in desperation, attempting to inflict maximum damage and to increase the evil in the world (Matt. 24:12).

Another explanation for global stress during the church age is provided by the very presence of the gospel in the world. A wicked world reacts adversely to the standards of righteousness and justice introduced by Christ's message. Although Christ is the Prince of Peace, the mere presence of his gospel creates a division between those who accept it and those who reject it (Matt. 10:34–36). A fallen world feels threatened by the intrusion of an opposing power destined to conquer it at the Parousia.

Consequently, Jesus taught the disciples that, in addition to the distress that would multiply randomly in the world, they would suffer tribulation. This tribulation would take two different forms: the active persecution they would suffer at the hands of the pagan nations (Matt. 24:9–13), and the attempt by the deceivers, the Christ-pretenders, and the traitors to lead the disciples astray (vv. 4–5, 22–28). Although those two forms of satanic opposition are closely related, we shall survey their thematic development in the New Testament separately under the headings of "The Tribulation" (vv. 9–13) and "The Antichrist" (vv. 4–5, 22–28).

a. The Tribulation

Jesus predicted to his disciples that the sufferings and turmoil of the end times would afflict both believers and the world they lived in (Matt. 24:6–9). His immediate disciples would personally experience this "tribulation" because it would begin within their lifetime (vv. 8–9 RSV), and this tribulation period would extend from their own lifetime until the end (v. 13).

The church of Jesus Christ has experienced tribulation from its very beginnings in Jerusalem. Early Christian communities were taught that "through many tribulations we must enter the kingdom of God" (Acts 14:22 RSV). During most of its history, the faithful church has suffered opposition at the hands of an unrighteous world. Only in rare circumstances has it enjoyed periods of peace and freedom. In the midst of such favorable conditions, Christians are tempted to believe that, since they are being spared tribulation, the promised tribulation will be confined to a brief period of time just prior to the End. However, this has not been the belief of the church through the ages, and it was certainly not the belief of the church of the apostles as reflected in the New Testament.

Indeed, the doctrine of the tribulation is explicitly defined in the New Testament. The Greek word for "tribulation" (*thlipsis*) appears some forty-five times in the New Testament, although it is often translated in current versions with words such as "persecutions," "trials," "distress," and "suffering." Its Hebrew equivalent is used only a few times in the Old Testament and never in its prophetic books. Neither the Old nor the New Testament justifies reading a concept of terminal tribulation in the disputed and hapaxic passage about the seventieth week in Daniel (Dan. 9:27). Jesus used that very text to describe not a terminal tribulation, but the destruction of the Jerusalem temple in A.D. 70, which his original disciples would see with their own eyes (Matt. 24:15; Mark 13:14; Luke 21:20–24; "When *you* see...").

More generally, Jesus taught that the world's natural response to the preaching of the Gospel was to inflict "tribulation" and persecution on his followers (Matt. 13:21). Since this tribulation would begin within the lifetime of his immediate disciples, Jesus prepared them to face it personally. He told them that they would be delivered "up to tribulation," be put to death, and "be hated by all nations for [his] name's sake" (24:9 RSV). The fall of Jerusalem would be a part of the "great tribulation," requiring them to flee the city (vv. 20–21). By extension, the "great tribulation" would provide the pattern for the tribulation that would be part of the experience of believers through the ages until the time of the Second Coming. It is only after the "tribulation" of those days, the period that stretches from the days of the apostles until the Second Coming, that the Son of Man will return and gather to himself all the elect (vv. 29, 31).

Soon after Pentecost, the predictions of Jesus regarding the forthcoming tribulation were fulfilled in the lives of his apostles and of the Jerusalem church. They experienced repeated persecution, ending with the "tribulation" that scattered the church away from Jerusalem at the time of Stephen's death (Acts 8:1; 11:19). The tribulation was likewise part of Paul's experience. He used that very word to describe his sufferings in Asia where he almost died (2 Cor. 1:8). The churches that Paul established were likewise going through the same "tribulations" (2 Cor. 4:17; 8:2; 1 Thess. 1:6, 3:3, 7; Heb. 10:33).

When John sent his Revelation to the seven churches of Asia Minor, they were also going through the "tribulation" (Rev. 1:9). The church in Smyrna was the special target of a "tribulation" that was to be intensified for a time represented by "ten days" (2:9–10). And at the very end of time, all believers who ever lived— people "from every nation, tribe, people and language"—will be gathered as a great multitude before the throne of God (7:9 NIV). They are the redeemed who, throughout history, "have washed their robes and made them white in the blood of the Lamb" (v. 14). They will have come out of the same "great tribulation" that engulfed the lives of the apostles and that has been, since then, the lot of the majority of Christ's followers throughout the course of history.

Christians who happen to live in peace and security do not realize that they enjoy exceptionally privileged circumstances while most Christians in other places go through the fires of tribulation. In every age and in most places, true believers have been a beleaguered, persecuted minority. It is commonly estimated that more Christians have died for their faith in the twentieth century than during all the previous centuries combined. During the 1915 "forgotten holocaust" alone, one and a half million Armenian Christians were massacred in their homeland by the Ottoman Turks in a systematic genocide, a horror surpassing the magnitude of Hitler's holocaust of the Jews in proportion to each people's total population at that time. Even at the end of our tormented twentieth century, Christians are experiencing the tribulation in more countries around the globe than in countries where they enjoy freedom. For most believers, beginning with Christ's apostles, his promise has been and is being tragically confirmed in their lives: "In the world you have tribulation" (John 16:33 RSV).

The point of this discussion is that Jesus had specifically warned his immediate disciples about the forthcoming tribulation that would be a part of their experience as his followers. In order to dramatize his disciples' involvement in the tribulation, Jesus repeatedly used the "you" form of address, thus making it clear that the tribulation would affect them personally and not just some distant generation of people (Matt. 24:9,20–21). That same tribulation would extend through the time of the church until the Parousia when the Son of Man returns with power and glory "immediately after the tribulation of those days" (v. 29 RSV, NASB). Accordingly, the authors of the New Testament who wrote about the possible imminence of the Parousia in their day were convinced that the tribulation was enough of a reality tragically present in their own experience to justify their belief that the Parousia could happen at any time during their lifetime or after it.

b. The Antichrist

In the Olivet Discourse, Jesus closely associated the tribulation with the rise of Christ-pretenders and false prophets (Matt. 24:5, 23–24) who would perform "great signs and wonders" (v. 24 RSV). We note again that Jesus gave this teaching to his original disciples and that it concerned them as well as future generations of believers. He exhorted the disciples, again in the "you" form of speech, not to be led astray by the claims of impostor christs who would appear in their day (vv. 4, 23, 25–26). Once again, it is evident that Jesus anticipated this form of deception to begin within the lifetime of his disciples.

Three other books of the New Testament expanded Christ's teaching on this subject, traditionally described as the doctrine of the Antichrist. We shall now survey those three texts to determine whether the early Christians detected any evidence of the presence of Antichrist in their own day or whether they considered it entirely an event of the future.

2 Thessalonians 2:1–12. The teachings about the doctrine of the Antichrist contained in this passage fall under two categories: some are clear and others are more difficult to understand.

Among the clear teachings is the fact that Paul describes two manifestations of Antichrist: one is an evil, anti-God system, and the other is its personification in a single God-usurper. The organized system is described as the "rebellion" (v. 3) and the "mystery [or secret power] of lawlessness" (v. 7 RSV). The person representing this force is designated as the "man of lawlessness," the "man of sin," or the "son of perdition" (v. 3), who opposes and usurps divinity; such descriptions are conveyed in language borrowed from the ancient prophets (v. 4; see Ezek. 28:2; Dan. 11:36).

It is also clear in this text that the twin evils of the Antichrist as a system and as a person constituted a reality present and active in Paul's day. Because the Antichrist was already a matter of concern for the Thessalonian Christians, Paul had personally given them this teaching while he was among them (v. 5). At the time when he wrote, he referred to the Antichrist in the present tense—as a reality active in his day (v. 4). He stated specifically that the Antichrist was already present "now," at the time of writing, though not yet revealed (v. 6). Likewise, the antichrist system was "already at work" at the time of writing (v. 7 RSV). Though both the antichrist person and system were being temporarily restrained, they were alive and well in Paul's day. With the eventual lifting of the restraint, Paul asserted that they would then come out in full force, only to be destroyed without effort at the Parousia of the Lord Jesus (vv. 8–9).

Paul's discussion of the Antichrist in this passage contains indications as to when the Thessalonians could expect him to come out in the open. When released from his restraint, he would make victims of some of the people in Paul's own day—people who "refused to love the truth and so be saved" (v. 10 RSV). At the time of writing, God was already sending upon them a strong delusion (v. 11) because they did "not believe the truth" but, instead, "delighted in wickedness" (v. 12 NIV). As a result, they had left themselves open to the Antichrist's deceptions. In other words, Paul did not describe the followers of the Antichrist here as belonging to a future generation; rather, they were his contemporaries, already conditioned to be receptive to his impending manifestation.

This text clearly teaches, then, that the antichrist duality was already present and active in Paul's day, though not yet fully deployed. A more difficult question in his discussion has to do with the identification of the Antichrist, of the antichrist institution, and of the restrainer. Some brief comments on this issue follow.

Theories abound for the identification of Paul's Antichrist in 2 Thessalonians. The following is presented as one option that seems to account for all the evidence. In this passage, Paul makes use of at least two recognizable models to characterize him.

The first model is Judas Iscariot, the disciple who turned traitor. The designation "son of perdition" (v. 3 RSV) had earlier been used by Jesus in reference to Judas (John 17:12 RSV). Paul may be using this expression to denounce the onslaught on the Christian community of apostate defectors about whose false teachings he forewarned the Thessalonians (2 Thess. 2:3; 3:6) and several other churches, including the Ephesian church (see 2 Tim. 3:1–5). This interpretation also sheds light on the cryptic reference to the "restrainer" (2 Thess. 2:6–7). There is evidence in the New Testament that Paul considered himself a God-appointed bulwark of the church against incipient heresies (Acts 20:29–30). What he is reported to have taught in Ephesus, he is likely to have also taught in Thessalonica, warning the church that when his ministry (the "what" of 2 Thess. 2:6) would terminate because of his removal (the "who" of v. 7), the heretics would come out in the open.

The wording of the passage indicates that the other model used to personify the Antichrist is the tyrant model, drawn from Ezekiel 28:2 and Daniel 11:36; both of these refer to totalitarian leaders who become religiously oppressive because of aspirations to self-deification. When Paul was in Thessalonica, he was denounced to the civil authorities as preaching subversion against Caesar, "saying that there is another king, Jesus" (Acts 17:7 RSV). This pitting of Caesar against Jesus is historically documented in the practice of emperor worship during New Testament times and in the ensuing persecutions. This activity of the Antichrist explains why Paul refers to him as taking "his seat in the temple of God" (2 Thess. 2:4 RSV). These oppressive powers were attempting to bring the Christian community (the true temple of God; see 2 Cor. 6:16; Eph. 2:21) in subjection to themselves through persecution (see 2 Thess. 1:4). In other words, the models used for the depiction of the Antichrist in 2 Thessalonians were drawn from the circumstances of Paul and the church to which he was writing.

1 John 2:18–19, 22; 4:3; 2 John 7. John's epistles contain the most precise and explicit statements about the Antichrist; they are the only books in the Bible that actually use the word "antichrist," thus revealing the essential nature and motivation of both the person and the system. The antichrist theme in these epistles contains two basic teachings. The first has to do with the timing of the appearance of Antichrist and the other with his identification.

The teaching relative to the *timing* begins with two direct declarations about the possible imminence of the End at the time of writing, "It is the last hour" (2:18). John's readers had been taught that the Antichrist would come before the End (2:18; 4:3). Now that the Antichrist was present, they could deduce that the End might occur at any moment. Not only had he come into their world but he had come in full force. There were "many antichrists." Like an invading army that enters a country and spreads out to occupy it, the Antichrist had entered the world and multiplied. This invasion made it an even more compelling sign that the End could occur imminently. Therefore, John emphatically repeated: "It is the last hour" (2:18). What Jesus had predicted (Matt. 24:24) and what Paul had confirmed (2 Thess. 2:3–4) had now become a reality in John's day. Antichrist had broken all restraint. He had brazenly come out and expanded his evil presence in multiple expressions, like a slithering monster with many heads.

John's teaching about the *identity* of the Antichrist is also consistent with that of Jesus and Paul. According to Jesus, many false prophets and false Christs would rise to lead the disciples and the "elect" astray (Matt. 24:5, 11, 24). Likewise, John described the Antichrist as having the faces of apostates and heretics. Some had been in the community of believers under false pretenses (1 John 2:19), because they denied the Father and the Son as the Christ (v. 22). They were deceivers who had gone out into the world because they refused to acknowledge Christ and his incarnation (2 John 7). This teaching also agrees with Paul's description of the Antichrist as the master deceiver who would cause people to reject the truth and to believe falsehood (2 Thess. 2:10–11). Paul had perceived the presence of Antichrist expressed also through an organized system. Likewise, John described the multiple manifestations of Antichrist in his day as the widespread "spirit of antichrist," of whose arrival his readers had been forewarned (1 John 4:3).

Revelation 13:11–18. This text represents the last body of teaching in the Bible on the doctrine of the Antichrist. The immediate context introduces a trinity of evil: the "great dragon" (symbolic language for Satan, 12:3, 9), the beast out of the sea (representing political power at the service of Satan, 13:1–10), and the beast out of the earth (representing the religious establishment at the service of the first beast, vv. 11–18). This second beast is subsequently identified as the "false prophet" (16:3; 19:20; 20:10), who leads people into worshiping falsehood (13:12). It performs "signs" (vv. 13–14) and deceives people through wonder-working powers (v. 14). It masterminds an organized system of religious and economic persecution that had become a frightful reality for many churches when the book of Revelation was written (vv. 15–17).

Revelation 13 concludes with the mention of the secret name of the beast, represented by a code number: 666 (v. 18). It is the key to economic survival within the organized system of opposition set up by the false prophet (vv. 16–17). This number has often inflamed the imagination of Christians as they have tried to decipher it in order to predict the future. However, the text itself suggests that such efforts are utterly wasted. After all, John addresses his book to "the seven churches that are in Asia" (1:4). The messages it contained were primarily intended for them and were intelligible to them. While Revelation has a universal and permanent relevance to all churches throughout the ages, its relevance is always dependent on how the originally designated readers of those books were intended to understand the message they contained.

Regarding the number 666, John extended an urgent invitation for his original readers in the seven churches to crack the code and to identify the human reality it represented. He gave them four clues to put them on track and to suggest that they could figure out who stood behind the number (v. 18): (1) "This calls for wisdom" NRSV). This was John's signal for his readers in Asia to gather their wits and to be sharp. (2) "Let anyone with understanding." John invited the most knowledgeable and the most discerning among his original readers to take notice. (3) "Calculate the number of the beast." The name hidden behind the number could then be figured out through sagacious judgment. (4) "For it is the number of a person." The meaning of the number was decipherable. Therefore, the Christians in Asia were able to decode the identity of the figure represented by the number.

Several theories have been elaborated as to the identity of Antichrist in John's day. Such speculations are not the concern of this study. Suffice it to conclude that, like Paul and John in his epistles, the author of Revelation considered that Antichrist as designated by the 666 symbol was active and identifiable in his own day.

This brief survey of the New Testament teaching on the theme of Antichrist has shown the existence of some continuity and of some variations from author to author. The continuity is the recognizable presence and activity of the Antichrist in their own day. The variations concern the identifications of the Antichrist as "many false Christs" in Matthew, as the "lawless one" in Thessalonians, as the "many antichrists" in John, and as the "beast" in Revelation. These differences show that the concept of the Antichrist refers to a flexible and changing historical reality that represents the perennial incarnations of the "activity of Satan" (2 Thess. 2:9), both as recurring personifications of evil and as a dominant figure.

The intent of the New Testament teaching on the Antichrist seems twofold. It warns believers of all times to expect opposition, persecution, and deception during their own lifetime so that they can overcome them (Matt. 24:13; 2 Thess. 2:2; 1 John 2:24; 2 John 7; Rev. 13:10). Second, it comforts Christians by assuring them of the ultimate victory of Christ over Satan and his emissaries. Thus, the days of tribulation will be shortened for the sake of the elect (Matt. 24:33). At his coming, the Lord Jesus will slay the lawless one (2 Thess. 2:8). Both beasts were seen by John thrown alive into the lake of fire (Rev. 19:20). The doom of Satan is sure.

The New Testament information about the Antichrist was not provided for future generations of Christians to stimulate their curiosity about the occult presence of Satan's allies in the world or to entice believers to engage in endless guesswork about the identity and the whereabouts of antichrists. Since Satan will remain active until the End, the Antichrist and antichrists will keep appearing until the Parousia. They were present in New Testament times. Their influence will probably become even more manifest as history draws nearer to the End. The New Testament message to Christians in all ages is to guard themselves against deceptive ideologies and to rest assured of the ultimate victory of their sovereign Lord over the power of Satan, even in its most virulent manifestations.

The end result of this survey of the three signs set by Jesus as preconditions for his return is that they were considered to have been accomplished within the lifetime of the apostles. Consequently, the churches of the first century were justified in waiting for the End as the next eschatological event to occur without the need for further developments to make it possible. The Parousia could have happened at any time during or after their day. Its occurrence was and still remains potentially "imminent."

This belief of the early church in the possible imminence of the Parousia precludes the addition of any other signs to the three indicated by Jesus. He told the twelve disciples that they would see the three signs fulfilled within their generation and that, as a result of this fulfillment, the Parousia would be near, ready to happen even within their generation (Matt. 24:33–34). Revelation, the last prophetic word in the Bible, proclaimed to the seven churches of Asia that Christ could return at any moment within the time frame of their lives (Rev. 1:1, 3; 3:11; 22:6–7, 10, 12, 20). This message remains as valid for today's churches as it was for the churches of the first century.

4. Parousia Behavior

The Olivet Discourse deals with one more concern relative to the time issue: the appropriate response of believers toward the possible imminence of the Parousia. Jesus knew that the anticipation of the end of the world drove the pagans into a frenzy of sign seeking and date setting. He strictly forbade his followers to engage in such behavior. The most extensive part of the Olivet Discourse is devoted to making this point clear. Jesus gave his disciples five illustrations to define the appropriate attitude of his followers toward the nearness of the End (Matt. 24:32–25:13), and two more to define the appropriate activity for his followers in anticipation of the End (25:14–46). These seven illustrations will be surveyed in sequence.

The Parable of the Fig Tree (Matt. 24:32–36). The budding of

247

the fig tree meant that summer was near and that it could break forth at any moment. Jesus was telling his disciples (using the "you" form of address) that *they* would see all the signs accomplished within their own lifetime. As a result, *they* would know that the Parousia was near, "at the very gates" (NRSV), ready at any moment to burst in on the scene of history. Jesus went on to declare solemnly that their own generation would still be alive when "all these things," meaning all the signs preliminary to the Parousia, would take place.

Of course, the apostle James died before the fulfillment of "all these things" was completed (Acts 12:2), but Peter, John, and believers who belonged to their generation saw the signs that announced the nearness of the Parousia. They expected it to happen perhaps within their lifetime, though Jesus denied anyone except the Father the ability to pierce the secret of the timing of the Parousia (Matt. 24:36). Today, the signs are behind us. Only the Parousia lies ahead of us.

The Great Surprise in Noah's Time (Matt. 24:37–42). When the Flood happened unexpectedly, some were saved by entering the ark and the rest of humankind were swept away into destruction. "So will be the coming of the Son of Man." Some will be taken into salvation (see also v. 31) and the rest will be left for judgment, mourning their loss in the midst of the collapsing universe (see vv. 29–30). The Lord told his disciples, and through them, all believers, to be ready and to watch for his coming at any time because no one would be able to predict the exact time of his return (v. 42).

The Parable of the Thief in the Night (Matt. 24:43–44). A burglar strikes at the most unexpected time. Likewise, the Parousia will happen at a time that the disciples or any future generation of disciples will be unable to predict. The apostles Paul and Peter understood this parable to refer to the unpredictable suddenness of the coming of "the day of the Lord," when the universe will be destroyed in judgment (1 Thess. 5:2–3; 2 Pet. 3:10). The Parousia will be a universal and terminal surprise. Therefore, the first disciples and all disciples after them must be ever ready for it to happen at any time.

The Parable of the Faithful Servant (Matt. 24:45–51). Because the servant does not know when the master will return, he carries out his duties diligently. When the master returns unexpectedly, the servant is found faithful and is rewarded. A second servant, however, becomes unconcerned about the master's return and is caught revelling instead of working and watching. Because of his carelessness, he is thrown out and destroyed. Likewise, the

Parousia will favor those who live expecting it, but it will mean judgment for those who live as if it were never to happen.

The Parable of the Ten Maidens (Matt. 25:1–13). Five maidens took their participation in the forthcoming celebration seriously enough to prepare for it; the other five were flippant about it and found themselves shut out. Again, Jesus told the disciples and, through them, Christians in all ages to be on the watch because no one would be able to predict the time of the End.

The Parable of the Talents (Matt. 25:14–30). Jesus now defines in this parable the activity that is appropriate for his followers before the Parousia. The possible shortness of time should not be a pretext for them to lead passive, unproductive lives. On the contrary, the prospect of the Parousia should provide the incentive to invest productively all the abilities God has entrusted to his people. While Christians must constantly be on the alert for the Parousia to happen at any time, they should also prepare for the possibility of it happening only "after a long time" (v. 19 NRSV).

The Last Judgment (Matt. 25:31–46). The previous parable illustrated Christ's requirement of active involvement and full use of resources for kingdom purposes during the interim period. This description of the last judgment defines the nature of the activity demanded by Christ. Those who will inherit the coming kingdom are the ones who act selflessly and with compassion toward people in need. It will be revealed to them that their good deeds have a profound meaning as the outward manifestation of a living faith. While helping the needy, they are really serving him, who has identified with the needy in order to help and save them. Those, however, who shut their hearts and do not follow Christ in servanthood by helping people in need will be separated and receive punishment.

The main emphasis that Jesus made in this message to the disciples was that since they were utterly unable to predict the time of the End, they should be waiting, watching, and working during this interim period. Because all the conditions and signs had been fulfilled in the disciples' lifetime, they could rightfully wait for Jesus instead of waiting for signs. This message remains unchanged for today's disciples. We should wait and watch for the return of Christ as if it could happen today—because it could. But we should also do kingdom work as if the Parousia may not happen for a million years—because it may not: "No one knows . . . but only the Father" (Matt. 24:36). What may seem to be a long delay from a human perspective may be a very short period in God's view of time (2 Pet. 3:8). Even if there is a long delay, it is a delay of grace for the benefit of humans (v. 9). In the meantime, the Lord is ready, "at the very gates" (Matt. 24:33).

II. THE PAROUSIA AS AN ABSOLUTE EVENT

Will the world come to a brutal end with a big bang or will it agonize in a long whimper? Will history suddenly reel upon itself and collapse into eternity or will it teeter from crisis to crisis toward a slow death? Will the Second Coming bring time to a sudden halt or will the End happen through a succession of eschatological events that will unfold over long periods of time?

These questions have been given different answers by people who scan the pages of the Bible. As we study this subject, we will take into account Old Testament data, but always keeping in mind that the final meaning of the Old Testament is to be found in the New Testament, since Christ is and has the final and complete word of God. Jesus knew the eschatological teachings of the Old Testament. He interpreted them, clarified them, and incorporated them into his own teaching on the subject of the End.

The New Testament contains some three hundred eschatological references. They unanimously teach that the End will be one cosmic, total, undivided, abrupt, instantaneous, and unitary happening rather than a series of long, drawn-out developments. In other words, the New Testament describes the End as an absolute event rather than as a multi-stage process. The Parousia happens once, not several times, and there is only one Second Coming, not repeated second comings!

1. The Teaching of Jesus

a. Matthew 13:24–30, 36–43, 47–50

The lesson in both of these parables is the same. The weeds and the good grain coexist in the field until harvest time. The good fish and the bad fish are in the net together until it is hauled out. Evil and good will remain in this world side by side until the End. Only then will they be separated. Evil will be forever eradicated and destroyed, while the righteous will shine in the heavenly glory of the Father's kingdom. The separation will happen at one time and it will be final.

b. Matthew 24:29–31, 37–42

This passage gives Jesus' own description of his return and of some of its accompanying features. As such, it carries a compelling authority that provides the basic pattern for the description of the

End in other books of the New Testament. Jesus incorporated prophetic teachings from the Old Testament in his prediction of the End, taking into account prophetic material from the Old Testament and integrating it into his understanding of the end times. Obviously, Jesus' model teaching on the End is normative for Christians.

- The tribulation period that extended from the time of the apostles through the church age will lead directly to the end of the world and the Parousia (vv. 29–30). The apostles experienced "tribulation" (v. 9) and witnessed the "great tribulation" of the fall of Jerusalem in A.D. 70 (v. 21). The "tribulation of those days" will continue until the End and will lead, without transition and "immediately," to the Second Coming and the collapse of the universe (v. 29).

- At the coming of Christ, the universe will self-destruct. The solar system will disintegrate and the galaxies collapse (v. 29). As the sun goes dark, life on this planet becomes extinct. Without the sun, the world comes to end.

- In the midst of this cosmic collapse, Christ will come from heaven "with power and great glory" for all the nations of the earth to see and mourn. He will come with three theophanic elements: the clouds of heaven, the angels, and the trumpet call, indicating God's manifest involvement in the Parousia (v. 30).

- All the redeemed (the "elect") will be gathered to their eternal destination (Matt. 24:31). Both in Matthew and in the rest of the New Testament, the "elect" consistently refers to all believers, both Jews and Gentiles (vv. 22, 24; Luke 18:7; Col. 3:12; 2 Tim. 2:10; Tit. 1:1; 1 Pet. 1:1–2).

- The unsaved will be "swept away" in this final conflagration like the wicked who were destroyed by the Flood in Noah's day (Matt. 24:37–42). The Flood and the Parousia impact the world with judgment. They both entail catastrophic destruction that results in the gathering of the saved and the punishment of the lost. At the Flood, the saved were gathered in the ark. At the Parousia (this word is used in vv. 37 and 39), the saved will be gathered by the angels (v. 31). Of two men in the field and two women at the mill, one will be taken to salvation and the other left to destruction (vv. 40–41). This will happen at the "coming of the Son of Man" (v. 39), when the "Lord will come" (v. 42) with power and great glory to gather his elect while the nations of the earth will mourn because of their impending destruction (vv. 30–31). Not only will the wicked be swept away to judgment, but heaven and earth are also destined to pass away (v. 35).

In summary, Jesus describes the End as one great unitary event revolving around his Parousia. At his coming, the nations will see him, the righteous will be saved as the upside of the End, the wicked will be destroyed as the downside, and the world will come to an end.

2. The Teaching of Paul

a. 1 Corinthians 15:23–26, 51–57

In 1 Corinthians 15, Paul's discussion of the End is limited to various aspects of the final resurrection of believers, an event that manifests Christ's ultimate victory over death (v. 54). But what he presents in it supplements other eschatological teachings of the New Testament.

The resurrection of the dead and the simultaneous "change" of those living at that time from this life to immortal life will happen "in a flash, in the twinkling of an eye, at the last trumpet" (v. 52). This feature of the general resurrection is consistent with Jesus' reference to the "loud trumpet call" that signals the gathering of the elect (Matt. 24:31). Paul defines precisely when this final resurrection as victory over death will occur (1 Cor. 15:23–26)—at Christ's "Parousia" (v. 23). God has already put everything under Christ's feet (v. 27; cf. Eph. 1:20–21). Consequently, Christ reigns, but his jurisdiction is not yet complete. It requires one more victory, when he also puts "all his enemies under his feet" (1 Cor. 15:25), including death itself, the "last enemy" (v. 26). At the final resurrection, death will "be swallowed up in victory," the victory will be complete, and the End will have come.

In keeping with the teaching of Jesus, the End is viewed in this passage as an event complete in itself. The Parousia triggers the destruction of death through the resurrection, and it signals the completion of the kingdom. The Parousia is the End; there is no indication in this passage of long delays between various components of the End.

b. 1 Thessalonians 4:14–5:4

In this passage, Paul explains to his readers the relationship between the Parousia and the resurrection of the elect. Jesus had described the End as an event that would be concurrent with his second coming (see Matt. 24:27, 37). On that basis, the Thessalonians understood that they, as the "elect," would be gathered in heaven at the time of the Second Coming. They became dismayed, however, when some of their fellow believers started dying before the Parousia. They thought that these deceased believers had been judged in the flesh like unbelievers because they suffered death.

Paul made it clear to his readers that his answer to their concern was not his idea but one that he had received "by the word of the Lord" (1 Thess. 4:15). He assured them that to be alive at the time of the Parousia would give no one an advantage over believers already dead (see v. 15, where the word "Parousia" is used). At the coming of the Lord, the dead in Christ would rise first and would be taken up with believers still alive; together they would enter eternity and be with the Lord forever (vv. 16–17).

The pattern of eschatological events described here by Paul bears a striking resemblance to Jesus' own description of the Parousia in the Olivet Discourse (Matt. 24:29–31, 37–42). In each account, the Parousia is a universally manifest event, not a secret visit. Christ descends visibly and audibly from heaven, announced by the "archangel's call" and "the sound of the trumpet of God" (v. 16 RSV; cf. Matt. 24:30). The redeemed ascend to "the clouds to meet the Lord in the air" (1 Thess. 4:17), the same clouds are present in Jesus' description (Matt. 24:31). All believers, newly risen or still alive at the time of the Parousia, will be caught up together to be with the Lord forever (1 Thess. 4:17), in conformity to Christ's message that the angels "will gather his elect from the four winds, from one end of heaven to the other" (Matt. 24:31 RSV).

In each account, there is also a downside, described in similar language. According to Paul, destruction will come upon the wicked suddenly, as unexpectedly as a thief in the night (1 Thess. 5:2). Likewise, Jesus predicts that destruction will come upon the world at the coming of the Son of Man as unexpectedly as the Flood in Noah's day and with the same surprise effect as a thief in the night (Matt. 24:37–44). Unbelievers will be falsely secure, celebrating their peace and their safety when sudden destruction will come upon them and there will be no escape (1 Thess. 5:3; cf. Matt. 24:38–39).

The numerous parallels between Paul's description of the Parousia and Jesus' model statement in the Olivet Discourse indicate that Paul was referring to the gathering of believers as part of the sudden, universal, and conclusive event of the End. For Paul, the Parousia (1 Thess. 4:15) and "the day of the Lord" (5:2) referred to the same event (cf. 1 Cor. 1:7–8).

3. The Teaching of Peter—2 Pet. 3:1–15

In this passage, the apostle Peter is addressing the mocking of people who were challenging belief in the Parousia because it was not happening soon enough. They claimed that history was at a standstill because nothing ever changed in this world (vv. 3–4). Peter addresses the criticism with the ringing affirmation of the "promise of his coming" ("Parousia," v. 4) at the "day of judgment" (v. 7) or "the day of the Lord" (v. 10), when the heavens and the earth will be destroyed by fire and godless people will be destroyed (v. 7). These are different expressions for the catastrophic end of the world and its replacement with a new reality (v. 13).

Peter's view, like Paul's, is consistent with that of Jesus in the Olivet Discourse. According to Jesus, the universe will disintegrate at the Parousia and the wicked will be swept away in judgment (Matt. 24:29, 39–41; cf. 2 Pet. 3:7). Peter even uses Jesus' parable of the thief in the night to illustrate the unpredictability and the suddenness of the Parousia (2 Pet. 3:10; cf. Matt. 24:42–44). Here again, the Parousia and the Day of the Lord are one and the same, bringing about the total and instantaneous termination of history without long delays of time between its various components.

4. The Teaching of John—The Book of Revelation

Some people regard the book of Revelation as a predictive timetable of future global events. This was not, however, the stated purpose of the author of Revelation. According to 1:1, the book is the God-given "revelation of Jesus Christ." This can mean that the book is the revelation given *by* Jesus Christ or is the revelation *about* Jesus Christ. The contents of the revelation show that the latter meaning is not excluded, for Christ is at the forefront of the whole book as the lowly crucified Lamb who becomes the supreme ruler and brings history, time, the nations, evil, and death under his dominion. This *christology* provides the key for the understanding of Revelation, for it shows how the principles of divine government intersect with the wild forces of history to manifest Christ's ultimate sovereignty over them and to associate the church with Christ's victory over the opposition.

The opening sentence also indicates who the intended readers of the Revelation are: "to show his servants." These "servants" are the believers in the seven churches of Asia whose needs and circumstances the book addresses. Whatever we think Revelation may mean to us in our day, we must first ask what meaning it had for its original readers in the seven churches.

Finally, Revelation 1:1 shows "what must soon take place." There is no reason for not taking the "soon" literally. The purpose of this book was to show the Christians of Asia in the first century what was to happen "soon" in their day. This does not mean that it has no relevance to the present or to times yet to come. It means that, whenever we interpret Revelation, the first questions should be, "What was the relevance of the text at the time of writing? What did it mean to the Christians in the seven churches?"

To complicate matters further, it is evident that Revelation was not written in straight, ordinary language. Rather, it was couched in a style that was current at the time and that pertained to a kind of writing called *apocalyptic literature.* One of the features of such writings is that their authors expressed ideas in images and symbols that formed a sort of secret code language. Consequently, to understand this book, we must first do research and learn as much as possible about that form of language in the first century. For example, comparing our Lord to a slain animal whose head is covered with seven horns and seven eyes would be blasphemous if it were interpreted literally (5:6). The explanation that the eyes are the seven spirits of God causes even more confusion, since the Scripture teaches that there is only one Spirit of God. However, once the value of symbols such as lamb, seven, horns, eyes, and spirits is recognized in the context of the genre of apocalyptic literature, the imagery acquires depth, beauty, and meaning. Unfortunately, many popular treatments of Revelation betray a total lack of awareness on the part of their authors for such requirements.

Since Revelation deals with the Christian understanding of history, we may rightly expect it to deal with the doctrine of the End. Indeed, it touches on this subject several times. We will probe the question whether John's view of the End in Revelation is consistent with the other authors of the New Testament discussed above or whether he adds a new dimension to it.

John ponders the torments and the convulsions of history that humans bring on themselves by their stubborn determination to go their own way instead of yielding to God's sovereign will. In the course of his visions, John is led on six different occasions to describe the End, using various forms of imagery that illustrate the same theme of the consummation of all things. We will now survey these to determine whether John conceives of the End as a unitary event or as a multi-stage process.

The Sixth Seal (Rev. 6:12–17). This vision of the End is consistent with that of Jesus in the Olivet Discourse (Matt. 24:29–30). In both, the universe collapses as the galaxies disintegrate, the sky vanishes, and the earth is dislocated. The sun going dark and the stars of heaven falling on the earth spell the complete obliteration of the earth several times over. The galactic bombardment of falling stars predicted in this text will bring history to a sudden and total resolution. A mere brush with a fraction of one falling star would incinerate the whole earth. As the final disaster takes place, there is universal awareness that it signals the great day of the wrath of God and of the Lamb. For all practical purposes this could have been the end of the book of Revelation, for there is nothing left but a gaping cosmic black hole where the earth used to be. Yet John resumes his visions in order to interpret history and the End from another perspective.

The Seventh Trumpet (Rev. 11:15–19). In this vision, history has come to its resolution in that Christ has permanently established his dominion over the kingdom of the world and has begun to reign for ever and ever. The opposition has been defeated and eternity has replaced time. The courts of heaven interpret the inauguration of Christ's eternal reign in terms of an upside and a downside. The downside is that the wrath of God has come upon the raging nations that were destroying God's good earth. Upon them comes a theophanic lightning, earthquake, and hailstorm, and they are destroyed. The upside is manifested in the rewarding of the prophets, of the saints, and of God-fearing people in all stations of life. Their blessing is to glimpse the security of their covenant within the very presence of God. Again, the book of Revelation could close on this final tableau since everything has been said and done and history has come to a complete halt. But John moves on to describe another aspect of the end of history.

The Two Harvests (Rev. 14:14–16). In this vision, the End is viewed from the perspective of the final judgment. The harvest of the world is fully ripe since history has fulfilled its purpose. In one fell swoop, the earth is reaped by one like a son of man seated on a cloud. On the upside, he garners the wheat that belongs to him. The downside harvest is entrusted to an angel whose improbable task is to collect the grapes of wrath with a sickle. The earth is harvested again, but this time, the grapes of the earth are crushed in the great winepress of the wrath of God. On the stripped earth, there remains only a sea of coagulating blood.

The Seventh Bowl (Rev. 16:17–21). Out of a cosmic theophany comes the shout signalling the End: "It is done!" Immediately, the cities of the nations collapse, the islands are gone, and the mountains disappear. Upon whoever is left standing on whatever remains of the earth fall hundred-pound hailstones as men curse God and as their idolatrous leader must take a downside toast to the fury of the wrath of God.

The Birds' Feast (Rev. 19:11–21). This vision portrays the downside of the End as a confrontation between the armies of heaven and the armies of the earth. However, the contest is too one-sided for any battle to take place, and there is no military engagement. The leaders of the armies of the earth are captured and thrown into hell, while the rest of the unbelieving world are killed by the word of him whose mouth holds a sharp sword with which he strikes the nations. He is also the one who treads the winepress of the fury of the wrath of God. All the birds are called to eat the flesh of all people, free and slave, small and great. When the great supper of God's wrath is ended, there is no one left on earth but fat birds gorged with human flesh.

The City and the Lake of Fire (Rev. 20:11–21:4). The End is represented as a final judgment. Once again, heaven and earth disappear; this time, they take off and there is no place for them to go. Thus, they pass away. In their place come a new heaven and a new earth with the new Jerusalem, the Bride of Christ, at the center. But there is also a downside: the lake of fire that receives death and all the dead not listed in the Book of Life.

The event described in each one of these six visions is the same: the end of history. The imagery varies to illustrate the horrific grandeur of the climactic termination of all earthly things. Despite this diversity, one theme remains constant: the End is an absolute event, undivided and complete in itself. In his renditions of the visions of the final consummation, John agrees fully with Christ's teachings and with the other eschatological authors of the New Testament.

Among all the eschatological references in the New Testament, there is one that stands out by its singularity in regard to the concept of the End as an absolute event. It is the only text where the notion of a multi-stage approach to the End can be found. A summary and discussion of the passage follow.

The Millennium (Rev. 20:1–10). The primary focus of this passage is the extermination of Satan—out of the ten verses that comprise it, seven deal with his demise. The defeat of Satan is meted out in two phases. In the first phase, a thousand years pass, during which Satan is bound and sequestered so that he is unable to deceive the nations. Then, in the second phase, Satan is released; he resumes deceiving the nations and organizes them into a coalition that is easily defeated as fire from heaven consumes the nations. Satan is thrown in the lake of fire, where he joins his associates, the beast and the false prophet, to be tormented forever. The importance that this topic of the defeat of Satan has for the author of Revelation can be appreciated by reading the two parts of the story as one (vv. 1–3, 7–10).

The middle three-verse unit tells the story of what happens to Christians who died by decapitation. They come to life for the "first resurrection" and reign with Christ for a thousand years, presumably the same thousand years as those of Satan's incarceration.

This segment of three verses has given rise to a huge amount of controversy disproportionate to its size. The various interpretations that have been offered for this passage may be summarized in three basic views. Through most of church history, the thousand-year reign of Christ (the *millennium*) has been interpreted to refer to the present age of the church: that is, the time between the first resurrection, when the power of Satan is limited because of the spiritual resurrection experienced by believers, and the End, when their bodies will also be resurrected. This is called the *amillenarian* or *nonmillenarian* view, because the chronology of the thousand years is interpreted in figurative terms. A slightly differing version of this view interprets the reign of the saints with Christ as referring to their participation in the rule of Christ in heaven after their physical death within the present age.

According to the second view, the *postmillenarian* interpretation, the thousand years represent a period of peace and righteousness on earth that will be brought about through the beneficial influence of the gospel upon society. Then, when time comes to its end, Christ will return to inaugurate eternity. This view is called postmillenarianism because the Parousia is thought to happen after the millennium on earth.

According to the third interpretation, called *premillenialism*, Christ will return upon the earth (the Parousia) to reign for a period of a thousand years marked by peace and righteousness, after which the End will come. This theory of an earthly millennium was formulated in the latter part of the second century A.D. It soon fell out of favor, only to be revived by fundamentalist and conservative churches primarily on the North American continent. This view is called *pre*millenarian because, according to it, the Parousia will take place *before* the establishment of a millennial earthly kingdom, during which utopian conditions will prevail upon the earth. Because it separates the Parousia from the End by an intermediate period of at least a thousand years, this interpretation requires a multi-stage view of the Second Coming.

The profound disagreements that surround this passage among interpreters of the Bible who respect and uphold it as divine revelation indicate that this particular text does not yield its meaning easily. Indeed, it presents several difficult features that must be taken into account if this text is to be used for doctrinal purposes. Those difficulties are amply discussed in the voluminous literature that exists on this subject. A listing will suffice here.

1. The text is found in an apocalyptic document filled with numerous figurative elements. Some are used in this passage itself: key, bottomless pit, great chain, dragon, serpent, thrones, the beast, Gog and Magog, sand of the sea, and lake of fire and brimstone. The question naturally arises as to whether the notion of a thousand years falls in the same category of metaphors or whether it should be interpreted as literal chronology.

2. From the very first lines of Revelation, John makes it clear that chronology is not his concern, nor is he interested in building a timetable for future history. Like the other authors of the New Testament, he believes that the End will always be imminent. From the very start, he gives an assurance to his readers that the time is near (1:3) and that the predictions contained in Revelation will "soon take place" (v. 1). Christ exhorts the embattled church in Philadelphia to stand firm because he is coming soon (3:11). Likewise, the book closes with the promise that the predictions it contains will "soon take place" (22:6), while the Lord proclaims three times his victorious affirmation. "I am coming soon" (vv. 7, 12, 20). It seems obvious that John was more interested with the Parousia itself than with matters that had to do with its timing.

This observation extends to the chronology of the book as a whole. We discovered above that Revelation contains six scattered accounts of the End. This fact alone makes it impossible to run a chronological sequence through it. Considering John's efforts to indicate that chronology was not his concern in this book, it is amazing that all the schools of interpretation mentioned above structure their understanding of Revelation 20 in terms of chronology.

3. Another difficulty stems from the fact that the text provides no clear indication of *where* the thousand-year reign of Christ takes place. Thrones are mentioned in connection with it (20:4–5), but in the book of Revelation, thrones belong exclusively in heaven (1:4; 3:21; 7:17; 8:3; 14:3, 5). Moreover, the reign of Christ is generally described in the New Testament, and especially in Revelation, as the *kingdom*, a present reality within believers and in heaven (Luke 11:20; 17:20–21; John 18:36; Rom. 14:17; 1 Cor. 15:50; Col. 1:13; Rev. 1:6, 9; 5:10, where there is good manuscript evidence for reading "they reign on earth"). The fact that the location of the millennial reign is not specified in Revelation 20 has contributed to much of the discussion about this passage.

4. The precise identification of the resurrected souls who reign with Christ for a thousand years constitutes a major difficulty. The

text is clear that the souls who come to life at the first resurrection to reign with Christ for a thousand years are the believers who have been beheaded for their testimony to Jesus and to the word of God. Beheaded martyrs represent a limited number of Christians throughout history. The text limits their number even more by supplying the added requirement of their noninvolvement in worshiping the beast or receiving its mark. Those two conditions confine the participants in Christ's reign to the martyrs by decapitation during the time of the beast, whenever that may have been or may still be.

The rest of the dead did not come to life until the end of the thousand years. To compound the problem even further, Christ's millennial co-regents are also designated as "priests of God and of Christ" (v. 6). These two designations of kingdom and priesthood are attributed to all believers in Revelation and are not limited to beheaded martyrs (1:6; 5:10). Of course, it is possible that the beheaded ones represent all the martyrs symbolically, or all the believers, or all the believers of one generation. But once the principle of symbolic language is accepted in a matter as important as the participants in Christ's reign, who will say that it cannot also be extended to the language that pertains to its duration and location?

5. Another serious difficulty that arises when the thousand-year reign of Christ is interpreted as a temporal rule over the earth is its connection with the story of the release of Satan in 20:7–10. As soon as he is released from the pit, he goes out to deceive the nations and to gather them for battle. Like one man, the nations turn against Christ and march across the breadth of the earth to destroy the embattled saints and the city that remain loyal to him. The thousand-year reign of Christ on the earth, therefore, turns out to have been a dismal failure, an exercise in futility, the greatest evangelistic fiasco of all times. His unhindered benevolent rule of ten centuries results in a massive and universal revolt against him.

This difficulty has been recognized and answered with the argument that the final revolt against Christ only shows the depth of the depravity of the human heart. But the questions remain: If Christ were to reign for a thousand years with Satan out of the way, what would be left for him to reign over but the human heart? How could Christ reign successfully over humans for a thousand years, only to have them finally reject him and rise up against him? What would be the meaning of a thousand-year reign over the nations if they end up taking sides with Satan as soon as he appears after an absence of a thousand years? Does not the final rebellion demonstrate that there was no genuine reign but only a cover-up for latent rejection? More pointedly, how could Christ expect his disciples to "go and make disciples of all nations" in the present age and in the face of satanic opposition if he will be unable to disciple the same nations in a thousand years with Satan tied up and out of the way? The notion of a perfect kingdom excludes by definition the possibility of its failure. The Scripture consistently presents the reign of Christ as eternal and unassailable. The theory of an earthly reign of Christ that ends in failure is a contradiction that cannot be supported from any passage of Scripture.

6. By far, the greatest difficulty presented by a chronological interpretation of Revelation 20:4–6 arises out of the fact that such a theory would be based on a spectacular biblical *hapax* (see pages 19–20), as this teaching is found nowhere else in the Bible. Indeed, this is the only text in Scripture that may be interpreted as predicting a temporal millennial reign of Christ. This fact alone does not invalidate the teaching of the hapax if its meaning were generally agreed upon in the history of Christian interpretation. But the difficulties listed above and the agelong debates between the several opposing schools of thought relative to the meaning of this text show that this hapax is unclear and that its meaning is hotly disputed among interpreters of the Bible.

Not only is the text unclear and debated, but it also contains references that, if interpreted in chronological fashion, contradict other clear teaching in non-hapaxic texts of non-apocalyptic books of the Bible. For example, let us examine the doctrine of the resurrection. Revelation 20 states that the beheaded martyrs came to life at the beginning of the thousand years while the rest of the dead did not come to life until the thousand years were ended— the "first resurrection." The resurrection at the end of the thousand years would presumably be the second resurrection. Thus, the passage contains the notion of a two-stage resurrection, with the phases occurring at least one thousand years apart. But many other passages of the Scriptures teach a single resurrection for both the righteous and the wicked: Daniel 12:2; John 5:28–29; 6:39–40, 44, 54; 11:24; Acts 24:15; 1 Corinthians 15:23–24, 51– 52; 1 Thessalonians 4:16–17. For Paul and John as for Jesus, the resurrection is a unitary event, a feature of the last day, simultaneous with the End. Since Revelation 20:4–6 is an unclear and contested hapax, a proper handling of this text requires that we humbly recognize our lack of understanding and that we refuse to press the text into service by forcing on it schemes not clearly suggested in the passage itself. Such a text may well have had relevancies and meanings for its author and his readers that are lost for us today.

A conservative approach to passages such as Revelation 20 would respect the secrets of the text while recognizing one's own limitations as interpreter. There is plenty of material in the Bible that is clear and unencumbered by hermeneutical contention so that it lends itself readily to exegetical use. The few difficult hapaxic statements like the one in this chapter beg to remain unexploited for teachings they cannot yield. Restraint and caution should characterize our approach toward them.

Sometimes, when the study of the details of a biblical passage proves unrewarding, an overall survey of its content may yield useful teachings. This is the case with Revelation 20. Everyone agrees that, whatever else the passage may teach in its minutiae, its overall message is a resounding affirmation of the sovereignty of the Lord Jesus Christ. Satan is manipulated at will, thrown around like a wet rag, defeated, and destroyed. The nations also fall under Christ's control, so that even a universal coalition between them and Satan is doomed to failure.

Finally, Christ is master over life and death. Those first Christians who initially received this book could be comforted with the knowledge that when Satan killed Christians and seemed to gain the upper hand, he was really defeating his own purposes. He was sending the martyrs on to claim Christ's victory over him. Certainly, whatever else the beheaded martyrs' involvement in Christ's reign may signify, it teaches that the church participates in the victory of Christ despite appearances to the contrary. This is a recurring theme of the book of Revelation (for instance, 2:26–27; 3:21; 12:10–11; 14:4; etc.).

Regardless of the eschatological scheme one adopts, it is of paramount importance that the absolute character of the Parousia be preserved. The object of the Christian hope is not a millennium, however it may be understood, nor any other component of the End, but "the glorious appearing of our great God and Savior Jesus Christ," the majesty and the intimacy of the church being gathered for eternal communion with him (Titus 2:13 NIV). To be genuinely biblical, eschatology must be defined in terms of the Parousia, not built around a hypothetical millennium.

Many Christians who believe firmly in the second coming of Christ do not adhere to any millenarian school, whether it be amill, postmill, or premill. It behooves Christians who do make a commitment in this regard to give no greater importance to their concept of the millennium within the overall framework of their theology than it had in the theology of the early church as reflected in the New Testament. This means that they should emphasize only that which is emphasized in the New Testament, that they should teach clearly only what the New Testament teaches clearly, and that they should exercise extreme caution with that which remains unclear in the New Testament.

III. THE PAROUSIA AS A UNIVERSAL EVENT

Having defined from Scripture those matters relative to the timing and the duration of the Parousia, we now turn to the issue of its location and scope. As Jesus was speaking to the disciples about the End, they asked, "When?" (Matt. 24:3), but they also asked, "Where, Lord?" (Luke 17:37). We will now survey the Scripture's answer to this last question.

Jesus addressed this matter of the place of the Parousia through several forms of teaching. He warned the disciples against deceptive attempts that would be made to localize his Second Coming. People would come claiming that Christ had returned secretly in one place or another, out in the open or in seclusion (Matt. 24:23, 26). Christ commanded his followers not to believe such reports about a secret Parousia because the real Parousia would be as universally evident as lightning when it flashes across the sky (v. 27, where the word "Parousia" is used). Jesus went on to affirm that at his return, *all* the tribes of the earth would mourn because they would see him coming in the clouds of heaven "with power and great glory," surrounded by angels, and universally heralded with a "loud trumpet call" (vv. 30–31). No place will be hidden from its explosive manifestation. The Parousia will impact the entire world; it will miss no one.

This teaching of the Parousia as a universal event is also confirmed in the writings of the apostle Paul. For him, the Parousia and the resurrection it triggers are part of the End when the victorious Christ destroys the opposition and transfers the kingdom into eternity (1 Cor. 15:23–27; "Parousia" is used in v. 23). It affects the whole universe as *every* rule, authority, and power are destroyed by its occurrence. At the sounding of "the last trumpet," all the resurrected dead and every living believer will be summoned to their eternal abode; Christ himself will shout a cry of command, and the archangel will give out a call (1 Thess. 4:15–17; cf. 1 Cor. 15:51–52). The sound of the last trumpet, the cry of command, and the archangel's call denote an event of universal proportions.

John's view of the universality of Christ's second coming is also consistent with Christ's teaching. When Christ comes with the clouds, "every eye" will see him, "even those who pierced him," and all "the tribes of the earth will wail" because of him (Rev. 1:7 NRSV; cf. Matt. 24:30–31). Here too, the Second Coming is a universal event, witnessed by the totality of the world's population.

On this basis, the New Testament defines the effects of the Parousia as two concurrent happenings of universal significance. The first, positive or upside, we shall call the "universal renewal"; the other, negative or downside, will be called the "universal removal."

1. The Universal Renewal

When history is consummated and creation is liberated from its bondage to decay and brought into the glorious freedom of the children of God (Rom. 8:21), then the victorious Christ, sitting on the throne, will proclaim, "See, I am making all things new. . . . It is done!" (Rev. 21:5–6 NRSV). This new creation brought forth at the Parousia is the new community on earth as it becomes the eternal community in heaven. According to Scripture, this transition of God's community from the temporal world to eternity will happen at the Parousia in two closely connected movements: the "resurrection" and the "reunion."

a. The Resurrection

The damage that the Fall caused at the beginning, the Resurrection will reverse at the End. The Fall thwarted God's purposes; the Resurrection will restore them to his original intent. The Fall drove humans away from God; the Resurrection will bring them close to him. The Fall disrupted God's image in human life; the Resurrection will make it perfect once more. The Fall gave Satan his greatest victory; the Resurrection will hand him his greatest defeat.

The Resurrection should not be seen as a cosmic magic act or as an eschatological extravaganza. It is a logical necessity rooted in God's own self-definition. As the apostle Peter put it in reference to Christ's own resurrection, "it was impossible for death to keep its hold on him" (Acts 2:24 NIV). Likewise, it will be impossible for death to keep its hold on those who belong to Christ. For Paul, the logic of the Resurrection is unassailable: Death came from one man to all his descendants; life comes from another man to all who belong to him (1 Cor. 15:21–23). God as the author of life loves life and hates death, the devourer of life. He has already proven his mastery over death in the resurrection of his Son. At the return of Christ, he will exercise his total mastery over death by destroying it and by releasing from its grasp all those who belong to him through faith.

Paul defined the Resurrection as the transformation of our lowly bodies to become like Christ's glorious resurrected body, and its purpose as Christ's plan to bring all things under his control (Phil. 3:20–21). In this sense, the final resurrection will only implement a positional resurrection that has already been obtained for believers with Christ's own resurrection (Col. 3:1–4). This "change" will affect not only the dead who will be brought to life at the Parousia but also the believers who will be alive at that time. They will be changed from this earthly life into the resurrection state "in a moment, in the twinkling of an eye, at the last trumpet" (1 Cor 15:51–52 NRSV).

This talk of a physical resurrection for the bodies of people dead for a long time, some for thousands of years, raises a host of biological problems. The bodies of most people who have died are not in tombs any more. They have disintegrated and become scattered throughout the environment. Through the ecological processes of the earth, they have been recycled many times over in an inextricable interpenetration of living things and beings through the constant recombination of atoms and molecules. At the resurrection, how can those overlapping bodies be separated from each other to form whole persons?

The Scripture's answer to such objections is straightforward: The body that is sown in death is not the same as the body that God gives at the resurrection (1 Cor. 15:37–38). There is continuity between the earthly body and the resurrection body insofar as God's image invested in each individual's personhood is preserved. But the resurrection causes a metamorphosis that enables resurrected bodies to acquire properties suited for God's mode of existence. The resurrection is much more than dead bodies reconstituted and resuscitated. It is a total transformation, a new creation making that which died perishable, in dishonor, and in weakness into a "spiritual body" raised immortal, glorious, and powerful (vv. 42–44). It is the victorious release from death's crippling, deforming grip on beings designed by God to be free, pure, and beautiful, and their instant remaking into "the image of the man from heaven" (vv. 47–50).

b. The reunion

In his farewell discourse, Jesus tried to comfort his disciples by promising that he would return to claim them for himself and would take them to remain with him eternally in the Father's house. To reassure them, he committed himself, in language they could understand, to prepare a safe place for them so that they could all be reunited together in ample celestial facilities with no fear of a housing shortage (John 14:1–2).

This gathering of believers with Christ at the Parousia is sometimes called the "Rapture." We will avoid using this term for three reasons. The first is that this word is often used to refer to a secret ascent of believers into heaven at a time prior to and separate from the End. Such a notion does not square with the biblical data presented earlier in this chapter. Second, the word "rapture" has a limited meaning that conveys only the idea of a "carrying away"; it suggests neither the reason for nor the destination of the gathering of the elect. Third, the word "rapture" is not found in the Bible. Of itself, this fact does not invalidate its use. However, the Scripture offers a beautiful word that describes the same event: "the gathering" or the "great gathering." This word conveys not only the idea of "carrying away" but it also suggests its purpose—to meet the Lord and be with him forever. Jesus himself used this word in the Olivet Discourse when he predicted that, at the Parousia, the angels would "gather his elect from the four winds" (Matt. 24:31; Mark 13:27 NIV).

Both Jesus and Paul taught about the gathering for the purpose of bringing comfort to believers. Jesus wanted to comfort his followers because they were shattered at the thought of losing him. Paul wanted to comfort the Thessalonian Christians because they thought they had forever lost their deceased fellow-believers. In both cases, Christ's followers were grieving the loss of community relationships dear to them. Jesus exhorted them to check their emotions and not allow their hearts to be troubled (John 14:1–3). Likewise, Paul told the believers not to grieve like pagans who have no hope, but to comfort one another with teachings that he had himself obtained from the Lord (1 Thess. 4:13, 18).

Jesus promised his followers that he would restore their community by taking them to be with him and with the Father. Paul also referred to the restoration of community. At the Lord's coming, all believers together would meet the Lord in heaven and remain with him forever (1 Thess. 4:17). In the teachings of both Jesus and Paul, the purpose of the great gathering is the reunion of the church into one heavenly community for all eternity. Both also expressed the joy, the intensity, and the ecstasy of the gathering through the imagery of a wedding (Matt. 22:1–14; 25:1–12; Luke 14:15–25; 2 Cor. 11:2; Eph. 5:27). In each case, the imagery suggests the ultimate embrace of love (Eph. 5:32).

The symbolism of the church gathered together from all places and all the ages as the bride of Christ is likewise developed in the book of Revelation. It first appears under the imagery of the 144,000 "who had been redeemed from the earth" (Rev. 14:1–5), representing collectively a virginal spouse unsullied by adulterous relationships (v. 4). This touches back to the 144,000 "servants of our God" from the tribes of Israel who are "sealed" into salvation (7:3–8).

Some Bible interpreters take Revelation 7 to refer to a last generation of believing Jews rather than a symbol of the church as the real children of Abraham, because it enumerates 12,000 for each of the twelve tribes of Israel. However, such an understanding creates an unbearable problem by positing an error in the Bible. According to the text, the 144,000 are taken "from all the tribes of Israel." But only eleven tribes are enumerated, since Joseph has a double portion of 24,000 (Manasseh was Joseph's son). To make matters worse, the tribe of Dan is omitted altogether, despite the fact that it is the first tribe named in the last tribal listing in the Old Testament (Ezek. 48). Actually, through the subtle device of announcing all the tribes of Israel and naming only eleven, the author of Revelation was telling his readers to watch for a broader meaning to his story. The use of conventional numbers strictly limiting the "servants of our God" to 144,000 individuals (1000 x 12 x 12), and the positioning at the top of the list of the tribe of Judah from which Jesus the Savior came, indicate that the author was describing in true apocalyptic language the fullness of the people of God.

John goes on to present the same reality of the complete church by describing the people of God as having passed through the "great tribulation" of the ages and as having entered into the presence of God to worship him and to be comforted by him (Rev. 7:9–17). They are also servants of God (v. 15a) and come from "every nation, tribe, people and language" (v. 9 NIV). This inclusiveness and the size of the "great multitude that no one could count" suggest that they are the believers from every nation that ever was, the church of all times that has made its way through the ages to be ushered to its final and glorious destination. Historically, most commentators have agreed that the 144,000 and the great multitude are two representations of the church, one on earth when it is prepared for the tribulation of persecution, the other in heaven as the eternal community.

The Lamb/bride pairing continues with one more depiction of "a great multitude in heaven" celebrating the wedding supper of the Lamb, because "the wedding of the Lamb has come, and his bride has made herself ready" (Rev. 19:1–9 NIV). To make sure that his readers understood the symbolism of the bride as the church,

John deftly described her garments as the "righteous acts of the saints" (v. 8).

Finally and climactically, the preeminence of the church in God's eternal purposes is celebrated by John with the vision of the bride as the new Jerusalem (Rev. 21:1–4). Heaven and earth have passed away and been replaced by a new reality. In the middle of it appears the "Holy City, the new Jerusalem, coming down out of heaven from God, prepared as a bride beautifully dressed for her husband" (v. 2 NIV; see also vv. 9–12) She is the dwelling of God with humans, "for the old order of things has passed away" (v. 4).

Ideally, a city is a community of people gathered in one place. In this text, however, the emphasis is not only on the oneness of the city, but even more on the communion of the city with God. "He will live with them. They will be his people, and God himself will be with them and be their God" (21:3 NIV). The love relationship between God and his gathered people could not be described with greater intensity. "Only those whose names are written in the Lamb's book of life" are in the city (21:27). Christ's servants "will serve him," they "will see his face" and "they will reign for ever and ever" (22:3–5). This is indeed what theologians call "the final state of the righteous."

The city bears "the names of the twelve tribes of Israel" and "the names of the twelve apostles of the Lamb" (21:12, 14). Thus, the imagery of the city shows the oneness of God's people gathered as a spiritual community, old and new covenant together, believers from all nations joined into one body as the bride of Christ. The coded value of the measurements (12,000 stadia long and 12 x 12 cubits thick) and the magnificence of the materials with which the city is made suggest the utter perfection of the bride of Christ, finally presented "as a radiant church, without stain or wrinkle or any other blemish, but holy and blameless" (Eph. 5:27 NIV).

The question may be raised as to why the church gathered in heaven as a collectivity of resurrected spiritual beings is represented in Revelation 21 by a physical object such as a city. The very same question may be raised about the depiction of the Lord Jesus in the same text as an animal and as an object (i.e., a Lamb and a lamp in v. 23). In both cases, what matters is the spiritual meaning of the objects, not the physical objects themselves. The Lamb symbolizes the self-sacrificing Savior, and the lamp images the truth he reveals. But Jesus is neither a lamb nor a lamp. Likewise, the city represents the people of God in its completion. The church comes out of the hands of God as his supreme creation, and it is "for ever and ever" (22:5).

John's use of imagery is justified to describe in human language such a sublime reality as the church gathered in heaven. If the New Jerusalem were to be conceived in physical terms, it would not be a city. What is described in this passage is an immense mass of solid gold shaped as a cube 1400 miles high, a vertical dimension equivalent to 255 times the height of Mount Everest or as high as the upended distance between Chicago and the Florida Keys. At its base, the cube would stretch from the Black Sea in the Ukraine down south to the Sudan in Africa, and from Greece in Europe all the way to Iran in Asia. The cube and its shadow would obliterate a good section of the earth's geography, including all of the Middle East.

It was probably to guard against such irreverent interpretations that John planted clues in his description of the vision to indicate that its human *meaning* was important, not the physical object itself. Some of the clues appear in the form of material impossibilities, such as the fact that jasper (which is opaque green) becomes "clear as crystal" (21:11), and that each of the twelve gates of the city is made of a single pearl (21:21). The city has only one street and, like the rest of the cube, the street is made of pure gold, but the gold is as transparent as glass (21:21, 18). Of course, a pearl that is as large as a city gate ceases to be a pearl, and gold is no longer gold when it is transparent as glass. The city has a river, but that river flows in the middle of its only street. It also has a tree, but the tree stands on both sides of the river at the same time (22:1–2). Such parabolic references indicate that neither the city nor its lamp were meant to be understood as physical objects. They represent the great reunion in eternity of the church gathered in the embrace of divine love.

2. The Universal Removal

The tragic downside of the end-time events will also be played out on the Last Day. According to Scripture, there will be a negative counterpart to the universal renewal in a purging of the universe by fire, removing everything that has been trashed by Satan, sin, and death. It will consist of two developments: the resolution of the presence of evil and the retribution by judgment. The Scripture defines this double elimination of all that falls under God's rejection the "removal of . . . created things," so that there will remain only that which escapes God's judgment (Heb. 12:25–27 NRSV), the church in heaven.

a. The resolution of the presence of evil

Scripture compares the great gathering of the new community from this earth into eternity to labor pains that produce new life. Both history and the created world are pregnant with the church (Matt. 24:8; Rom. 8:22). They will strain and suffer until its safe passage into eternity is complete. Once the church has made the transition to its final destination and history has fulfilled its grand purpose, what will happen to this world? The Scripture answers this question with the promise of the final resolution of evil, predicting that evil itself and everything contaminated by it will be purged by fire. The Old Testament described this cosmic clean-up as the expression of God's wrath let loose on the Day of the Lord. As he proceeded with the creation of the world, God put in place the heavens and the earth, the sun, the moon, and the stars. The End will affect the same universe in reverse order with the undoing of creation: The sun and the stars will become extinct, the moon will become dark, and "the earth will be shaken out of its place" (Isa. 13:13 NRSV; Joel 2:30–31). It will be "the great and terrible day of the LORD" (Mal. 4:5 NRSV).

Jesus associates this unravelling of creation with "the coming of the Son of Man," when the celestial bodies will collapse (Matt. 24:29–30) and the earth will experience a sudden devastation similar to that of the Flood in Noah's time (vv. 38–39). With the gathering of the community of the elect, the physical universe will have served its purpose. Its contamination by evil will have made it unusable and unpreservable so that its deliverance from torment through incineration will be the most merciful thing that could happen to it. The wrath of God is not directed at his own creation but at the evil that has infiltrated it like the spreading of a generalized malignancy (13:30, 40–41, 49–50).

For Paul, the Day of the Lord will come as a sudden destruction from which there will be no escape (1 Thess. 5:2–3). But this destruction will not be confined to the physical world; it will also involve the destruction of every rule, authority, and power, including the ultimate enemy, death itself (1 Cor. 15:23–26). The sin-polluted environment will be purged, along with the sin-polluters themselves, the spiritual forces of darkness that pitted themselves in rebellion against God.

Peter's predictions about the Day of the Lord present it as a universal conflagration of "the heavens and earth that now exist" (2 Pet. 3:7 RSV). The heavens will disappear with a big bang, the elements will dissolve in flames, and the earth will go through fire (v. 10). Because everything unredeemed will disappear into

270

physical nothingness through this cosmic cremation (v. 12), the universe will be replaced by a new evil-proof reality (v. 13). In other words, this world has been so thoroughly corrupted by satanic infestations that it has become terminally diseased. God mercifully recognizes the loss and concentrates on the new community that he gathers to himself just before the End.

Revelation's references to the End contain the same features but, predictably, they are more graphically presented. Sun, moon, and stars disintegrate, and the earth explodes while its inhabitants scurry for cover and, finding none, clamor for their own extermination (Rev. 6:12–17). Their prayer is answered in a parallel vision as they are crushed under a celestial bombardment while the earth and its cities vanish under their feet and mountains and islands fly off into space (16:17–21). In yet another vision, fire comes down from heaven to consume them while the author of all evil is forcibly immersed in the ultimate baptism of fire (20:9–10), where he is joined by his grisly inventions, death and the kingdom of death (vv. 13–14). Satan, evil, and death disappear into eternal oblivion, out of the presence of God.

b. The retribution by judgment

Tragically, a similar fate awaits those who have mistakenly bet on Satan winning the battle for eternity by siding with him in this life. The testimony throughout Scripture is that judgment awaits them.

When he introduced Jesus as the Savior to the world, John the Baptist described him as the dispenser of the greatest blessing in the gift of the Holy Spirit and as the cause of the greatest loss on account of the Last Judgment. Drawing on harvest imagery, John likened Christ to the farmer who sifts the grain from the waste in order to keep the former and to dispose of the latter (Matt. 3:11–12). Jesus used a similar parable to describe the eschatological judgment of the wicked. He described them as "the sons of the evil one," planted in the world by the devil. At the "end of the age," "everything that causes sin and all who do evil" will be gathered by angels in a sort of reverse, downside reunion and be thrown into the fire like a bunch of weeds (13:24–29, 36–43).

The authors of the New Testament affirm the notion of the destruction by fire of those who oppose God in this life (Heb. 6:7–8; 2 Pet. 3:7; Rev. 20:15); judgment is a universal moral necessity (Mark 9:43–48; Rom. 2:5–11; Heb. 9:27; 10:26–27). By far the most concise and descriptive definition of hell to be found in the Bible is provided by Paul as he considers the effect of just retribution that the Parousia will have on the godless (2 Thess.

1:7–10). His vision of the fate of the lost is consistent with the teaching of Jesus in that retribution will befall them on the "day" when Christ returns for his "saints" (v. 10). Two sorts of disasters engulf the godless: They suffer the punishment of "everlasting destruction," and they are excluded or "shut out" from the presence of the Lord (v. 9). The "destruction" suggests complete extinction of beings, the return to nothingness of that which had been originally created by God out of nothing. However, the shutting out suggests complete separation from God in eternity of those who chose to remain separated from him during this earthly life. In other words, one form of punishment suggests instant annihilation, and the other, the suffering of eternal separation. If there seems to be a tension between those two ideas, it may be because we tend to conceive of eternity in earthly time-bound terms instead of defining it in relation to the non-temporal quality of the transcendence that characterizes spiritual existence outside of and beyond time.

The victims of the retribution are defined in two broad categories: those who do not know God and those who do not obey the gospel of our Lord Jesus (v. 8). They are the indifferent and the unconcerned on one hand, and the rebellious and the rejecting on the other. In each case, their fate beyond this life results from choices made within this life. Again, the Scripture teaches that humans are responsible for their decisions. Whether they have related to God in this life or whether they have chosen not to do so will affect their standing toward God in the afterlife. In other words, God allows the indifferent and the rebellious to have it their own way both in this life and in the next. It is not fair to say that God consigns anyone to hell. He does not; people make that choice for themselves.

Obviously, Scripture deals with this topic with measure and restraint. It never justifies the lurid, sometimes almost gleeful depictions that are made of hell with sweeping determinations as to who belongs there. In fact, the Bible sternly forbids Christians to play God by deciding for him who will ascend to heaven and who will descend into hell (Rom. 10:6–7). Instead, each believer is called to examine only his or her own heart and to determine whether the profession made with one's lips is consistent with the convictions of one's heart so as to confirm one's salvation (vv. 8–11). Only God has the right to judge other people since only he knows the secrets and the inner motives of each individual (2:13–16). Jesus himself warned those who blithely consign other people to hell against the dangers of surprise reversals on Judgment Day (Luke 13:23–30). He taught them that performing spectacular ministries was no substitute for doing the will of God (Matt. 7:21–23), and he graphically described the eternal ruin of religious people who neglect to act justly, to love mercy, and to walk humbly with their God (Matt. 6:14–15; 18:21–35; 25:31–46; Luke 12:16–21; 16:19–31; cf. Mic. 6:8).

IV. CURRENT VIEWS ON THE END TIMES

There exists such a wide variety of views on eschatology, ranging from its virtual denial to incredibly imaginative and complicated scenarios for the End, that it might be more useful to describe theological attitudes toward the doctrine of the end times rather than attempt to catalogue the different views.

1. Anti-eschatological Attitudes

Some theologians think that the notion of a divinely initiated climactic end to history should be softened and expressed in terms that do not imply supernatural interventions and a radical termination of earthly life. Some interpret the eschatological data of the Bible in personal existential terms, equating the Parousia to one's transition from life on this earth to eternity through the experience of death. More often, eschatology is viewed as an extension of the historical process into a future shaped by the church's involvement in establishing God's kingdom on earth. In this case, issues of peace and justice, of global survival, and of political, social, and economic development are viewed as eschatological objectives yet to be attained. This identification of eschatology with outcomes within history generally stems from attitudes of indifference and even denial toward the biblical teachings on the end times.

2. Indifferent Attitudes

Biblically founded Christians generally approach the end times teachings of Scriptures with an attitude of respect. Their belief in the Parousia finds expression in their institutional statements of faith and in the teaching and preaching ministries of their churches. Quite frequently, however, their adherence to eschatological beliefs remains formal and theoretical, with no recognizable impact on lifestyles and values. Yet, as noted in this chapter, the Scriptures make it consistently clear that the practical object of the Christian hope is to promote the cultivation of lives of holiness devoted to selfless pursuits and sacrificial deeds of compassion. Because of the nearness of the End, the lifestyle of Christians should be an imitation of that of the Lord Jesus and should be free of self-centered concerns (Rom. 13:11–14; Tit. 2:11–14; Heb. 10:23–25; Jas. 5:7–9; 1 Pet. 1:13–16; 2 Pet. 3:11–12, 14).

Faith in the "blessed hope" naturally results in an attitude of detachment from a world that may disappear at any moment and in a commitment to ministry opportunities that may vanish instantly. Yet far too much evidence indicates that faith in the Second Coming does not necessarily result in Christians being less materialistic, less consumerist, and less media controlled than their unbelieving neighbors. Obviously, it is possible to believe in the Parousia and to live as if it were never to happen.

3. Obsessive Attitudes

If some Christians believe in eschatology without passion, others make it an obsession. Throughout the centuries, groups of believers have sporadically been seized by a spirit of apocalyptic fervor that led them to read signs of the nearness of the Parousia in contemporary events and to predict the impending end of the world. Despite the fact that they have been consistently proven wrong, this kind of *predictionism* has become institutionalized in our day. As a phenomenon characteristically North American, many Christians engage in sign-seeking and date-setting by attempting to match current historical events with bits and pieces of biblical texts drawn mainly from the prophetic books of the Old Testament, for the purpose of demonstrating that "prophecy is being fulfilled before our own eyes." They have spawned specialized multi-million dollar publication and media industries that flourish with every flare-up of the Middle East crisis. But the predictions are always proven wrong, and the eschatological jigsaw puzzles must be rearranged for the next international outbreak.

Such attempts to outguess God's timing are specifically forbidden in Scripture. According to the New Testament, Christians are not to look and wait for signs but rather for the Lord himself. The real purpose of prophecy is to encourage Christians to "watch and pray" (cf. Mark 13:35, 37; 14:38) and to live "lives of holiness and godliness, waiting for and earnestly desiring [alternate translation] the coming of the day of God" (2 Pet. 3:11–12 NRSV). Consequently, Christians ought to plan for ministry as if the Parousia might not happen in a million years, but they should also watch and pray as if it were to happen today—because it could.

RESOURCES

For further study on the doctrine of the end times, see the following resources:

Alan F. Johnson and Robert E. Webber. *What Christians Believe: A Biblical and Historical Summary*. Grand Rapids: Zondervan, 1989, pp. 415–61.

Gilbert Bilezikian. "Interpreting Apocalyptic Literature." Pp. 267–99 in *The Literature and Meaning of Scripture*, eds. Morris A. Inch and C. Hassell Bullock. Grand Rapids: Baker, 1981.

William C. Crockett, John Walvoord, Zachary Hayes, and Clark Pinnock. *Four Views on Hell*. Grand Rapids: Zondervan, 1992.

George Ladd. *The Last Things*. Grand Rapids: Eerdmans, 1978.

DISCUSSION QUESTIONS

1. Is Parousia the name of a rock group or a country in South America?
2. Can the observation of signs enable humans to predict the time of the end?
3. When will the Tribulation happen?
4. What form does the Antichrist take according to the New Testament?
5. Is hell eternal suffering or eternal death?

General Index

Abortion, 138, 154, 223
Abraham, 63–64, 71, 143, 150–53, 178–81, 191–93, 267
Agnosticism, 47
Antichrist, 242–47
Apocalyptic, 255
Apocrypha, 12
Ascension, 76, 89
Asceticism, 162–63
Atheism, 47
Atonement, 144
Augustine, 138
Authority, 6–9, 129, 197–202, 205

Baptism, 65–66, 207–9
Baptism of the Spirit, 90–94, 110, 164
Bibliolatry, 21
Bishops, elders, deacons, 200

Calling, 149
Canon, 11–12
Celibacy, 125
Charisma, 107
Charismatic, 109
Church discipline, 197, 200
Clergy, 190, 200–202
Confession of faith, 195
Conversion, 158–60
Councils, 11–12, 81–82
Covenant, 88, 97, 143, 178, 220
Creation, 31, 53, 58, 61

Dead Sea Scrolls, 13
Death, 127–32, 157, 204–12
Divorce, 223

Election, 149
Eschatology, 230
Evangelical, 225
Evangelism, 213–17
Exaltation, 73
Expiation, 144

Fall, 127
Free will, 40–46, 164
Fundamentalism, 225

Gentile mission, 237–38
Glossolalia, 93–94, 111–15, 164

Head, headship, 80–81, 130, 190
Heavenly Jerusalem, 191–94
Holiness of God, 32–34

Holocaust, 138, 241
Humiliation, 62

Image of God, 119–27
Immanence, 31, 48
Imminence, 231, 249–50
Incarnation, 58, 60, 62–63, 66
Inerrancy, 10
Inspiration, 10, 88
Interpretation, hermeneutics, 14–20, 229–30
Israel, 151–61

Justification, 145

Kenosis, 59, 87
Kingdom, 67, 109, 256, 259, 261

Legalism, 163, 197
Liberal, 224
Liberation theology, 169
Logos, 58–59
Lord's supper, 101, 209–12
Love, 34–35, 52

Male and female, 121–22, 126
Messiah, 182
Millennium, 257–63
Ministry, 107, 154–56, 213–24
Miracles, 67

New community, 5

Omnipotence, 28
Omnipresence, 27
Omniscience, 29
Oneness, 88, 95, 97, 129, 123–24, 132–33, 137, 184–91, 194, 199, 202, 212, 268
Ontology, 32, 121
Ordinances, 207
Ordination, 190–91, 200

Paraclete, 97–99, 104
Parousia, 230
Pelagius, 138
Pentecostal, 109
Pharisees, 68–69
Predestination, 149–56
Predictionism, 274
Preexistence, 57–58, 62
Priesthood of believers, 200, 206
Problem of evil, 35–45, 65
Process theology, 170

Scripture Index

RESOURCES

Vision,   Training,   Resources,

This resource was created to serve you and to help you in building a local church that prevails! It is just one of many Willow Creek Resources copublished by the Willow Creek Association and Zondervan Publishing House.

Since 1992, the Willow Creek Association (WCA) has been linking like-minded, action-oriented churches with each other and with strategic vision, training, and resources. Now a worldwide network of over five thousand churches from more than eighty denominations, the WCA works to equip Member Churches and others with the tools needed to build prevailing churches. Our desire is to inspire, equip, and encourage Christian leaders to build biblically functioning churches that reach increasing numbers of unchurched people, not just with innovations from Willow Creek Community Church in South Barrington, Illinois, but from any church in the world that has experienced God-given breakthroughs.

Willow Creek Conferences

In the past year, more than 65,000 local church leaders, staff, and volunteers—from WCA Member Churches and others—attended one of our conferences or training events.

Conferences offered on the Willow Creek campus in South Barrington, Illinois, include:

Prevailing Church Conference—Foundational training for staff and volunteers working to build a prevailing local church; offered twice each year.

Prevailing Church Workshops—More than fifty workshops cover seven topic areas that represent key characteristics of a prevailing church; offered twice each year.

Promiseland Conference—Children's ministries; infant through fifth grade.

Prevailing Youth Ministries Conference—Junior and senior high ministries.

Arts Conference—Vision and training for Christian artists using their gifts in the ministries of local churches.

Leadership Summit—Envisioning and equipping Christians with leadership gifts and responsibilities; broadcast live via satellite to sixteen cities.

Contagious Evangelism Conference—Encouragement and training for churches and church leaders who want to be strategic in reaching lost people for Christ.

Small Groups Conference—Exploring how small groups can play a key role in developing authentic Christian community that leads to spiritual transformation.

Prevailing Church Regional Workshops

Each year the WCA team leads seven, two-day training events in cities across the United States. Workshops are offered in topic areas including leadership, next-generation ministries, small groups, arts and worship, evangelism, spiritual gifts, financial stewardship, and spiritual formation. These events make quality training more accessible and affordable to larger groups of staff and volunteers.

Willow Creek Resources

Churches can look to Willow Creek Resources for a trusted channel of ministry tools in areas of leadership, evangelism, spiritual gifts, small groups, drama, contemporary music, financial stewardship, spiritual transformation, and more. For ordering information, call 800-570-9812 or visit www.willowcreek.com.

WCA Membership

Membership in the Willow Creek Association as well as attendance at WCA Conferences is for churches, ministries, and leaders who hold to a historic, orthodox understanding of biblical Christianity. The annual church membership fee of $249 provides discounts for your entire team on all conferences and Willow Creek Resources, networking opportunities with other outreach-oriented churches, a bimonthly newsletter, a subscription to *Defining Moments* monthly audio journal, and more.

WillowNet (www.willowcreek.com)

This internet service provides you with access to hundreds of Willow Creek messages, drama scripts, songs, videos, and multimedia suggestions. The system allows you to sort through these elements and download them for a fee.

Our website also provides detailed information on the Willow Creek Association, Willow Creek Community Church, WCA Membership, conferences, training events, resources, and more.

Willow Creek Association
P.O. Box 3188
Barrington, IL 60011-3188
Phone: 800-570-9812
Fax: 888-922-0035
Web: www.willowcreek.com